'A TRACT FOR OUR TIMES'

'A TRACT FOR OUR TIMES'

A Retrospective on Joe Lee's *Ireland 1912–1985*

edited by

MIRIAM NYHAN GREY

UNIVERSITY COLLEGE DUBLIN PRESS
PREAS CHOLÁISTE OLLSCOILE BHAILE ÁTHA CLIATH
2024

First published 2024
by University College Dublin Press
UCD Humanities Institute, Room H103,
Belfield,
Dublin 4

www.ucdpress.ie

ISBN 978-17-3-90863-74

CIP data available from the British Library

Typeset in Dublin by Gough Typesetting Limited
Text design by Lyn Davies
Printed in England on acid-free paper by
CPI Antony Rowe, Chippenham, Wiltshire.

Contents

For Anne

Foreword

While this volume commemorates the publication in 1989 of a groundbreaking work in modern Irish history, it also celebrates the career of a distinguished historian and public figure. John Joseph Lee is among the great historians of his generation and during a 50-year career that took him to Dublin, Cambridge, Cork and New York, gained enormous admiration and esteem as teacher, writer, university administrator, parliamentarian and public intellectual.[1]

This volume originated in a 2018 conference at the Royal Irish Academy which brought academic colleagues and former students together to consider the context, content and impact of *Ireland, 1912–1985: Politics and Society* on Irish historiography, on understanding Irish history, and on public discourse, then and since. Unusually, for the time, the work became a bestseller, was soon a standard teaching text and, still in print, has now attained classic status. This collection of essays pays tribute to a valued text but also to some of Professor Lee's interests and strengths as well as offering reconsiderations of transformative events.

I am honoured to write this foreword. Not only was Professor Lee my lecturer, supervisor, mentor, and a friend, but, as for many others, his work fostered my intellectual development as a historian. Prior to publishing *Ireland 1912-1985*, his innovative and provocative *The Modernisation of Irish Society* (1973) had provided young historians with a tantalising menu for future research. When *Ireland 1912-1985* followed, it was understandably acclaimed as a magisterial synthesis though it also drew criticism of an apparent neglect of women's experiences: I once pointed out to Joe that, ironically, the omission provided historians of women with a great lecture on the theme of *Cherchez la femme*. But any criticism or suggestion of oversight must be placed alongside his hugely influential essay 'Women and the Church since the Famine' in the seminal *Women in Irish Society: The Historical Dimension*, co-edited by his good friends and colleagues, Margaret MacCurtain and Donnchadh Ó Corráin, (1978), having previously reached a countrywide audience as a Thomas Davis lecture broadcast. Some 20 years later, in a commentary on what by then was a well-established field, Maryann Valiulis and Mary O'Dowd noted that as the first academic collection on women's role in Irish society, it set an agenda that subsequent historians, intellectuals and activists profitably followed. When asked what work she would most like to be remembered for, Margaret MacCurtain, chose that volume because its essays were 'an expression of the vitality of the intellectual and creative energy of the 1970s', a trait that would remain characteristic of Joe's work.[2]

J. J. Lee's belief in the importance of international and comparative contexts expanded to include an American dimension when he moved in 2002 to the Glucksman Chair of Irish History at New York University. Not so well-known to an Irish audience is his contribution there to Irish and Irish-American historiography in a transnational context. Among his key

---

1   I am very grateful to Dr John Logan for his help and guidance in writing this piece. Dr Logan is a friend as well as former PhD student of Joe's when the latter was in University College Cork.
2   Maryann Gialanella Valiulis and Mary O'Dowd (eds), *Women and Irish History* (Dublin, 1997), p. 7.

achievements while at NYU was co-editing, with Marion R. Casey, the 706-page volume *Making the Irish American: History and Heritage of the Irish in the United States*, (2006). Another is his chapter, 'The Irish Diaspora in the Nineteenth Century' in Lawrence M. Geary and Margaret Kelleher's collection, *Nineteenth Century Ireland: A Guide to Recent Research* (2005). It remains of immense value because of its penetrating analysis of the concept of the diaspora and of what it meant to be Irish abroad. A provocative questioning of a firmly established narrative, and a characteristic emphasis on a rigorous interrogation of evidence, significantly progressed diaspora studies. Although Joe's frequently voiced, 'No New York, No America, No (Easter) Rising', remains debatable, it originated as a prodding typical of his wish to interrogate simplistic explanations of historical complexities.

As a diligent and generous colleague and then as a public intellectual, J. J. Lee's impact on Irish education went beyond historical scholarship. At UCC, he served as Dean of the Faculty of Arts (1976–9) and College Vice-President (1982–5). He served four terms as a member of the College Governing Body and on many of its committees. He was elected by the convocation of university graduates to the Senate of the National University of Ireland to serve from 1992 to 1997. His immense energy led to further engagement in the public sphere when he represented the National University in Seanad Éireann between 1993 and 1997. During these 'public years' a weekly column in the *Sunday Tribune* and subsequent publication of *The Shifting Balance of Power: Exploring the 20th Century* (2000) contextualised many complex events for a wide and loyal readership.

While this is an academic tome, it would be remiss not to record what his many friends and colleagues have experienced: J. J. Lee is the best of company in any setting, intimate or public. His sense of humour and fun, his fairness, integrity, acuity but also self-deprecating nature, will always enrich an event. It would not be amiss for any aspiring historian to model their career on his. There is much, much more to be said about his immense contribution to Irish life and of the role of his wife, Anne and their three children in supporting and sustaining that. For now, his innovative approach to historical scholarship, his generosity of spirit and action, and his integrity distinguish a singular role in the academy and in Irish public life.

Professor emeritus Bernadette Whelan, MRIA
Limerick, January 2024

INTRODUCTION

'I wanted to explain my country to myself'
Joe Lee, *Irish Times*, 26 Oct. 1991

On the occasion of his retirement from New York University in 2017, J. J. (Joe) Lee's contributions to the academy and public life were celebrated by Ireland's first citizen, Uachtarán na hÉireann, Michael D. Higgins. Higgins, speaking to the domestic and international impact of Joe's magisterial 1989 monograph, Ireland 1912-1985: Politics and Society (Cambridge University Press) observed that Lee had penned a 'classic of history-writing and an incisive, sometimes unsparing, analysis of the independent Irish state and its economic travails and tribulations'.[1]

Not only had he written a classic, but Lee also managed with *Ireland 1912–1985* to transcend the reach of the academy to become widely popular and controversial by general readers. All historians aspire to write a book that is intellectually significant while reaching a popular audience, but only a few manage to scale Lee's heights, especially in the way it did in late 1980s and early 1990s. The landmark monograph, along with its sharp, honest and quick-witted author, instantly caused a sensation. Cambridge University Press were caught somewhat off guard by the success and in time had to go to over a dozen reprints, selling close to 35,000 copies, some achievement for a book on Irish history of a hefty scholarly format. In the *Irish Times* it was observed that even those 'who never read history ploughed through its 754 pages'.[2] A compulsive read, it quickly also became compulsory reading. Awards followed, including an Aer Lingus-*Irish Times* Prize for Literature.

For a country that has undergone so much change since the late 1980s one might wonder how *Ireland 1912–1985* stands the test of time. Not long after the publication Ireland experienced a dramatic decade beset with revelation after revelation, marked by significant levels of secularisation and demographic change. On top of the changed Ireland is the range of archival material that has become available, especially since the turn of the century. But the reality is that no scholars since have 'matched the quality of his writing and the depth of his analytical probing of politics and policy formation in the formative decades of the Irish State'.[3]

Joe Lee, born in Kerry in 1942, was educated by the Franciscans at Gormanston and went on to University College Dublin (UCD) to take a Double First in History and Economics.

---

1 New York University, 'Glucksman Ireland House to Celebrate Professor J. Joseph Lee's Fifteen-Year Tenure as Director', 21 May 2018, (https://www.nyu.edu/about/news-publications/news/2018/may/glucksman-ireland-house-to-celebrate-professor-j—joseph-lee-s-f.html) (11 Apr. 2024)
2 *Irish Times*, 2 Nov. 1991.
3 *Irish Times*, 20 Apr. 2019.

After a short stint at the Department of Finance he resumed his academic trajectory with a National University of Ireland (NUI) Travelling Scholarship which brought him to the Institute for European History in Mainz and from there to Cambridge's Peterhouse as Fellow, Tutor, Lecturer and Director of Studies. In 1974 he became Professor of Modern History at University College Cork (UCC) and from 2002 until 2017 he was Director of New York University's Glucksman Ireland House. As a sought-after public intellectual, a Sunday columnist and a member of Seanad Éireann, Joe produced five monographs, five edited collections, and a stunning 101 scholarly articles.

Much ink has been fittingly spilled about *Ireland 1912–1985*, especially in scholarly settings, and many aspects of its reception are taken up eloquently in the pages to follow. The purpose of this collection is to honour Lee's contribution to historical scholarship by gauging the perspicacity of *Ireland 1912–1985* as a historical analysis and commentary. No less importantly this collection measures the applicability of the work's historiographical and methodological approach to more recent history. Many of the scholars who write in this collection were schooled in history with *Ireland 1912–1985* as a touchstone text and each author approaches the subject differently depending on their own field of expertise.

In a variety of ways the contributors help us to understand how a text of significant intellectual calibre could provoke a lively national public discourse at the close of 'a disenchanting decade ravaged by economic failure, emigration and cultural civil wars'.[4] Of course, *Ireland 1912–1985* was not spared some criticism, much of which is succinctly summarised in Diarmaid Ferriter's 2019 *Irish Times* column.[5] Yet the overwhelming consensus is that Lee's work marked a historiographical turning point and broke new ground in Irish historical scholarship by combining contemporary observation with historical analysis. Lee's emphasis on tracing Irish development within a comparative framework, and especially in relation to European experiences, was ahead of the curve. By leaning into deeper statistical analysis of trends he probed the process and methodology which were then part of Irish historical scholarship. Paying close attention to leadership, in terms of both personality and style, his acerbic and iconoclastic approach enabled his challenging conclusions to transcend the ivory tower. Above all, Lee deployed a close and questioning exploration of the sources then available to frame his research for *Ireland 1912–1985*. Appropriately, given his commitment to teaching and mentorship of younger scholars, the collection is bookended with a foreword and an afterword by two of his former students. Bernadette Whelan pursued a stellar career as a widely-published and respected academic, while Daniel Mulhall's pursuits would lead him to the highest level of Ireland's diplomatic corps into coveted appointments such as the ambassadorships to the United Kingdom and United States.

✶✶✶✶✶✶

The collection opens with a piece drawing on a combination of oral history testimony and documentary sources in *A Portrait of the Historian as a Young Boy*. Here Marion R. Casey lingers on the Castlegregory of Lee's youth in an elegant attempt to add nuance to our

---

4   *Irish Times*, 20 Apr. 2019.
5   Ibid.

understandings of rural Irish society in the first half of the twentieth century. Perhaps what is more remarkable is how little Lee had self-consciously drawn on his own 'Ireland' in the pages of *Ireland 1919–1985* and how, in her act of interviewing him, Casey uncovers how Joe compartmentalised his engagements– an act, no doubt, framed by the pressure of striving for objective and scientific historical enquiry and the top-down viewpoint of the book. Casey closes the chapter noting that 'Castlegregory may have rendered the Ireland of his boyhood as a simple plane for Joe, but the heft and dimension that J. J. Lee, historian, gave modern Ireland was in his own family too'. This chapter richly demonstrates the individual historian's personal experience as an influencer and shaper of approach, philosophy and methodology.

Richard McMahon and Niall Whelehan further enable us to understand the younger scholar Lee by charting his intellectual evolution, early writings and historiographical influences. This chapter provides vital historical context in our understanding of the type of history Lee would come to write, culminating magisterially in *Ireland 1912–1985*. McMahon and Whelehan nimbly unpack Lee's 'flurry of activity in the late 1960s', leading to an 'accompanying historiographical call to arms' by way of the 1973 publication of *Modernisation and Irish Society 1848 to 1918* (Gill and Macmillan). Their conclusions apply just as much to *Ireland 1912–1985* as they do to his earlier contributions, when they note that his writing was 'critical, iconoclastic, and robust in its assessments of the forces and personalities at the heart of Irish economic, social and political life'.

The distinguished economic historian Cormac Ó Grada follows with 'Tríocha Bliain ag Fás: Some Reflections on a Classic'. Deftly drawing on economic analysis, an approach much studied and revered by Lee himself, Ó Grada also looks at Lee's interventions on indigenous Irish business in *Ireland 1912–1984* as well as in his earlier monograph, *Modernisation and Irish Society*. Noting how the present shapes almost all historical writing, Ó Grada concludes that *Ireland 1912–1985* is 'a book for the ages', while also warning that without care it may also prove to be 'as relevant and as provocative'.

In 'The Lash of the Liberators: Ireland 1912-1985 on Independence' Anne Dolan notes that she 'grew up with this book' and that she has 'clearly been shaped by it to the core'. Her penetrating analysis of the themes and reception of the book demonstrate the very type of engagement Lee always hoped to provoke and one can't help but imagine him taking much pleasure from Dolan's example, especially when she takes on a much-debated theme of the book, begrudgery. After all Lee himself had stimulated an interrogation on how 'possession' dominated 'performance', thereby providing context to how we frame 'begrudgery' in the Irish past and present.

In obliquely asking what our purpose of engaging with the past is, she pushes readers into important reflection:

> Given the anger of *Ireland 1912–1985*, happiness, even brief and at best cheeseparing, might well seem a whitewash, a papering over the cracks, when there is still so much to be brought out into the light. To be outraged, appalled, even defiant of the past, or to meet it on the measure of its own defiance rather than our own, to be confused by its wayward capacities for great hatreds, great cruelties, and great joys just as we might hope to confound out successors in a century's time when they dare to reduce us to dull outlines of our much more muddled selves.

Many themes expounded by Dolan also appear in Diarmaid Ferriter's 'Touting for Respectability' one which follows in what seems like an appropriate pairing of scholars highly influenced by Lee. In locating *Ireland 1912–1985* in its historiographical context Ferriter interrogates many of the book's grand themes which touch on aspects of class, the role of the Church, the public sphere, as well as, of course, political underpinnings. In the process, he draws out the many varied ways in which the book remains an essential guide to understanding both Ireland in the twentieth century, as well as our present. His reminder that *Ireland 1912–1985* caused the great stir 'precisely because of the mix of contemporary observation and historical analysis' is fitting in the context of great scholarship possessing an innate propensity to be provocative.

It has been asserted that emigration was 'the most volatile component of population change throughout the twentieth century'. The role of emigration in modern Irish history, and Lee's contributions to that significant demographic consideration, is taken up by his former UCC-colleague Andy Bielenberg. In particular Bielenberg is interested in the extent of conflict-related migration during and after the Irish revolutionary period. Since Lee had jettisoned the traditional approach of scholars to look at emigration within certain chronological constraints so there is a refreshing degree of continuity in the analysis in *Ireland 1912–1985*. The role of emigration, as a social escape hatch and controller, is underscored, while Lee's 'identification of the fundamental continuity in emigration of this under-privileged strats of rural migrants from the late nineteenth century through to the 1960s' was a particularly salient topic for the Irish public in the late 1980s.

In the penultimate chapter by historian of the Irish language Nicholas M. Wolf takes on an aspect of Irish history that is especially dear to a man whose mother tongue was Irish. Wolf opens the chapter with an important observation in that non-specialists may not be aware that *Ireland 1912–1985* 'had a significant influence on how researchers analyse the history of the language, in particular its status in the nineteenth century'. Primarily, Wolf connects the framework for interpreting the history of the Irish language presented in *Ireland 1912–1985* to the debate over language and identity. A compelling analysis, Wolf concludes by reminding readers of the need to respond to Lee's insistence 'that we move beyond received explanations to think harder about how culture operates'. All this seems especially resonant in consideration of the complex reasons for language shift and the evolution of the minority rights approach to the protection of the language.

The collection is drawn to a close with Gearóid Ó Tuathaigh's dynamic historiographical assessment of the theme of leadership, which he defines, in this context as 'the capacity for exerting influence in shaping and driving crucial choices in public policy calculated to serve the national interest'. The depth and breadth of Ó Tuathaigh's engagement is quickly evident in a piece that considers Lee's assessment of Irish leadership, as well as the historiography on the topic since. Ó Tuathaigh is interested in how Lee's take has been challenged or revised and it serves as a timely provocation as to the tangible impact something that can feel somewhat remote can have on the lives of ordinary citizens. In the process Ó Tuathaigh implicitly draws our attention to a challenge laid down by Lee for scholars to also 'perceive the inter-relationships' in interrogating the linkages across cultural, social, spiritual, intellectual and economic fields.

By way of conclusion, it is interesting to return to the immediate aftermath of the book's publication. As a testament to the popular interest in what he had to say Lee appeared on the iconic *Late Late Show* in early 1990 with another two intellectual heavyweights, Galway's Professor Gearóid Ó Tuathaigh and Trinity College Dublin's Professor Terence Brown. In a 35-minute slot, which was partly a follow-up to a radio segment Lee had also done with Gay in April 1989, it is evident that the broadcaster was deeply engaged with Lee's hypotheses. With Lee taking the lead in setting out his stall, so to speak, the trifecta of scholars responded to Gay and then engaged with the audience, both live in the studio and via telephone. Lee's intervention was not only being parsed in the highest echelons of scholarly scrutiny, but it clearly also had the nation talking. After the *Late Late Show* the book topped the paperback nonfiction bestseller list, where it would dominate for quite a while and Lee's appearance on television did not go unnoticed in scholarly circles. In the *Sunday Independent* the following weekend historian Ronan Fanning penned a piece carrying the headline that inspired the title of this collection, noting that: 'Few books, and still fewer works of scholarship, are given access to the national audience at Gay Byrne's command. Why should this one do so? Why is it so important?' In part, Fanning answered his rhetorical questions:

> 'Joe Lee, in short, is a man with a mission who has produced a tract for our times. Hence the appropriateness of his being granted access to the Late Late Show, that most coveted of Ireland's secular pulpits'.[6]

In a similar vein literary scholar Declan Kiberd noted in the *Irish Press* that on television 'Lee had spellbound the audience'. If *Ireland 1912–1985* was to bring Irish history and Lee to a wide audience, then the *Late Late Show* feature amplified that impact by bringing his work into the sitting rooms of the length and breadth of Ireland.

For the many thousands of readers influenced by his provocative intervention in *Ireland 1912–1985* Joe had succeeded in activating a lively debate which still resonates. As an academic and a public intellectual he made massive contributions to national life in Ireland and far beyond Irish shores. There is no doubt that his monumental monograph elevated his profile but more importantly to the man himself was how the reception of *Ireland 1912–1985* demonstrated that 'ordinary' Irish people could appreciate and debate complex history when they read it. If in writing the book he wanted to explain his country to himself, as he retrospectively observed in 1991, in the process he had also eloquently explained it to us all. *Buan an fear ina dhúiche féin.*

---

6   *Sunday Independent*, 21 Jan. 1990.

A Portrait of the Historian as a Young Boy

Marion R. Casey

When Joe Lee was confirmed by Bishop William J. Philbin in Ballinasloe, Co. Galway, he took the name Gregory. This was not a nod to St Gregory the Great, the patron saint of students and teachers, although that would, in hindsight, have been a prescient choice for the young man who would become a major academic.

The first years of Joe's life were spent in Castlegregory, Co. Kerry, or 'Castle', as those raised in its bosom called the little village on the Tralee Bay side of the Dingle Peninsula.[1]

J. J. Lee, the historian, was moulded by a youthful experience of country life far from the centre of Irish power and long before exposure to the pedagogy of the university and the archival paper trail. Therefore, we might ask, to what extent did the intellectual acumen and professional discipline required to chronicle modern Ireland also dampen curiosity about Joe's own roots? Could his family's background and their time in Castlegregory have offered further understanding of twentieth-century Irish politics and society?

★★★★★★

The first three chapters of *Ireland 1912–1985* chart the country's public policymaking as a newly-independent state, at the time when Joe Lee's mother and father were coming of age. His parents were natives of County Galway: Cáit Burke from Oughterard and Tom Lee from the city of Galway. Socially, their stories reveal a stratum of Ireland that was still largely undocumented by historians when their son published his magnum opus in 1989.

'You're asking me questions that I've never actually thought of,' Joe reflected when I pressed him about his mother's people, questions 'that are actually central to knowing a bit more about my own background.' According to Joe:

> All I know about [my Burke grandmother] is that I've seen her pictures, handsome pictures, which tells straight away: if there is a handsome picture of somebody, painted in 1917, there was money in that background ... I'm only going on snatches of conversations. I never sat down with my parents – I don't think Irish children did in that age – to discuss their family origin in that sort of way. She was the daughter of a strong farmer, and my grandfather was an agricultural labourer. Agricultural labourers and the daughters of strong farmers did not marry. You know, that's crossing a class divide – it's not called class in Irish folklore, Irish verbal

---

1   Collection of the Lee Family, Joe Lee Oral History with Marion R. Casey, 8 Jan. 2018, audio, 49:24. This essay is principally drawn from two oral histories conducted with Joe Lee in New York City in 2017 and 2018, as well as 20 years of conversations as his friend and colleague at Glucksman Ireland House, New York University.

culture, but there was a very sharp class divide between landless labourers and farmers of any type, particularly strong farmers … She must have been a woman of great sense of character because I can't imagine that was regarded as a good match for her. She's marrying down in a way, right? And there are very few strong farmers who would allow their daughters to marry in any way [like that], unless the daughter was extremely strong-headed.[2]

Despite Joe's assumptions, class may not have been as great a factor after all when 36-year-old Martin Burke married 30-year-old Annie Geoghegan around 1910. 'Memory can mislead as well as lead,' observed fellow historian Richard White.[3] In 1895 the Midland Great Western Railway Company opened a line from Galway to Clifden via Oughterard, creating high demand for accommodations, for anglers who wanted to fish on Lough Corrib and tourists exploring Connemara. Annie's mother, Catherine Geoghegan (b. 1851), and grandmother, Catherine Holleran (b. 1813),[4] were both widows who ran a hotel on the Main Street (Faugh West) from at least the turn of the century,[5] one of three in the town.[6] John Geoghegan, Annie's father, had been dead since 1890, so he couldn't object to the marriage; perhaps his aging wife was actually happy with the match. Joe only remembers a very fine house in Oughterard with thirteen bedrooms, 'a lovely field going down to the river behind [and] an orchard along the way', as well as an island in the lake where the Burkes grazed cattle. But none of it ever registered with him in any economic sense. 'I'm thinking about this for the first time in my life … I just took it for granted as a young kid,' he said, wondering aloud if his grandfather was a hired man for the Geoghegans, at the same time recalling that 'there are still fields in Oughterard, or there were, that were shown to me as belonging to him.'[7] *Him* not *her*.

---

2   Collection of the Lee Family, Joe Lee Oral History with Marion R. Casey, 7 Apr. 2017, audio, 15:06–17:25.

3   Richard White, *Remembering Ahanagran: A History of Stories* (New York, 1998), p. 4.

4   Catherine Halloran [sic] is recorded in the same place (townland of Kilcummin) in Griffith's Valuation in 1855. How she survived the famine is lost to history: the local population dropped by more than 3,000 between 1841 and 1851, and a graphic account of the Hollerans in March 1847, recorded by the Protestant rector of Kilcummin, survives: 'In the house of John Holleran I found his wife very unwell. I never had seen a more frightful scene than this poor man's family. I cannot conceive anything living so worn and wasted away as the children.' Murt Molloy, 'The Famine Part 6: Condition of Oughterard Poor 1847', Oughterard Heritage: A Community History of Oughterard, Co. Galway, https://www.oughterardheritage.org/content/topics/the-great-famine/the-famine-part-6, accessed 21 Jun. 2021. 'Population of Oughterard, Co. Galway', The Great Irish Famine Online, https://www.arcgis.com/apps/MapSeries/index.html?appid=8de2b863f4454cbf93387dacb5cb8412, accessed 21 Jun. 2021.

5   'Katherine [sic] Holleran, House 26 in Faugh West (Oughterard, Galway)', *Census of Ireland 1901*, http://www.census.nationalarchives.ie/pages/1901/Galway/Oughterard/Faugh_West/1394902/, accessed 21 Jun. 2021; 'Catherine Geoghegan, House 26 in Fough [sic] West, Main St. (Oughterard, Galway)', *Census of Ireland 1911*, http://www.census.nationalarchives.ie/pages/1911/Galway/Oughterard/Fough_West__Main_St_/471485/, accessed 21 Jun. 2021.

6   This was most likely Murphy's Hotel, later known as Egan's Lake Hotel or the Connemara Lake Hotel. The only other hotel on Main Street was the Angler's, operated by the Naughton family. Mary Kyne, 'Porter's Views of Oughterard', Oughterard Heritage, https://www.oughterardheritage.org/content/topics/porters-view-of-oughterard-1900s, accessed 21 Jun. 2021; 'Oughterard and Connemara: Travel and Transport to the 19th Century', Oughterard Heritage, https://www.oughterardheritage.org/content/topics/transport/oughterard-and-connemara-travel-and-transport-to-the-19th-century, accessed 21 Jun. 2021.

7   Lee, Oral History, 7 April 2017, 17:36–22:51.

In the 1911 census, Mrs. Geoghegan, 'hotel keeper', is listed as the head of the household, living with her son-in-law Martin Burke, 'farmer', not 'agricultural labourer'. Even if Martin was a *cliamhain isteach* – a man who marries into a farm that a woman has inherited (perhaps along with the hotel in this case) – it seems likely that Joe's mother and her parents were part of the west of Ireland's comfortable middle class. Annie Geoghegan Burke died in January 1919 during the influenza pandemic, when Cáit was just a year old.[8] Her portrait therefore took on a special significance for young Joe because it filled her absence in the family, as did the presence of Martin's sister Helena who moved to Oughterard from Inishdoorus, the island in Lough Cong where the Burkes had farmed for generations, to raise his four young children (Ann, Mary, Michael, Kate/Cáit).[9] The memory of that portrait reveals a complex network of relationships that was far more enduring than any class transgression.

The documented labourer was actually on Joe's paternal side. Thomas Lee and Ellen (née O'Sullivan) Lee, Joe's grandparents, raised a large family in Bohermore in the eastern part of Galway City. Thomas was said to have been in the British Army. 'It's interesting, it's only now that it begins to come back to me,' Joe commented in 2017, during Ireland's Decade of Centenaries, when there was an effort to be more inclusive about the history of 1912–1922.

> That was never spoken of. I only discovered that afterwards. Because, of course, that went very much out of fashion once we became independent. There were 150,000 Irish in the First World War, or maybe 200,000 ... but you did not talk about that obviously. It did not occur to me but now, because I'm much more familiar with historiography and so on, I realised that – I won't say there was repression – but you just didn't speak about it.[10]

However, Thomas Lee was 44 years old when the First World War broke out, with a young and growing family.[11] He could have been part of the Connaught Rangers' 3rd Reserve Battalion since their recruiting depot was nearby, at Renmore Barracks. But it is far more likely that, if he served at all, it was before 1905, while he was a single man, which suggests the Boer War rather than World War I. While conflation is not uncommon when relying on shards of memory, in this case the story seems to have been coloured by retroactive political sensitivities.[12]

---

8   Geoghegan/Burke, Kilcummin Cemetery, Oughterard, County Galway, Ireland, Memorial ID 127918914, Find A Grave, https://www.findagrave.com/memorial/127918914/martin-burke, accessed 21 Jun. 2021.

9   'Helena Burke, House 2, Inishdoorus (Island), (Cong, Galway)', *Census of Ireland 1911* http://www.census.nationalarchives.ie/pages/1911/Galway/Cong/Inishdoorus__Island_/469430/, accessed 21 Jun. 2021; Tomas O Flatharta, 'Inishdoorus/Inis Dubhruis,' Galway County Heritage Office, https://heritage.galwaycommunityheritage.org/content/places/joyce-country-places/joyce-country/inishdoorus, accessed 21 Jun. 2021; Lee, oral history, 7 April 2017, 23:38.

10 Lee, Oral History, 7 Apr. 2017, 02:39.

11 'Thomas Lee, House 24, Bakermore, part of Galway East,' *Census of Ireland 1911*, http://www.census.nationalarchives.ie/pages/1911/Galway/Galway_East__Urban/Bakermore__part_of_/454081/, accessed 21 Jun. 2021.

12 No military service record for Thomas Lee could be located. In 1901 he was an unmarried 29-year-old employed in a draper's shop who was living with his elderly parents, John and Margaret Lee. House 32, Bohermore, Galway Urban, Co. Galway, *Census of Ireland 1901*,

Every summer Joe and his parents made the long journey from Kerry to Galway: first, by bus from Castlegregory to Tralee, then by train to Limerick, and another train for the last 60 miles to Galway City. On those trips, Joe met his first Americans, who were flying into Shannon Airport, which was only as old as himself. 'My mother tells me my first love was a three-year-old American girl. She and I apparently hit it off great waiting at the train station at Limerick.'[13] But, like lots of Irish families at the time, the Lees had a genuine American connection. Five aunts went to America. Two of them – Monica and Kathleen – emigrated as nuns, dying in 1943 and 1945, respectively. A third, Bridget, became a Franciscan who trained as a nurse and then worked for many years in Texas and Connecticut. Theresa later left religious life and married in Boston; her sister, Margaret, married in Trenton, New Jersey. 'You're actually making me think about people I never knew in many ways,' Joe gently accused me.[14]

The Lee boys had a different trajectory. The eldest, John, rose high up in the Electricity Supply Board (established 1927); Tom (Joe's father) became a policeman; Tony became a doctor; Michael joined the Franciscans and, as Brother Humilis, spent World War II at St Isidore's College in occupied Rome. Joe knew these uncles well and he was especially close to Humilis, so it appears that the male perspective girded his understanding of the extended Lee family experience in modern Ireland.

> If you've got a big family of nine[15] and if you're – now I'm only surmising – if you're presumably striving to be middle class, or are middle class, or are petty bourgeoisie in that sense, and all the rest of it – whatever my grandfather worked at, he had enough to obviously raise a family, to give them some education – because all that takes education, you know. And education was not free beyond primary school, beyond National School, beyond the age sort of 14 at the outside of it, maybe 12, 13, depending on how bright you were to get through sixth class. And that depended partly on the accident of your ... year of birth and things like that, when you entered school.[16]

Framing the Lee siblings in this way certainly demonstrates the pathways available for large families in urban and rural Ireland after independence: emigration, religious life, the civil service, and, far more rarely, a profession. However, it is interesting that the adult success of his father and uncles led Joe to presume that his Lee grandfather – listed as a 'general labourer' in the 1911 census – had middle-class aspirations for his sons, when the ambitions of his Burke grandfather, even if achieved through a strategic marriage, had

---

http://www.census.nationalarchives.ie/pages/1901/Galway/Galway_Urban/Bohermore__part_of/1373073/, accessed 21 Jun. 2021.

13   Lee, Oral History, 7 Apr. 2017, 00:24.

14   Carmenati Family Tree, Ancestry.com, https://www.ancestrylibrary.com/family-tree/person/tree/152092497/person/352016047460/facts, accessed 21 Jun. 2021; Lee, oral history, 7 April 2017, 30:25.

15   It appears that Joe only knew nine of the Lees. There were two others: Nellie, who died young in 1930, and Kevin, who emigrated to North Lincolnshire, England, sometime after 1958. Carmenati Family Tree, Ancestry.com, https://www.ancestrylibrary.com/family-tree/person/tree/152092497/person/352016047460/facts, accessed 21 Jun. 2021.

16   Lee, Oral History, 7 Apr. 2017, 29:53–30:50.

just as much consequence for the next generation.[17] The women in their lives no doubt understood family economics and dynamics differently.

Joe thought it was a very American question to ask how his parents met. 'You see, you would never talk about things like that,' he said. 'Genealogy is driving the Irish economy, Joe,' I said.[18] The *Connacht Tribune* announced the wedding of 35-year-old Garda Thomas Lee, then stationed in Carraroe, to 23-year-old Katie Burke in the parish church in Oughterard on Thursday, 10 October 1940.[19] By then, who was marrying up or down was seemingly no longer relevant. 'History is the enemy of memory,' observed Richard White.[20]

******

'Malaise: 1945–1958' is the title of Chapter 4 of *Ireland 1912–1985*. It covers the period of Joe's own youth but at a remove from it that is quite astonishing. This was a period in Ireland in which the mechanics of government were still being refined, especially in the wake of the 1937 Constitution and the Second World War. The chapter demonstrates the ways in which personalities in specific departments – Seán MacEntee, J. J. McElligott and Seán Lemass, or Finance, Local Government and Industry and Commerce, for example – were managed, finessed, or circumvented under Fianna Fáil. The policy issues ranged widely: budget austerity, trade unions, children's allowance, industrial efficiency. But, at the local level in the far west of Ireland, the need for clean drinking water and sewerage was more urgent.

According to the 'Castlegregory Notes' in the *Kerry Champion*, the appalling condition of the public road, the progress of crops of onions, carrots and sugar beet, fluctuating prices at the monthly cattle fair, and the challenges of transporting the catch of fishermen to market were more relevant to local life than arguments in Dáil Éireann. In July 1942, the month Joe Lee was born, the 'Notes' author lamented:

> Of all the irregular little towns in this country I daresay Castlegregory comes first. No two houses are the same height. No two adjoining houses are covered with the same kind of roof. Some of the streets are fronted by unsightly ruins, cowsheds are unsightly constructions. Some streets have a cement pavement on one side with cobblestones or earth on the other. In places the pavement is over five feet wide, then gets beautifully less till it completely disappears. It is a pity that we have no public authority to regulate building construction. If we had, the ends of some houses would not face the street, while others are turned broadside or with an acute angle.[21]

But through the eyes of a child, Castlegregory was wonderful. Joe lived in what he described as a 'good' two-storey house on the Main Street between the Garda barracks and St Mary's R. C. Church, a distance he estimated as no more than 300 yards.

There was a fine garden out at the back. I mean, one thing that was *flúirseach*, plentiful –

---

17 Joe's maternal uncle, Michael Burke, was a senior civil servant in the social welfare office in Clifden, Co. Galway. Ibid., 24:15–25:35.
18 Ibid., 10:08–11:24.
19 'Guard's Wedding', *Connacht Tribune*, 12 Oct. 1940, p. 10.
20 White, *Remembering Ahanagran*, p. 4.
21 'Castlegregory Notes: Town Planning', *Kerry Champion*, 18 Jul. 1942, p. 8.

flúirseach is an Irish word – was land. And so, there was a fine garden that stretched back, oh, in my memory, maybe 100 yards ... And then there were fields beyond that, farmer's fields ... You know, my abiding recollection [is of] ... rabbits, rabbits, rabbits everywhere, because this was before myxomatosis.[22]

There were, in fact, about 40 million rabbits in Ireland at the time, with an entire economy and diet for the rural poor that was centred on them.[23] Joe said, 'I loved rabbits. But they didn't impinge on me and my parents. They weren't farmers, so they weren't directly affected.'[24]

The Lees did not sow a kitchen garden or eat rabbit because Joe's father was one of four Garda Síochána officers based in Castlegregory. Joe was born during the Emergency, when wartime rationing saw empty shelves in the shops. In 1943 the village poor 'were deprived of meat, butter and eggs, found it impossible to get milk and were forced to survive on bread and black tea.'[25] Severe shortages of foodstuffs and price inflation continued into 1947. Nevertheless, Joe only remembered plenty of meat and potatoes on his dinner table. He was unaware of the extent to which his mother, who relied on the shops for her provisions, might have worried about shortages, or whether a guard's social stature and a wartime bonus of seven shillings per week somehow made all the difference.[26] The flu epidemic that closed the schools in the parish during the winter of 1946 also did not make an impression, suggesting that his parents shielded their son from any adversity at the time, which influenced the positive memories of Castlegregory he had later in life.[27]

'Castle was lovely but it was very rustic,' Joe reminisced, 'so it was a very self-contained existence ... We had to make our own entertainments, whatever they were. And they were not elaborate. You'd be doing hopscotch and jump, that sort of stuff.'[28] He attended the local national school where the headmaster was the former Gaelic footballer Pat 'Aeroplane' O'Shea, assisted by his wife, plus Mrs Rohan and Mrs Cummins.

Really, it was like an extension of home. You know, they were all friends with everybody, everybody knew them. And a village doesn't realise how tightly knit it is until you go and live outside it ... You're thinking of them as neighbours and friends, etc. And they're keeping in touch with your parents, normally with your mother, about how you're getting on, this sort of stuff. I'm probably making it sound more idyllic.[29]

---

22 Lee, Oral History, 8 Jan. 2018, 03:00–6:00. The description is of the townland of Martramane, Castlegregory Electoral District. Irish Townlands, https://www.townlands.ie/kerry/corkaguiny/killiney/castlegregory/martramane/, accessed 21 Jun. 2021.

23 Myxomatosis was a disease introduced to Ireland in 1954 as a 'progressive' farming scheme to cull the rabbit population. Michael Viney, 'A furry good history of the wild Irish rabbit', *Irish Times*, 7 Jan. 2017, https://www.irishtimes.com/news/environment/a-furry-good-history-of-the-wild-irish-rabbit-1.2924454.

24 Lee, Oral History, 8 January 2018, 5:52.

25 Martin Lynch, *The Land and People of Maharees & Castlegregory: A History 1560–1960* (Castlegregory,2016), p. 243.

26 Lee, Oral History, 8 Jan. 2018, 5:56–6:50; Lynch, *Land and People*, p. 244; Vicky Conway, *Policing Twentieth Century Ireland* (London, 2013), pp. 56, 59.

27 Lynch, *Land and People*, p. 243.

28 Lee, Oral History, 8 Jan. 2018, 32:25.

29 Ibid., 35:55.

Years later, after a lecture at Boston College, one of his classmates from Castlegregory, who had immigrated to Springfield, reconnected with Joe. It was an encounter that was deeply emotional for him because she brought him a photograph of his mother, one he had never seen before. He held back tears as he told me, 'I thought it was so lovely. You see, it's a strange – small villages are strange like that. You can have senses of obligation established even though, frankly, you have no obligation, you know, and 50, 60 years afterwards, they can still operate … It was just so, so, so sweet.'[30] For a boy growing up in Kerry, Gaelic football was more like breathing than mere sport. 'The one game you knew about was football,' Joe declared.

> The Castle team was quite a good team. Because it wasn't just Castle, it was Castle and the environs. Now, they had a dreadful playing pitch, it was almost – a side of a hill is putting it a bit strongly – but it sloped down near the sea … The slope was so pronounced that all the play was into one goal. So whichever side had the hill, had the ball eighty percent of the time in that half. And so, all you did was to position yourself behind that goal and you saw the whole thing.

He vividly recalled watching the future Kerry wingback Sean Murphy, from Camp, then only about 14 years old, play for Castle. 'He was a wonderful, wonderful natural footballer, because nobody taught you football … There was no coaching, there was no anything except go out and get the ball and belt it down the field … That fella [had] hands on him like, you know … the ball just dropped into them.'[31]

Published memoirs of Irish childhood are plentiful, varying from Alice Taylor's evocative *To School Through the Fields* to Frank McCourt's caustic account of poverty in *Angela's Ashes*. McCourt famously declared, 'the happy childhood is hardly worth your while.'[32] What then should we make of the way in which the mature historian Joe Lee perceived Castlegregory between 1942 and 1951? It hardly seems right to dismiss it as mere sentiment, and yet it is almost as if he saw his childhood through the same prism as De Valera's now famous 1943 radio address 'On Language & the Irish Nation':

> The ideal Ireland that we would have, the Ireland that we dreamed of, would be the home of a people who valued material wealth only as a basis for right living, of a people who, satisfied with frugal comfort, devoted their leisure to the things of the spirit – a land whose countryside would be bright with cosy homesteads, whose fields and villages would be joyous with the sounds of industry, with the romping of sturdy children, the contest of athletic youths and the laughter of happy maidens, whose firesides would be forums for the wisdom of serene old age. The home, in short, of a people living the life that God desires that men should live.[33]

From a nostalgic perspective, Joe was indeed that sturdy child, romping through fields full of rabbits and relishing everything his mother cooked for him. His fireside was warmed by hard turf that 'would have been coal if it could have been', from a high bog that looked out over the Atlantic: 'it was one of the loveliest places on God's earth … In that sense, it was

---

30   Ibid., 01:09:20.
31   Ibid., 37:28–39:58.
32   Frank McCourt, *Angela's Ashes* (New York, 1996), p. 11.
33   Éamon De Valera, 'On Language & the Irish Nation,' in *Speeches and Statements by Eamon De Valera: 1917–73,* ed. Maurice Moynihan (Dublin, 1980), p. 466.

heaven on earth.'[34] The Catholicism of his youth was a 'very, very, very religious milieu, not sanctimonious, but religious'.[35] His mother was devout, with a deep faith: 'She would have rosary beads and she'd be in church and all the rest of it … We're talking about a different world now. Yes, we are. My mother said to me, 'John Joseph, you're named after St John and St Joseph.' He was baptised in St Mary's in Castlegregory; the village tailor, Sandy Kelliher, was his godfather. 'Oh, Lord, you see, we were [such] close-knit families,' Joe said about the community. Or, in Alice Taylor's words, 'Neighbours came to our house and we went to theirs as freely as the birds flew across the sky; invitations were unheard of and welcomes unquestioned.'[36]

In *Ireland 1912–1985*, Joe – then a man in his forties – assessed De Valera's inability to 'move existing reality in the direction of his ideal [because] many of his policies directly subverted it'.[37] Ironically, even though Joe didn't connect his book with his own family history, Castlegregory during Joe's youth is proof of this. There were few quality-of-life improvements there while Fianna Fáil was in power.

Thomas Lee previously had been posted to the village of Shrule, Co. Mayo, population 1,005 according to the 1936 census.[38] Settling his new bride (whose hometown had nearly 500 residents) in Castlegregory in the 1940s – a village half that size and 16 miles from the nearest town – must have been quite an adjustment for the couple.[39] Conditions there made a 1945 visitor 'shudder' at 'the sight of green germ-laden pools of sewage flowing down the sides of streets' and declare that he 'had seen nothing as revolting in any little town compared to this.'[40] In January 1947 the *Kerry Champion* was still bemoaning the lack of government attention to local services that could have addressed soil erosion on the coast and flooded roads and waste management in Castlegregory.[41] 'The Castlegregory sewerage scheme which was to be put up for contract has apparently been left in abeyance,' the newspaper reported in May 1948. 'All the authorities agree that this scheme is very necessary, so it is hard to understand why it is not being advertised.'[42] It was late 1949 before funds were allotted to repair the roads and for officials from the Department of Agriculture to visit the village.[43] At the same time, the local chapter of Muintir na Tíre took up a house-to-house collection to buy kerosene lamps to light the streets during the winter – 'a long-felt want' – that 'met with a generous response.'[44] In fact, the village

---

34   Lee, Oral History, 8 Jan. 2018, 8:20.
35   Lee, Oral History, 7 Apr. 2017, 4:14-5:22.
36   Alice Taylor, *To School Through the Fields* (Dingle: Brandon Books, 1998, 2nd edn), p. 7.
37   J. J. Lee, *Ireland 1912–1985: Politics and Society* (Cambridge, 1989), p. 334.
38   Lee, Oral History, 7 Apr. 2017, 11:24; 'Shrule, Co. Mayo,' *Census of Ireland, 1936, Volume 1,* Table 11, Population, Area and Valuation of Each District Electoral Division, Urban District, Rural District and County, p. 115, Central Statistics Office, https://www.cso.ie/en/media/csoie/census/census1936results/volume1/C_1936_Vol_1_T11.pdf, (Ireland), accessed 21 Jun. 2021.
39   'Oughterard, Co. Galway' and 'Castlegregory, Co. Kerry,' *Census of Ireland, 1946,* Volume 1, Population, Area and Valuation of Each DED and Each Larger Unit of Area, pp 133, 137, Central Statistics Office, https://www.cso.ie/en/media/csoie/census/census1946results/volume1/C_1946_V1_T13.pdf, accessed 21 Jun. 2021.
40   *Kerry Champion,* 18 Aug. 1945, quoted in Lynch, *Land and People,* p. 261.
41   *Kerry Champion,* 11 Jan. 1947, p. 3.
42   Ibid., 15 May 1948, p. 3.
43   Ibid., 12 Nov. 1949, p. 1; Ibid., 26 Nov. 1949, p. 1.
44   Ibid., 29 Oct. 1949, p. 4; Ibid., 19 Nov. 1949, p. 4.

without public lighting at night was referred to in the 'Castlegregory Notes' as 'The Dark Hole of Calcutta.'[45] Joe remembers how the whole village came out to watch the lights go on; Sunday, 20 November 1949 'was the beginning of a new era.'[46] The *Kerry Champion* congratulated those who had undertaken the initiative and reported that funds would be raised to purchase four more lamps.[47] The sewage scheme finally arrived in 1949 too.[48]

Joe's parents were warm admirers of De Valera, so politically Kerry South was a copacetic move for the Lees since the constituency mainly supported Fianna Fáil. When his father 'was in uniform, he wouldn't talk politics at all' Joe recalled. 'He had to be in civilian clothes to even mention politics.' Joe did not know whether any of the Lees were involved in the national struggle. His father had been a young teenager during the War of Independence; the Black and Tans shot one of his neighbours in Bohermore in 1920. Obviously, they were not untouched by events at that time or during the subsequent civil war, but life was complicated.[49]

> Even though [my father] joined the guards when it would have been very much under Cumann na nGaedhael control, he always … felt that De Valera cared far more – which I think was true – cared far more for ordinary people than the head phalanx of Cumann na nGaedhael at that time, where you had, you know, you had a significant number of very well off people … Dad had a very intense sense of fairness in every aspect of his life, and I think he just applied that to politics as to everything else … He would keep off topics that he felt might be divisive. He had integrity, very much so.[50]

Besides, guards were not allowed to vote.[51]

Tom Lee's silence was wise because support for national politics shifted during his tenure in Castlegregory, a period for Ireland in which there was increasing tension between the Gardaí and the IRA. Castle's contribution to the War of Independence was prominently commemorated by a Celtic cross, just steps from the Lee home on the corner near St Mary's, erected before a crowd of 900 in April 1934. It was inscribed with the names of the fallen from the Kerry No. 1 Brigade, 4th Battalion who were remembered annually thereafter. Anti-Treaty partisanship lingered in the area so that support for De Valera was only natural; his visit to Castlegregory in February, just before the 1932 election, had been the biggest public spectacle in the village since its centennial commemorations of 1798.[52] However, Fianna Fáil's tacit acceptance of partition and official suppression of the IRA quickly led to disillusionment. Michael A. O'Donnell, a former Sinn Féin member of the Kerry County Council, formed the Castlegregory branch of Cumann Poblachta na hÉireann in June 1936 and named it after John Casey, 'the first secretary of the local Sinn

---

45   *Kerry Champion*, 18 Mar. 1937, quoted in Lynch, *Land and People*, p. 260.
46   Lee, Oral History, 8 Jan. 2018, 19:57.
47   *Kerry Champion*, 26 Nov. 1949, p. 1.
48   Lynch, *Land and People*, p. 262.
49   Hugh Tully was shot in his house in St. Brigid's Terrace, Bohermore, Galway. 'Witness Statement No. 714, Thomas Hynes', p. 17, Bureau of Military History, Military Archives (Ireland), https://www.militaryarchives.ie/collections/online-collections/bureau-of-military-history-1913-1921/reels/bmh/BMH.WS0714.pdf#page=19, accessed 21 Jun. 2021.
50   Lee, Oral History, 8 Jan. 2018, 42:13.
51   Conway, *Policing Twentieth Century*, p. 62.
52   Lynch, *Land and People*, pp. 206–207, 209.

Féin Club [who had been] shot dead by Free State soldiers on 17 November 1922.' There was also rising support for the Labour Party after the election of Dan Spring as Teachta Dála (TD) for Kerry in 1943. By 1944, after the hanging of Charlie Kerins, 'De Valera was condemned in Kerry.'[53]

An Irish policeman in the 1940s was in regular contact with his community and had 'an exceptionally high level of local knowledge' that made him 'indispensable to the administration of the state.'[54] But the rank and file were largely unsupported by the Irish government when it came to salary and 'substandard accommodation.'[55] There were 7,500 guards in Ireland by 1948; they were always on call (an 88-hour week in rural areas), had two days off a month, were not paid for overtime, and had few prospects for promotion. A guard 'could be transferred to any part of the country with one week's notice.' Married men usually slept in the barracks every other night; there may have been some leeway about that in tiny Castlegregory, where Tom Lee rented a house only a few doors from the barracks.[56] The worst crime Joe remembered his father confronting in Castlegregory was an encounter he had while on night duty. 'I don't know what this country is coming to,' he said to seven-year-old Joe about a man out late on his bicycle without a light.[57] On reflection, Joe concluded that 'they were the straightest men, the most decent men you could find.'

★★★★★★

In his memoir, *Warrenpoint,* our late distinguished colleague at Glucksman Ireland House, Denis Donoghue defined a village as 'a community surrounded by fields: the people are farmers, or they serve farmers and their families as shopkeepers, nurses, doctors, teachers, priests. At Sunday Mass the men wear caps, not hats, and after Mass they stand around the church to chat, gossip, or stare at the hills.'[58] As a child, Joe Lee was unaware of the complexities of the agricultural economy that swirled all around Castlegregory, whose small businesses depended upon yields from the soil. Being the son of a transient, landless Garda bestowed a different relationship to the area than for those who farmed it. The long road to proprietorship had been dangerous and costly for former tenants; now, post-independence conditions, especially unforeseen debts, annually threatened their ability to hold on to precious acres.[59]

---

53   Ibid., pp. 210–211.
54   Conway, *Policing Twentieth Century*, p. 61.
55   Ibid., p. 64.
56   Ibid., pp. 59–60.
57   Lee, Oral History, 7 April 2017, 39:34–41:46.
58   Denis Donoghue, *Warrenpoint* (New York, 1994), pp. 9, 12–13. Denis's family background was similar to Joe's. His father, a native of Cloghernoosh, Beaufort, Co. Kerry, was an RIC sergeant stationed in Tullow, Co. Carlow, where he met and married the granddaughter of Bridget Coady, an 'egg exporter' who lived with her sons, Martin ('shop man provisions') and Lawrence ('farmer'). 'Johanna O'Neill, House 9, Bridge Street, Tullow Urban, Carlow,' *Census of Ireland 1911*, http://www.census.nationalarchives.ie/pages/1911/Carlow/Tullow_Urban/Bridge_Street/312880/, accessed 21 Jun. 2021.
59   White, *Remembering Ahanagran*, pp. 66–76, describes the Walsh family struggle to hold onto land near Ballylongford, Co. Kerry.

When Joe was a young boy, Castlegregory's principal farmlands set with crops were the Maharees, a flat isthmus in the Atlantic off the larger Dingle Peninsula. Vegetables from the Maharees had established a good reputation. According to a 1926 report in *The Kerryman*, 'the most industrious people in this county are in this sandy peninsula. We send deputations to Denmark and other countries to ascertain what their inhabitants wring from comparatively unproductive soils, but where is the country that supports a bigger population in comparative plenty and contentment in an area the size of this apparently sandy waste?'[60] This was confirmed by the local parish priest who observed in 1928 that an

> extraordinary spirit of industry … prevails through the length and breadth of the parish. Motoring through the parish these mornings between half-past six and seven o'clock, on the way to Stations, I have seen men and women, boys and girls, at this early hour, sometimes in heavy rain, working hard in the fields. The same persons I have seen still at work when darkness has fallen at half past six or seven in the evening.[61]

Among the challenges to a work ethic born of sheer necessity – in 1930, 80 farms of three acres or less in the Maharees were dependent upon growing potatoes[62] – was first and foremost disease. It was an issue that drew the attention of the Department of Lands, which suggested changing the seed and crop rotation, then finally that the land should be left fallow for several years. None of this relieved the economic insecurity of local families. Fianna Fáil was anxious to avoid reports of potato failure; Kate Breen, a 'personal friend' of De Valera and a member of the Kerry County Council who lived in Castlegregory,[63] downplayed distress among area farmers. Then the Great Depression exacerbated conditions until potatoes had to be abandoned altogether.[64] Where once the Scotch Champion variety had grown, soon sugar beet prevailed. It was a labour-intensive but good cash crop; in 1937 beet netted Maharees farmers £6,000. When the Castlegregory light railway line closed in the spring of 1939, the cost of transporting beet to Mallow, Co. Cork for processing increased. Still, nearly 300 acres of beet were sown in the early 1940s, fertilised with seaweed by hand. The reputation of the Maharees for industry was burnished by winning the All-Ireland Cup for the best sugar beet crop in 1940–1 and 1942–3. The *Kerry Champion* gloated in 1946 that 'the most efficient and up to date farming in this country is practiced in the Castlegregory area.'[65]

Onions were another alternative crop introduced to the Maharees in the 1930s by the Department of Lands and Fisheries, which subsidised the cost of its seed. In 1938 1,500 tons of onions yielded £15,000 for the district.[66] This was soon compounded, however, by the importation of foreign onions from Hungary as well as disease caused by the onion fly that undercut economic initiative. Locals sought advice on 'soil analysis, manurial and variety trials in 1943' when crops were rotting in the fields but received 'no help from the

---

60   *The Kerryman*, 31 Jul. 1926, quoted in Lynch, *Land and People*, p. 283.
61   *The Kerryman*, 27 Oct. 1928, quoted in Lynch, *Land and People*, p. 283.
62   Lynch, *Land and People*, p. 284.
63   'Served Ireland in War and Peace; Death of Miss Kate Breen Fearless Republican and Friend,' *Irish Press*, 28 Dec. 1937, p. 1.
64   Lynch, *Land and People*, pp. 283–286.
65   Ibid., pp. 288–290; *The Kerry Champion*, 2 Feb. 1946, quoted in Lynch, *Land and People*, p. 290.
66   Lynch, *Land and People*, p. 292.

Department.' As onion growing waned, carrot cultivation waxed until that market also collapsed in 1943.[67]

It was a similar tale with seaweed. The Department of Lands and Fisheries attempted to revive the production of kelp in the Maharees between 1927 and 1932. Promises were made but not kept to the satisfaction of local families who gathered, dried and burned the seaweed to increase its iodine content.[68] When lack of equipment, transport costs, export duties and competition from French trawlers impinged on the profitability of mackerel fishing in the 1920s, the government dole for the unemployed was supplemented by the labour of women and children who picked *carraigín* moss and *duileasc* to sell. During World War II, de Valera's daughter Máirín visited the area to encourage harvesting agar and 40 families in the Maharees held starvation at bay for a time in that way.[69] When all else failed, there was emigration to America or England; from the late 1930s, the Land Commission also transplanted whole families from the Dingle Peninsula to the Irish midlands. Twenty-three abandoned houses were a constant reminder to those left behind of those who disappeared from Castlegregory to resettle on farms in Meath and Kildare, far from the rhythm of life on the edge of the sea.[70] High rents for their vacated fields also generated anger in Castlegregory. Up the country, the Kerry migrants were sometimes resented by their new neighbours and still had to struggle to make their farms pay.[71]

Despite the willingness of locals to try any innovation to save their livelihoods, policy set in Dublin – even that which was inconsistent – often determined success or failure on the small tillage farms around Castlegregory. The Irish peasantry and the rural West may have been officially idealised, but agricultural efficiency there was thwarted by the politics of de Valera during Joe's childhood.[72] The mature Joe distilled this without ever knowing the precise details of how that played out among his neighbours and friends. 'It was all but impossible for an economy to expand rapidly on the basis of an agriculture that generated little increased output, that provided so limited a market for industrial products, and that operated in so seasonal a fashion that the bulk of its output was exported in a raw rather than a processed state,' he wrote. But by revisiting modern Ireland from the bottom-up (Castlegregory) rather than from the top-down (Dublin), Joe's general assessment that there was a 'dearth of enterprise' due to 'an absence of an adequate performance ethic in society' is perhaps not entirely fair.[73]

✶✶✶✶✶✶

Prior to the oral history he did with me, the 'autobiography' of Joe Lee appeared in the form of print and radio interviews. In those, the arc of his life moves very rapidly out of Castlegregory to follow his educational pathways: Ballinasloe, Gormanston, UCD, Mainz,

67   Ibid., p. 297.
68   Ibid., pp. 270–272.
69   Ibid., pp. 174–176, 273.
70   Ibid., pp. 302, 305–313.
71   Ibid., pp. 306, 308, 310, 313–314.
72   Lee, *Ireland 1912–1985*, pp. 231–232.
73   Ibid., pp. 528–530.

Peterhouse, UCC, NYU.[74] Yet, Castlegregory was actually the longest stretch in one place for Joe; even his time in Cork was broken every five or six years by a visiting professorship abroad.[75] In this sense, in the words of Alice Taylor, it was 'the nest from which [he] learned to fly.'[76]

The mountain that forms the picturesque backdrop to the village of Castlegregory is called Beenoskee, the 28th highest peak in Ireland. It is part of a range that forms the spine of the Dingle Peninsula, stretching west from Tralee for nearly 70 kilometres. My mother – born in 1931 – spent the first 19 years of her life directly on the other side of this range, as the crow flies, near the village of Annascaul. There is a 12-kilometre hiking path through Macha na Bó that figuratively connects Joe Lee with me. We ended up in the same place in life (via University College Dublin to New York University), but our Kerry origin stories are entirely different.

My family were small farmers for generations. Their long history in the area was stationary and regulated by the seasons, with little opportunity for social mobility. My grandmother was widowed young and raised seven children with the help of my great-grandparents, on a farm that was the grass of ten cows in the shadow of, and up the side of, another summit, Beennabrack. The townland's name translates as 'The Dead-end Place of the Dockleaves.'[77] One of my uncles got the farm, the other had to emigrate. One of my aunts became a nun in England, one married in the village after a stint abroad as a nurse, two others became civil servants in Dublin and Birmingham. Nothing out of the ordinary for West Kerry. Our only ancestral connection to the extraordinary was Jack Tadhg Kennedy who 'was very troublesome to the landlords' and whose sister, Bridget Kennedy Ashe, was the great-great-grandmother of the actor Gregory Peck.[78] I became only the second of my Kerry first cousins ever to go to university; my mother's immigration to New York in 1951 – around the time Joe moved from Castlegregory to Ballinasloe – made that possible.

Our understanding of how family history and local history are linked is now untethered from the top-down political approach Joe took in *Ireland 1912–1985*. Less than a generation separates us in age but the timing of my arrival at UCD came as the discipline of History was rapidly evolving and expanding in Ireland. In writing this essay, I had access to training in how to interrogate the past in a different way and to sources that were still years in the future when Joe wrote his big blue book. But he left a clue embedded in its preface: 'Ireland is a country where history is autobiographical and autobiography historical.'[79]

---

74   For examples, G. Henry, 'Peripatetic Professor', in *History Ireland* 3:2 (Summer 1995), https://www.historyireland.com/20th-century-contemporary-history/peripatetic-professor/, accessed 21 Jun. 2021; and the first four minutes of Joe Lee's half-hour interview with Miriam O'Callaghan, *Sunday with Miriam*, RTÉ Radio, 24 Jun. 2018, https://audiojunkie.co/podcasts/rte-sunday-with-miriam/episodes/professor-joe-lee, accessed 21 Jun. 2021.

75   Lee, Oral History, 8 Jan. 2018, 01:12:41.

76   Taylor, *To School*, p. 9, referring to Lisnasheoga, Newmarket, Co. Cork.

77   Paul Tempan, Irish Hill and Mountain Names, http://www.mountaineering.ie/_files/Paul%20Tempan%20Irish%20Mountain%20Placenames%20-%20Feb%202012.pdf, accessed 21 Jun. 2021; Rev. John Ashe, *Annascaul: Revisited and Reviewed* (Melbourne, Australia, 1949), p. 7.

78   'Witness Statement No. 1413, Tadhg Kennedy', p. 3, Bureau of Military History, Military Archives, https://www.militaryarchives.ie/collections/online-collections/bureau-of-military-history-1913-1921/reels/bmh/BMH.WS1413.pdf#page=1, accessed 21 Jun. 2021; Tomas Aghas, 'Letters to the Editor: Gregory Peck and Thomas Ashe' *The Kerryman*, 4 Apr. 1986, p. 18.

79   Lee, *Ireland 1912–1985*, p. xii.

When he described how Ireland was controlled by 'flint-minded men and women whose grandparents had done well out of the Famine and who intended to better themselves out of the Free State,'[80] Joe believed he owed his own career solely to the commitment of his parents – a gentle couple somehow apart from the deep recesses of the Irish past – to educating their only child. He framed his personal story consistently in terms of intellectual illumination, such as the good marks at school and the scholarships that got him to university and then beyond. Details like the 'unlinked bits of genealogical gossip' that lay buried underneath were then superfluous.[81] Nevertheless, over the course of the century following the Famine, women and men in Galway made life decisions that led to the birth of a child in Kerry in 1942. Castlegregory may have rendered the Ireland of his boyhood as a simple plane for Joe, but the heft and dimension that J. J. Lee, historian, gave modern Ireland was in his own family too.

Left to right: Maureen and Teresa Rohan, Michael and Anna Fitzgerald, and Joe Lee dressed as 'Little Boy Blue' at the 1948 Castlegregory Carnival. Collection of the Lee Family.

---

80 Ibid., p. 158.
81 Dan Barry, *Pull Me Up: A Memoir* (New York, 2004), p. 19.

MODERNISATION, NINETEENTH-CENTURY IRELAND AND THE EARLY WRITINGS OF JOE LEE[1]

Richard Mc Mahon and Niall Whelehan

The 1960s and early 1970s represented a *sattelzeit* of sorts in modern Irish history. There were growing demands and attempts to open the Irish economy to greater international trade and to attract foreign investment, marking a discernible shift away from the protectionist policies of previous decades. There was also a greater enthusiasm for state intervention in the national economy. An increased questioning of central tenets of Irish social and cultural life emerged – be it the place of organised religion, the role of women in Irish society, or Ireland's relationship with Britain and continental Europe. The growing demands for a more open and progressive society were heard amidst an increasing recognition that Ireland, to prosper, needed to 'modernise'. These modernising voices were not always welcomed, and there was often strong resistance to progressive forms of politics and to more open forms of economic and social development.[2] It was also a time when greater violent threats to the established constitutional order emerged, particularly north of the border, contributing to growing concerns about the stability of political arrangements on the island. This occurred within an international context where radical political action, including the 1968 student protests, sought to challenge established orders in the western world and European empires relinquished formal control over some non-European territories.

Irish historical studies were not immune to these wider forces in Irish and European society, particularly the questioning of dominant cultural practices and beliefs as well as the growing influence of radical politics. Conflict in Northern Ireland also increasingly influenced interpretations of the Irish past.[3] In the mid-twentieth century, 'technical history' had dominated academic historical writing, with a strong emphasis on in-depth research, using state archives to explore the political and diplomatic history of Ireland before 1900. This, in turn, led to the revising of key tenets of older nationalist histories. From the

---

1   For the purposes of this article, 'early writings' refers to works published between 1966 and 1973. The authors are grateful to Professor Alvin Jackson and Professor Gearóid Ó Tuathaigh for their comments on a draft of this chapter. All errors and opinions are our own.

2   For an overview of this period, see Brian Girvan, 'Stability, crisis and change in post-war Ireland, 1945–1973' in Thomas Bartlett (ed.), *The Cambridge History of Ireland*, Vol. 4: *1880 to the Present* (Cambridge, 2018), pp. 381–406.

3   For an assessment of the impact of Northern Ireland on the development of Irish historical studies, see Alvin Jackson, 'Irish history in the twentieth and twenty-first centuries' in Alvin Jackson (ed.), *The Oxford Handbook of Modern Irish History* (Oxford, 2014), pp. 3–21.

1960s onwards, however, there was a greater engagement with contemporary history and, if anything, a greater emphasis on questioning nationalist 'myth' and republican readings of history. New approaches rooted in comparative social and economic history also came increasingly to the fore (without adopting, in an Irish context, the radical forms it would take elsewhere). It was in this moment that Joe Lee emerged as an important figure in Irish historical studies. His early writings, from this time, marked him out as a historian who sought to offer new and distinctive interpretations of the roots of 'modern' Irish history.

******

Lee's approach to Irish history arose, in part, from a university education that was varied and cosmopolitan. He graduated from University College Dublin (UCD) in 1962 with a degree in history and economics. After a period working as a civil servant in the Department of Finance he returned to UCD to complete an MA in History, writing on railways in nineteenth-century Ireland under the supervision of Professor of Modern History T. Desmond Williams. Irish and European history were both relatively well established at the university, and Lee credits members of the academic staff of the department with having reasonably strong comparative approaches.[4] Williams, who was to prove a key influence on Lee's early career, combined the study of European and Irish history. He was first and foremost a historian of modern Germany with particular expertise in the 1930s and the development of foreign policy under Hitler's regime. Lee adopted his mentor's interest in German history in his early career, although he explored economic and social history in the long nineteenth century, in contrast to Williams's focus on diplomacy and politics. Williams, of course, also contributed to key debates on modern Irish history. He served as co-editor of *Irish Historical Studies* and edited volumes on modern Irish history including *The Irish Struggle, 1916–1926* and *Ireland in the War Years and After, 1939–51*. He provided a stirring defence of Irish neutrality and, although from a pro-Treaty and Fine Gael background, he, like Lee, admired aspects of de Valera's 'statecraft'.[5] He also contributed to the development of Irish economic and social history, famously co-editing a collection on the Great Famine as well as a ground-breaking volume on *Secret Societies in Ireland*, to which Lee contributed an influential article on Ribbonmen.[6]

With Williams' guidance, Lee embarked on a distinctive and distinguished postgraduate career outside of Ireland, beginning at the Institute for European History (IEG) in Mainz. Here, he engaged with comparative social science and economic history methodologies then emerging in Europe. This scholarly environment left an enduring impression on his

---

4   In a 1995 interview with *History Ireland*, Lee praised the European perspective offered by Kevin B. Nowlan, who also studied in both Germany and England. 'Peripatetic professor', in *History Ireland* 2:3 (Summer 1995), pp. 44–47. Other important early influences at UCD included Maureen Wall and, outside the history department, Patrick (Paddy) Lynch, a lecturer in economics. Both are discussed below.

5   James McGuire, 'T. Desmond Williams (1921–1987)', *Irish Historical Studies*, 26:101 (1988), pp. 3–7.

6   T. Desmond Williams (ed.), *The Irish Struggle, 1916–1926* (London, 1966); Kevin B. Nowlan and T. Desmond Williams (eds), *Ireland in the War Years and After, 1939–51* (Dublin, 1969); R. Dudley Edwards and T. Desmond Williams (eds), *The Great Irish Famine: Studies in Irish History* (New York, 1957); T. Desmond Williams (ed.), *Secret Societies in Ireland* (Dublin, 1973).

approach to history. The weight he placed on particular Irish developments was influenced by a familiarity with the historiography of corresponding themes in other European societies, particularly Germany, and his writing often drew parallels between Ireland and continental Europe. Perhaps this familiarity with different theoretical and methodological approaches sharpened the sense of impatience with Irish historiography that is discernible in his early writings.

The IEG in Mainz was founded in 1950 as an independent institute with the mission to conduct scholarly research on European history. A product of the post-war atmosphere, it aimed to facilitate cross-border academic collaboration and brought together doctoral and postdoctoral fellows from different backgrounds. The 24-year-old Lee was part of a cohort of *stipendiaten*, or fellows, that was cosmopolitan by the standards of then or now, including large numbers from communist countries, whose presence was facilitated by exchange agreements, making for a distinctive research culture. Among the 67 doctoral and postdoctoral *stipendiaten* present there during the years 1966–8, those from Czechoslovakia represented the largest group, followed closely by the USA and Germany itself, with smaller numbers from other Western European and Eastern Bloc countries, as well as Argentina, Chile, Cameroon, and one from Ireland.[7] It was a congenial environment for developing comparative perspectives.

Studying in Mainz was initially an isolating experience for Lee due to language barriers and infrequent trips home, as well as an academic culture that he found overly deferential. Yet as his German improved, he increasingly found the institute a stimulating environment. The institute was then, and still is, divided into two sections – 'universal history' and 'western religious history'. Lee was attached to the former, which encouraged international and comparative research. While he departed Mainz in 1968, he retained links with German historians, and he published research on the history of German labour, urbanisation and agriculture in the 1970s, and for a time he considered a monograph on a new economic history of modern Germany.[8] There are obvious differences between the histories of nineteenth-century Germany and Ireland, nonetheless a similar emphasis on population change, migration, and statistics can be found in his writing on both places. Lee also met Hans-Ulrich Wehler, the influential historian and pioneer of the 'Bielefeld School' of history that advanced an agenda for social history, not as a subfield, but as an all-embracing approach to history, incorporating comparative methods, elements of Marxism,

---

7   The IEG published the history of its fellowship programme in 2020 as part of the events marking its seventieth anniversary, https://www.ieg-mainz.de/en/studentships/fellowfinder, accessed 15 Nov. 2021.

8   Joseph Lee, 'Administrators and agriculture: aspects of German agricultural policy in the First World War', in J. M. Winter (ed.), *War and Economic Development* (Cambridge, 1975), pp 229–38; idem, 'Labour in German Industrialisation', in P. Mathias and M. M. Postan (eds), *Cambridge Economic History of Europe, Vol. 7*, Part 1 (Cambridge, 1978), pp. 442–91; idem, 'Aspects of Urbanisation and Economic Development in Germany, 1815–1914' in P. Abrams and E. A. Wrigley (eds), *Towns in Societies* (Cambridge, 1978), pp. 279–93.

and modernisation theory.[9] In 1978 Lee contributed a chapter to a volume edited by Wehler on German historiography in international perspective.[10]

In 1968, Lee transferred his National University of Ireland Travelling Studentship to the University of Cambridge, a move that was again facilitated by Williams and built on existing connections between UCD and Peterhouse College. Williams was a postgraduate there in the 1940s, and Herbert Butterfield, a fellow of Peterhouse, was the external examiner at UCD. Williams and Butterfield had met at UCD, and Williams's own move to Cambridge was aided by Robin Dudley Edwards, UCD's professor of modern Irish history. At the young age of 28, Williams, with Butterfield's backing, then moved back from Peterhouse to take up his position as Professor of Modern History at UCD.[11] He maintained strong links with the University of Cambridge throughout his life and continued a close and enduring friendship with Butterfield.[12] He also aided several UCD history students to undertake postgraduate research at Peterhouse College in the mid- to late-twentieth century, including Joe Lee.

By the time of Lee's arrival, Peterhouse was already home to a number of historians who were to emerge as leading figures in British social history and there can be little doubt but this had a profound impact on his approach to modern Irish history. Yet Peterhouse was renowned as a conservative college with a particular emphasis on political history and was, in that sense, a curious choice for Lee. A critique of forms of liberalism and, more obviously, the Whig interpretation of English history were, under the guiding influence of Butterfield, well-established features of historical research in the college from the 1930s. Butterfield's historical and political inclinations were rooted in a profoundly religious sensibility and in English conservatism.[13] There was obviously not too much sympathy among dominant figures within the college for modernisation theory and approaches to social history found in new universities such as Bielefeld or, indeed, Warwick in the UK, where there was a strong Marxist influence. Elements within the college in the late 1960s were highly reactionary. Most obviously, Maurice Cowling, a fellow of Peterhouse, was a mainstay of a Cambridge collective who shared Butterfield's original hostility to narratives of liberal progress and whose historical research focused on 'high politics', emphasising

---

9   Lutz Raphael, 'Bielefeld School of History', in James D. Wright (ed.), *International Encyclopedia of the Social and Behavioral Sciences*, Vol. 2, (2nd edn, London, 2015), pp. 553–8; David Blackbourn, 'Memorial: Hans-Ulrich Wehler (1931–2014)' in *Central European History* 47:4 (2014), pp. 700–15.

10 Joseph Lee, 'Britische Forschungen (1945-1975) zur modernen deutschen Sozial- und Wirtschaftsgeschichte' in Hans-Ulrich Wehler (ed.), *Die moderne deutsche Geschichte in der internationalen Forschung: 1945-1975* (Gottingen, 1978), pp. 48–63; Hans-Ulrich Wehler (ed.), *Moderne Deutsche Sozialgeschichte* (Cologne, 1968).

11 See McGuire, 'T. Desmond Williams'.

12 See Michael Bentley, *The Life and Thought of Herbert Butterfield: History, Science and God* (Cambridge: Cambridge University Press, 2011). Bentley does not offer an overly-positive assessment of Williams or of his connections with Butterfield.

13 For Julia Stapleton, for instance, Butterfield, in his historical writing and political thought, represented a 'fine expression of English conservatism'. Julia Stapleton, 'Modernism, the English past, and Christianity: Herbert Butterfield and the Study of History' in *Historical Journal* 5:2 (2008), p. 557.

narrow political self-interest over the power of political principle or ideology.[14] Cowling and others, including Michael Bentley and John Vincent, are sometimes credited with exercising at least some influence on the 'intellectual' development of Conservative politicians in the 1980s (with the benefit perhaps of providing *ex post facto* support for a perspective that places an undue emphasis on self-interest as a primary force in politics).

The influence of Butterfield and the UCD-Peterhouse connection on the development of historical research in Ireland has, of course, been a subject of much comment. Brendan Bradshaw regarded Butterfield's *The Whig Interpretation of History* as a touchstone text for Irish revisionism with the underlying Rankean approach permeating critiques of the grand narrative of Irish nationalist history.[15] 'Technical history', which lay at the heart of Butterfield's vision in the 1930s, was certainly in tune with the approaches adopted by Dudley Edwards and T. W. Moody when establishing *Irish Historical Studies*. The *weltanschauung* of historians at Peterhouse and among the pioneers of Irish historical studies was, in some respects, similar. As Jackson points out, prominent Irish revisionist historians, both Catholic and Protestant, in the mid-twentieth century, were, like their Butterfieldian counterparts in Cambridge, often steeped in and ultimately shaped by a deeply religious view of the world. Dudley Edwards was a progenitor of Irish revisionism and a devout Catholic, while religious adherence and a faith in 'Christian civilisation' were central to the lives of prominent figures such as Moody and J. C. Beckett.[16] In this sense, both historians at Peterhouse and prominent Irish historians were engaged in often pious critiques of narratives of progress, be they liberal or nationalist. The attachment to a form of 'technical history', which sought to eschew grand narratives and rooted historical understanding in detailed and ideally uncontroversial research, was arguably stronger within Irish than British historical writing in the mid-twentieth century.[17] Williams, who did much to guide Lee's early career, was shaped by his time at Peterhouse and, although there were differences in approach, he is often regarded as remaining, in the words of James McGuire, a 'good Butterfieldian'. He certainly placed a strong emphasis on political and diplomatic history and also on 'the role of personality', which is something that also emerges, in various guises, as a key factor in much of Lee's work.[18]

While there is an imprint of a Butterfieldian approach in his scholarship, it would nonetheless be hard to locate Lee within this tradition. He was clearly willing to plough a different furrow to both master and mentor. His early work was very critical of the

---

14   Richard Brent, 'Butterfield's Tories: "high politics" and the writing of modern British history' in *Historical Journal*, 30:4 (December 1987), pp. 943–954.

15   Brendan Bradshaw, 'Nationalism and historical scholarship in modern Ireland' in *Irish Historical Studies*, 26:104 (1989), pp. 329–351.

16   Jackson, 'Irish history in the twentieth and twenty-first centuries', pp. 5–6.

17   The extent of enthusiasm for 'technical history', of course, could vary from scholar to scholar and not all prominent Irish historians of the time fully embraced it. See, for instance, the discussion of the work of J. C. Beckett in Alvin Jackson, 'J. C. Beckett: Politics, Faith, Scholarship', *Irish Historical Studies*, 33, 130 (2002), pp. 145–146.

18   McGuire, 'T. Desmond Williams', p. 5. For a very different interpretation of Williams, see John Regan, *Myth and the Irish State* (Dublin: Irish Academic Press, 2013). Regan sees Williams as drifting far from the moorings of the 'technical history' advocated by Butterfield and rather regards him as pursuing a 'treatyite public history', which involved the ignoring of crucial evidence in pursuit of politically comforting but ultimately unsound historical narratives.

focus on 'high politics' in historical research. He decried the overwhelming emphasis on official documents and diplomatic history in an Irish context and suggested that Rankean approaches left little room for methodological innovation. If anything, he ultimately leaned more towards Burkhardt than Ranke. Lee, a Petrean, was not of the 'Peterhouse school'.[19] Too great a contrast also should not be drawn between historiographical traditions encountered in Germany and England. An emphasis on 'personality' in history was by no means a phenomenon found exclusively at Cambridge. While focusing on broad social forces and modernisation theory, Wehler also incorporated studies of the personalities of major figures in modern German history. Later, the major German historian Thomas Nipperdey, who Lee greatly admires, linked broad economic and social forces and political developments with an emphasis on the importance of individual action in his studies of nineteenth-century German history.[20] There was also much more to Cambridge and, indeed, Peterhouse in the 1960s and 1970s than figures such as Cowling. Whatever Butterfield's influence over Irish historical studies, and allowing for the tendency among some Irish historians to emphasise how political principle could be utilised to mask narrow self-interest, the overwhelming majority of Irish historians did not embrace a Cowlingite 'high politics' approach in the 1970s and 1980s, and it was something that Lee rejected.[21]

Of greater importance was that Cambridge and, indeed, Peterhouse were home to historians at the forefront of developing social history as a major force in British history and these historians, while generally eschewing more radical approaches, also rejected the exclusive and narrow ground of 'high politics' favoured by Cowling and others. It was among these scholars that Lee was to find his natural home. Indeed, if anything, he was fortunate to arrive at a vibrant time for those with an inclination towards the social and he had the opportunity to engage with some of the most important British social historians of the time. The Group for the History of Population and Social Structure at Cambridge was, for instance, cofounded by E. A. Wrigley and Peter Laslett in 1964, just a few years before Lee's arrival. Wrigley, a fellow of Peterhouse, became a key figure in English economic and social history, and his book *Population and History* is widely regarded as a classic.[22] He developed new and innovative statistical approaches and weaved issues of demography,

---

19 Cowling would later, amidst a rancorous and brutal dispute with Hugh Trevor-Roper, claim that Lee coined the phrase 'the Peterhouse School of History'. Maurice Cowling, 'A reply to Hugh Trevor-Roper', in *The New York Review of Books*, 10 Apr. 1986.

20 Thomas Nipperdey, *Germany from Napoleon to Bismarck: 1800-1866* (trans. Daniel Nolan, New Jersey, 1996).

21 Cowling continues to have admirers among modern British historians, see, for instance, Robert Crowcroft, 'Maurice Cowling and the Writing of British Political History' *Contemporary British History*, 22, 2, 2008, pp. 279–86. In contrast, it is difficult to identify modern Irish professional historians who consciously or openly acknowledge their adoption of his conservative 'high politics' approach, although the work of some has been noted as containing elements of this tendency. See, for instance, Brent's discussion of R. F. Foster's *Lord Randolph Churchill* (Oxford: Oxford University Press, 1981) in Brent, 'Butterfield's Tories'. See also the discussion of Foster and others in M.A.G. Ó Tuathaigh, 'Irish Historical 'Revisionism': State of the Art or Ideological Project?' in Ciaran Brady (ed.), *Interpreting Irish History: The Debate on Historical Revisionism, 1938-1994* (Dublin, 1994), pp 319–21. For Lee's reflections on this issue, see J. J. Lee, 'Gearóid Ó Tuathaigh' in John Cunningham and Niall Ó Ciosáin (eds.), *Culture and Society in Ireland since 1750: Essays in Honour of Gearoid Ó Tuathaigh* (Dublin, 2015), pp. 15–47, 32–33.

22 E. A. Wrigley, *Population and History* (London, 1969).

economy, and society together, and it is not difficult to detect similar concerns running through Lee's work in the 1960s and 1970s. Lee became friends with Wrigley and held him in high regard, and contributed an essay on German urbanisation to a collection edited by Wrigley and Philip Abrams.[23] Abrams, another fellow at Peterhouse, was a rising sociologist and on the editorial board of *Past and Present*. The distinguished American sociologist Edward Shils, a professor at the University of Chicago and a fellow at Peterhouse college from 1970–8, also influenced Lee's work. Shils placed an emphasis on intellectuals, political development and modernisation and Lee's later book *Ireland 1912–1985* admiringly cited his research.[24] Peter Laslett, who had originally studied at Peterhouse under Butterfield, is also regarded as a key figure in the development of the history of political thought at Cambridge and crucially as a major figure in the development of British social history. His book *The World We Have Lost* influenced a range of scholars working in the field of social history in Britain and beyond.[25] The combination of interests in social and political history became, albeit in a distinctive form, a defining feature of Lee's work on modern Irish history. And though emerging from a conservative society and academy, albeit ones undergoing considerable change, Lee found sufficient scope to carve out a more inquiring and liberal approach to the study of the past than many Irish historians at the time.

★★★★★★

The late 1960s and early 1970s were a productive time for Lee. He published numerous journal articles and reviews relating to the economic and social history of nineteenth-century Ireland and contributed robustly to debates on the development of Irish historical studies. These articles began to fill some gaps and recalibrate approaches to core questions of Irish history. The publications were situated within both a 'social' and 'European' turn in Irish historical studies, a turn that he did much to initiate, drive, and sustain over the course of his career. One of his first essays lamented that Irish historical research was 'more concerned with the state than with society', and his work in the 1960s and 1970s was characterised by a determination to challenge the supremacy of high political history and to introduce new questions about a variety of themes from demography, interpretation of statistics, economic change, migration, rural unrest, railways and beer.[26] These early publications also set the scene for the reinterpretation of key developments in modern Irish history in the light of wider processes of 'modernisation', a theme and concept that also lay at the heart of political and cultural debates in Ireland at the time.

His early published work on railways, emerging from his MA at UCD, revealed a strong commitment to economic and social history rooted in detailed empirical research. Indeed, those seeking a compelling account of the width of railway gauges in nineteenth-century Ireland will not, on reading the work, be disappointed. Two articles in *Business History*

---

23   J. J. Lee, 'Aspects of urbanisation and economic development in Germany, 1815–1914' in P. Abrams and E. A. Wrigley (eds), *Towns and Societies* (Cambridge, 1978), pp. 279–93.

24   Edward Shils, 'Intellectuals in the political development of the new states' *World Politics*, 12, 3 (1960), pp. 329–68.

25   Peter Laslett, *The World We Have Lost* (London, 1965).

26   Lee, 'Some aspects of modern Irish historiography' in Ernst Schulin (ed.), *Gedenkschrift Martin Göhring: Studien zur Europäischen Geschichte* (Wiesbaden, 1968), p. 441.

(1967) and *Irish Historical Studies* (1968) revealed, in their footnotes alone, a characteristic willingness to mine a wide range of sources including newspapers, parliamentary papers, and archival material generated by railway companies and business directories.[27] The work and importance of individual civil engineers and contractors was also stressed; for instance, the engineer, Sir John Macneill, and the contractor, William Dargan, emerged as key figures in the early construction of Irish railways.[28] Speculators also won praise for the beneficial economic effects of their risk-taking.[29] Stylistically, this early work on railways also revealed an occasional fondness for an eye-catching phrase. Surviving railway companies in the 1840s were described as 'cripples groping their way among the corpses' of their competitors.[30] His approach was also often accompanied by an iconoclastic tone and a skill for provocative generalisation that invited further examination. A memorable 1973 essay expressed puzzlement at how an 'autumnal haze envelops Grattan's Parliament in the popular imagination', when in reality it represents 'the bloodiest repressive institution in modern Irish history'.[31] This foray into eighteenth-century Irish history also indicated an early and admirable willingness to range across different centuries in pursuit of important research themes – something that was replicated, on a grander scale, through a later engagement with twentieth-century Irish history. In this sense Lee was similar to another significant influence on his early studies, Maureen Wall at UCD. She was a specialist in the history of eighteenth-century Ireland but also lectured and published on nineteenth- and twentieth- century Ireland, including the decline of the Irish language and partition, before her untimely death in 1972.[32]

Lee's writings from these years also placed a keen emphasis on the need for detailed analyses of social structure and its profound transformation in the nineteenth-century Irish context. A dissenting review article of Raymond Crotty's *Irish Agricultural Production* (1966) challenged, in substantial detail, the book's interpretation of statistical data for the nineteenth century. Crotty downplayed the demographic and economic impact of the Famine, Lee contended, by overlooking its most dramatic consequence, 'the revolution in the rural class structure'. This article was among the first to forcefully highlight the disappearance of the Irish agricultural labourer and the social consequences of this in the second half of the nineteenth century: 'The rural proletariat was not so much transformed as buried.... This radical change in the balance of the classes must surely count as more than a "tremor" in the demographic and social structure of rural Ireland'.[33] A 1968 article in the *Economic History Review* about marriage ages in pre-Famine Ireland again called for more critical awareness of these changes in rural society and criticised K. H. Connell for 'lumping labourers and farmers together under the obfuscatory term "peasant"', which concealed important class differences within rural society, not least in terms of marriage

---

27   Joseph Lee, 'The construction costs of Irish railways, 1830–1853' in *Business History,* 9:2 (1967), pp. 95–109; Joseph Lee, 'The provision of capital for early Irish railways, 1830–53' in *Irish Historical Studies,* 16:61 (1968), pp. 33–63.
28   Lee, 'The construction costs'.
29   Lee, 'The provision of capital'.
30   Ibid., p.35.
31   Joseph Lee, 'Grattan's Parliament' in Brian Farrell (ed.), *The Irish Parliamentary Tradition* (Dublin, 1973), pp. 149–159.
32   Tom Dunne, 'Maureen Wall', *Dictionary of Irish Biography* (Cambridge, 2009), www.dib.ie
33   Joseph Lee, 'Irish agriculture' in *Agricultural History Review,* 17:1 (1969), pp. 64–76; 65.

patterns. The same article chided other historians for seeing the 1841 Census statistics as a superior source to the oral witness testimony gathered by the '1836 Poor Inquiry'.[34]

A characteristic of his early published work was a critical approach to the work of other scholars, even those he otherwise admired. Some of the more iconoclastic essays from this period were aimed at Lynch and Vaizey's history of the Guinness brewery and their theory that the pre-Famine Irish economy was divided between a monetary zone and a subsistence, barter zone. In two swashbuckling essays – a 1966 review article, accompanied by an exchange of views with the authors, and a 1971 essay – Lee provided considerable counter evidence to their claims.[35] The idea of 'geographical dualism existed only to a very limited extent', he argued, while the authors' emphasis on monetary policy downplayed the importance of structural factors in influencing economic development. As with the critique of Connell, Lee lamented how the authors ignored the complexity of social structure, grouping 'farmers with cottiers and labourers under the conceptually useless terms "peasantry" or "country folk"'. One of the authors, Paddy Lynch, was an economics lecturer at UCD, a friend of Williams' and was held in high regard by Lee. But the essay didn't pull its punches, highlighting the 'major conceptual weakness' in the book's discussion of monetary policy.[36]

Lee was also not shy in offering provocative interventions on the nature and quality of general historical practice in Ireland. In Mainz he was invited to contribute to the *Gedenkschrift* for Martin Göhring, who had served as the director of the IEG until his death in 1968.[37] Lee's essay focused on Irish historiography and is suggestive of how the IEG might have influenced his views of methodological theory and Irish history writing. The essay opened by questioning why Nicholas Mansergh, then Smuts Professor of Commonwealth History at Cambridge, had labelled the developments in Irish historiography from the 1930s to the 1960s a 'revolution'. It was difficult to know whether a revolution had happened or not, Lee argued, since so few analyses of Irish historiography existed.[38] The essay linked what he considered to be the underdevelopment of Irish historiography to, among other factors, an early-twentieth-century generation of history professors and included unforgiving assessments of some of them, unfairly so in the case of Mary Hayden, the first professor of modern Irish history at UCD. The achievements and virtues of the *Irish Historical Studies* generation were praised; at the same time, the essay described the journal's positivist approach, in which 'Ranke has superseded Carlyle', as one that left little room for discussions of theory, historiography, methodology, intellectual history or periodisation. Unlike the '*Historische Zeitschrift*, the *Revue Historique*, the *American Historical Review*, and even the *English Historical Review*', the first issue of *Irish Historical Studies* 'was

---

34   Joseph Lee, 'Marriage and population in pre-Famine Ireland', *Economic History Review*, 21, 2 (1968), p. 284.

35   Joseph Lee, 'Money and beer in Ireland, 1790–1875', in *Economic History Review*, 2nd Series 19, 1 (1966), pp. 183–90.

36   Joseph Lee, 'The Dual Economy in Ireland 1800-1850' in T. D. Williams (ed.), *Historical Studies, viii* (Dublin, 1971), pp 191–201; 193, 196, 200.

37   Lee, 'Some aspects of modern Irish historiography', pp. 431–43.

38   Ibid., p. 432.

not introduced by a historiographical survey, but plunged into a Detailstudie after a three-page declaration of editorial intent'.[39]

In contrast to developments in Europe and North America, the essay argued, the 'primacy of the ministerial file' frustratingly continued in 1960s Irish history writing. Irish social history remained understudied despite the existence of rich primary sources. It was no coincidence, Lee continued, that the only major work of cultural anthropology on rural Ireland was written by an American, the 'only really challenging interpretation' of social structure in Irish politics was 'a Heidelberg dissertation', and the only systematic Marxist approach to Irish nationalism was by an Austrian.[40] He later remarked that German historian Peter Alter's 1971 study of Irish nationalism, along with the work of Erhard Rumpf, served as 'timely reminders of the insularity of much of the English language historiography of Ireland'.[41] The essay ended with a measured sense of hope and recognised that there were new approaches incorporating methodologies 'from other social sciences and exploiting the comparative method', citing the work of David Beers Quinn.[42] The essay could have gone further here; perhaps Lee's location in Mainz led to unfamiliarity with some research in Ireland. In the next years, new publications suggested the picture was a little brighter than the one presented in the essay.[43]

The culmination of this flurry of activity in the late 1960s and its accompanying historiographical call to arms was, in many respects, the publication of *The Modernisation of Irish Society* (henceforth: *Modernisation*) in 1973. Lee's first book skilfully applied different historiographical approaches to illuminate key themes in nineteenth-century Irish history. He defined modernisation as 'the growth of equality of opportunity' and applied the concept to post-Famine transformations in Irish society, highlighting changes in traditional rural life along with the emergence of new mentalities. The concept of 'modernisation' has, of course, come under heavy attack and fallen from favour since the 1970s, but Lee chose it with the aim of linking to international scholarship and perhaps to avoid the dead weight of older nationalist and unionist readings of Irish history.[44] Indeed, the title may partially allude to the idea of modernising Irish historiography itself, given the shortcomings lamented in earlier articles, by steering it towards developments in economics and comparative social science. These provided new frameworks within which he explored more conventional forms of political history.

---

39   Ibid., p. 441.
40   Conrad M. Arensberg, *The Irish Countryman: An Anthropological Study* (London, 1937); Erhard Rumpf, *Nationalismus und Sozialismus in Irland: Historischsoziologischer Versuch uber die Irische Revolution seit 1918* (Meisenheim, 1959); Erich Strauss, *Irish Nationalism and British Democracy* (London, 1951).
41   Joseph Lee, *The Modernisation of Irish Society, 1848–1918* (Dublin, 1973), p. x; Peter Alter, *Die irische Nationalbewegung Zwischen Parlament und Revolution: der Konstitutionelle Nationalismus in Irland 1880–1918* (Munich: Oldenbourg, 1971).
42   Lee, 'Some Aspects', p. 442.
43   For example a volume on Irish historiography did appear just three years later. T. W. Moody (ed.), *Irish Historiography, 1936–70* (Dublin, 1971). The sequel to this volume was edited by Lee: Joseph Lee (ed.), *Irish Historiography, 1970–79* (Cork, 1981). A string of publications by Louis Cullen appeared between 1968 and 1973.
44   Lee, *Modernisation*, preface (no pagination).

The book's early chapters engaged with questions raised in the articles discussed above regarding changing class structure, intracommunal social tensions, emigration and population decline, deploying a range of statistical evidence in the process. The Famine provided the starting point for the book. Lee asserted the unexceptional nature of the Famine years when viewed in the light of other 'pre-industrial' subsistence crises. Instead, what was exceptional or 'peculiar' was the 'long-term response' of Irish society to the catastrophe.[45] Here the book emphasised the profound change in social structure, which saw the increasing prominence and influence of farmers in Irish society, particularly farmers with larger farms. This, in turn, contributed to Ireland becoming a 'demographic freak' in its patterns of marriage. The age at marriage rose along with the proportion of the population who remained unmarried. This he attributed less to a revolution in attitudes as to the destruction during the Famine of many of those who were most inclined to marry earlier, namely labourers.[46]

Farmers, he argued, had, both pre- and post-Famine, generally sought to protect the value of the land they held by delaying and restricting marriage among their offspring. This pragmatic and, at times, severe approach simply hardened in the post-Famine decades as the range of possible marriage partners contracted and there was greater definition to the distinctions between different social groups. Or, as he put it, 'Farmers' children preferred celibacy to labourers'.[47] Lee also explored psychological explanations for Irish marriage patterns, stressing the influence of Irish mothers over their children, in particular their sons, and how resentment towards daughters-in-law (actual or potential) may have shaped family life and wider Irish society. In a similar, quasi-Freudian analysis, he linked celibacy to mental health problems, noting how 'celibate victims' of 'economic man' were consoled by the churches.[48] Wider cultural and institutional explanations for marriage patterns were given less credence, with, at times, the Irish mammy given greater agency than the churches. For Lee, the economic priorities of Irish farming families took precedence, and the churches 'merely reflected the dominant economic values of post-Famine rural society'. The clergy were simply 'powerless to challenge the primacy of economic man over the Irish countryside'. He also highlighted the similarities hidden behind the small differences between patterns of behaviour found in Catholic and Protestant communities in Ireland and how these patterns had a profound impact on the performance of the Irish economy.[49]

For Lee, the Irish economy underperformed. This was evident in agriculture, which 'made nothing like its potential contribution to economic growth'.[50] This was not due to a lack of commercialised forms of production, as Ireland had 'one of the most commercially advanced agricultures in the world'. Irish farmers, he noted, responded to demand, in particular international demand, by concentrating their energies on forms of pasture farming, and this, in narrow economic terms, proved profitable. However, profit did not inspire innovation, but rather stagnation and lack of initiative in achieving technological

---

45 Ibid., p. 1.
46 Ibid., pp. 3–4.
47 Ibid., p. 4.
48 Ibid., p. 6.
49 Ibid., p. 6.
50 Ibid., p. 9.

advancement. As a result, the full potential for growth was not reached. The shortfall was 'substantial', as narrow individual profit motives trumped the wider potential for growth.[51]

Nor was a lack of an adequate labour supply an inhibiting factor on economic development; if anything, a high level of supply discouraged innovation. Sufficient capital was also available, but there was, for Lee, a certain lack of initiative and aversion to risk, which inhibited investment in areas of the economy. There was also a reasonable infrastructure for industrial expansion with a reasonably well-developed market economy and 'one of the densest' railway networks in the world. He linked a familiarity with commercial and market forces to literacy and again saw Ireland as well-positioned. He claimed that, even before the Famine, Ireland was a 'remarkably literate' society and that engagement with the market economy was by no means lacking. Literacy and engagement with commercial life increased in the post-Famine decades but, aside from the drinks industry, the market was dominated by imports. This, for Lee, reflected a real and genuine failure to develop native industries in much of the country – particularly clothing industries.[52]

Why did the Irish economy fail to reach its potential? Lee's answer lay, to some degree at least, in the 'quality of businessmen'. He rejected historical interpretations which downplayed the importance of entrepreneurial initiative, seeing it as crucial to economic development. It was the innovations of, often British, businessmen that he saw driving the expansion of shipbuilding in Belfast, and he bemoaned the dominance of the respectable professions (in particular, law and medicine) in drawing talent away from business and industry in much of the rest of the country. He was critical too of the 'state' and the worldview of commentators, officials and politicians who, in his view, were too often ignorant of Irish circumstances and who too readily applied English models to Irish problems with often ruinous consequences. Abstract economic thinking trumped the ability to gather and interpret reliable evidence too frequently. He reserved particular ire for those who interpreted economic development in the light of legal training, attributing to them a tendency towards abstraction and poor analysis.[53]

State interventions were 'timid' by continental standards. The book was highly critical, for instance, of state intervention in the field of education. Those who ran the system, rather than the system itself, contributed to the 'slow mental death' which left students 'incapable of prescribing for the ills plaguing Irish society'.[54] The schools were 'powerless' when it came to tackling deep-rooted sectarian feeling: indeed, it is notable how Lee often saw institutions as 'powerless' to combat wider social forces, while individuals had considerable potential to reshape economic life and social development. It was, for Lee, ultimately a failure of intellect and initiative that contributed to the failures of Irish society: poor economic growth was 'due more to intellectual irresponsibility than to political ill-will'. These intellectual shortcomings deprived Ireland of the 'state initiatives' that constituted the 'only hope for sustained economic growth' and offer proof that it was 'less the lack of mineral than of mental resources' that inhibited growth.[55] This analysis is striking for

---

51   Ibid., pp. 10–11. These arguments anticipated some themes of *Ireland 1912–1985: Politics and Society* (Cambridge, 1990).
52   Lee, *Modernisation*, pp. 11–14.
53   Ibid., pp. 20–22.
54   Ibid., p. 31.
55   Ibid., p. 35.

its emphasis on individual and intellectual initiative, within broader state structures, in shaping economic life. The influence of economic and social forces were acknowledged but ultimately regarded as ripe for manipulation through human initiative and intelligent action, an argument which would surely have appealed to those looking and calling for greater intervention and initiative in Irish economic life at the time in which Lee was writing.

Modernisation did not seek to replace political history with economic and social history, rather it sought to integrate different historical approaches within the one study. In the realm of politics and culture, it is striking that the focus of the book rested on themes that would have had considerable contemporary relevance in the late 1960s and early 1970s, namely, the role of the Catholic Church in Irish society, unionism, nationalism, the development of Irish republicanism and sectarian conflict in Ulster (particularly Belfast). On the Catholic Church, the book emphasised how, like other institutions, it was able to achieve a powerful position when serving the interests and expressing the priorities of its adherents, but it held limited sway when at odds with the 'popular will'. This is exemplified in his discussion of the Land League, which downplayed the Catholic Church's role and he contended that deference to ecclesiastical authority was weak compared to earlier decades. Similarly, his discussion of Parnell was dismissive of the clergy's role in his downfall. Rather the book firmly emphasised the loss of Irish public support due to a growing sense that Parnell had lost political influence. It was ultimately the hostile reaction of Gladstone and the nonconformist wing of the Liberal party, not initially that of the Catholic Church, that was the major factor in his defeat.[56] For Lee, 'priests, even when they presented a united front, could influence the voters only in the direction in which they wished to go'.[57] Similarly, in the context of the Plan of Campaign, 'papal condemnation' proved 'ineffective' and it was money rather the spectre of the crozier that undermined the movement.[58]

If institutions merely reflected popular opinion (though the book paid insufficient attention to how institutions shaped such opinion), then key personalities emerged as dynamic. Lee shone a positive light on Paul Cullen's role in the development of Irish Catholicism in the nineteenth century, presenting him as a pragmatic figure who skilfully managed to maintain a deep connection and allegiance to Rome while simultaneously eschewing 'the spirit of the Syllabus of Errors'.[59] The impact of his reforms, portrayed as emphasising merit over birth, was heralded as contributing to a modernising and reforming spirit in the country. Here, in a careful, perhaps even ingratiating, approach to the history of the Catholic Church in Ireland, the book offered a historical precedent for the benefits of steady and pragmatic reform, an analysis, which may again have appealed to, or at least chimed with, those interested in encouraging reform as a means of strengthening the power and position of the Catholic Church in Ireland and elsewhere at the time.

The analysis of sectarianism was imbued with an enthusiasm for the potential of modernisation processes to overcome the debilitating conflicts of the past. He noted the

---

56   Ibid., p. 115.
57   Ibid., p. 120.
58   Ibid., p. 114. For a notable critique of Lee's interpretation of the role of the Catholic Church in nineteenth-century Ireland, see, J.S. Donnelly, 'Review of *The Modernisation of Irish Society, 1848-1918, by Joseph Lee*', *Irish Historical Studies* 1976, 20 (78), pp. 206–212.
59   Ibid., p. 47.

potential benefits of industrialisation and urbanisation in overcoming the 'rural roots of prejudice' but conceded, quite rightly, that ultimately they 'became instead powerful agencies for the perpetuation and accentuation of sectarian animosity'. He lamented in particular that Belfast in 1857 missed 'the final entry to the modernisation highway and continued to grind relentlessly around the traditional track for the rest of the century.'[60] This constituted a relatively rare excursion into the territory of Irish exceptionalism. It also fed into (perhaps largely revisionist) narratives, which stressed the integral nature of sectarianism in Irish life and the persistence of traditional (rural) quarrels in direct contradiction to the obvious benefits of enlightened (urban) modernity. This reading of Irish sectarianism, with its focus on Belfast, perhaps too quickly and untypically abandoned the benefits of a comparative framework. It rather isolated Belfast from wider British and even Atlantic contexts where the forces of 'modernity' also often coexisted with and complemented those of deep religious convictions and where deep sectarian animosity also lived quite happily, if less violently, in industrial cities.[61]

The book was occasionally critical of leading nationalists in the late-nineteenth century but displayed some admiration for broader nationalist movements. Michael Davitt was portrayed as somewhat naïve. Parnell, while admired for effective leadership, exceptional political skill and as a moderniser, was regarded as having limited intellectual merits. Local agitators were presented in a sympathetic light. James Daly, the editor of the *Connaught Telegraph*, was depicted as highly effective in mobilising support for the Land League.[62] Lee's account of Fenianism was quite dismissive of its organisational capacities, nonetheless he regarded the movement as helping to 'broaden petty horizons' and, in the 1870s and 1880s, 'infusing constitutional politics with a vigour and determination lacking hitherto'.[63] The Land War was presented as a crucial turning point in processes of modernisation and a considerable proportion of the book – two of its six chapters – dealt with the agitation of 1879–82. The emergence of the Land League in County Mayo was rooted in an economic crisis but was also driven by a 'vigorous leadership cadre' and by a 'revolution of rising expectations' among the wider population in the post-Famine decades. He saw it as a movement from below, arguing that for 'the first time in Irish history the masses came on to the political stage as leading players rather than extras'.[64] Crucially, the movement reflected a fundamental change in Irish society whereby traditional forms of economic and social interaction, rooted in deference to the claims of birth, were overturned. A new consciousness emerged as people began to conceptualise society in abstract rather than strictly personal terms, with critiques of 'landlordism' appearing, whereas before, Lee argued, critiques of individual landlords prevailed. The Land War marked 'the definitive modernisation of the peasant mind' and 'constituted a revolution in mentalities which the deferential famine generation could scarcely credit'.[65] The agitation was remarkable too for

---

60 Ibid., pp. 52–3.
61 For a history of sectarianism in nineteenth-century Belfast with a strong comparative dimension, see Mark Doyle, *Fighting Like the Devil for the Sake of God: Protestants, Catholics and the Origins of Sectarian Violence in Victorian Belfast* (Manchester, 2009).
62 Lee, *Modernisation*, pp. 69–70.
63 Ibid., pp. 57–58.
64 Ibid., pp. 70–72.
65 Ibid., p. 96.

both its rural roots and its underlying organisational sophistication. Lee was more sceptical, however, about the fundamental economic achievements of the movement, noting that it brought limited improvement in agricultural output and there was no transformation in the fortunes of ordinary farmers. Yet the predictions of economic ruination made by the defenders of the status quo proved unfounded and were, he argued, rooted in an even more limited analysis of the prevailing circumstances than that provided by reformers.[66]

As the book moved toward the twentieth century it discussed political developments and leaders in considerable depth. Douglas Hyde, Patrick Pearse and James Connolly all received lengthy treatment, as did the 1916 Rising. Hyde fared badly, and he and the Irish Ireland generation had, Lee claimed, mistakenly equated 'modernisation with anglicisation' and failed to recognise how the developments they resisted at the turn of the twentieth century were 'occurring more or less simultaneously in all European countries, without in the least involving their "anglicisation"'.[67] This rather partial assessment of Hyde failed to recognise his enthusiasm for elements of 'modernisation', of which his language movement was a part, something which Lee later acknowledged in the preface to the 2008 edition of the book.[68] The underlying distinction drawn between 'anglicisation' and 'modernisation' also, in hindsight, appears rather crude. It does not engage sufficiently with how patterns of mass consumption, state intervention and cultural expression, while displaying characteristics found elsewhere in Europe, were also profoundly shaped by English thought and culture. The claim, moreover, that the increasing adoption and dominance of the English language was 'not crucial' is debateable.[69] In contrast to Hyde, key figures involved in the 1916 Rising were commended by Lee. Connolly was deemed 'the most remarkable man of his generation in Irish politics' and was notable in a wider European context too as 'the only unskilled labourer among European socialist intellectuals, and one of the few intellectuals among European trade unionists'.[70] Pearse was considered a moderniser, particularly on matters of education and for emphasising merit over birth. While prone to 'logical confusion', he was relatively sophisticated in his thinking and could not be categorised as 'reactionary'. Lee, indeed, presented a reasonable case that the logic of organising a rising during the First World War was sound (if the principle that a rising was justified is accepted). He also refuted any suggestion that the Rising was fundamentally rooted in a flawed romanticism; rather, the 1916 Proclamation was 'dedicated to the modernisation of Irish society' and had 'promised equality of political, social, economic, and religious opportunity'.[71]

******

There are strands of Lee's work on Ireland in the long nineteenth century that fit within

---

66   Ibid., pp. 99–105.
67   Ibid., p. 140.
68   Joseph Lee, *The Modernisation of Irish Society, 1848–1918* (Dublin, 2008), preface (no pagination).
69   Lee, *Modernisation* (1973), p. 139.
70   Ibid., p. 151.
71   Ibid., p. 155. This reading of Pearse clearly contrasted with revisionist interpretations published in the same decade, for example, Ruth Dudley Edwards, *Patrick Pearse: The Triumph of Failure* (London, 1977).

already well-established approaches in Irish historical studies, and historical writing generally, in the mid-twentieth century. There was an attachment to detailed empirical research and often a keen focus on central political developments. The 'personality' (particularly the intellectual strengths and weaknesses) of key figures looms large in the narrative, perhaps reflecting some of Edward Shils' influence. This approach arguably also fits within a broad Butterfieldian framework and reflects the influence of certain dominant figures at Peterhouse and UCD. There was certainly no outright rejection in Lee's early work of the methods advocated by the founding fathers of Irish historical studies in the early to mid-twentieth century. At the same time, there was no mere acceptance of the status quo. Rather Lee engaged in a progressive and open questioning of elements of existing practice. In the 1960s and 1970s he continually sought improvement through more innovative approaches to the Irish past – be it through more rigorous statistical analysis or an emphasis on comparative approaches, which were then married to more conventional historical and political narratives. The combination of the comparative perspectives of some at UCD, the more sustained engagement with comparative methodologies and social science in Mainz, and the new social history of some historians at Peterhouse is evident. There was also to be no embrace of more radical or even Marxist readings of history that were current and, in some spheres, dominant in the 1960s and 1970s. Lee did not want to overthrow the established order, rather he was keen to modernise it.

In this sense, it may be possible to locate him within a new generation of historians working in Ireland in the 1970s and 1980s. Like others at the time, and later, his work brimmed with challenges to conventional nationalist interpretations and was accompanied by controversial and contentious debates. *Modernisation* certainly aimed to provoke, and from the outset it included expressions that may have seemed sacrilegious from orthodox nationalist perspectives. The first page declared, 'there was nothing unique, by the standards of pre-industrial subsistence crises, about the famine'. A few pages later the reader is told that 'The Irish farmer behaved as a rational economic man, and, after the wave of famine evictions ebbed, it was he, not the landlord, who drove his children and the labourers off the land'.[72] His work on Ribbonmen also countered traditional nationalist narratives which conceptualised the nineteenth century as a battle between predatory Anglo-Irish landlords and rebelling tenants. Rather Lee placed the focus firmly on the struggles between tenants and labourers in the early- to mid-nineteenth century. This interpretation proved highly influential, although it was not based on quite the same level of rigorous research as his earlier studies.[73]

In the late 1960s and early 1970s, Lee also offered one of the most unabashedly liberal voices in Irish historical studies. He continually asserted the central role of the individual in historical processes, attributing considerable agency to key and important figures such as Paul Cullen and Charles Stewart Parnell, but also regional figures such as James Daly. The failure of economic and social progress was generally attributed to a failure of intellect and initiative. Businessmen, speculators and risk-takers were regularly praised for making a tangible difference to economic and social life. His continual faith in statistical analysis and the necessity for judicious assessment of the evidence shines through. He tended to

---

72   Lee, *Modernisation* (1973), p. 1, 10.
73   Joseph Lee, 'The Ribbonmen' in T. Desmond Williams (ed.), *Secret Societies*, pp. 26–35.

stress, even if implicitly, how individual intellectual endeavour, rooted in an analysis of the evidence, can aid the progress of human societies. While he recognised the power of social and economic forces to shape history, they alone did not determine its course.

Lee's critique of nationalist 'myth' and embrace of elements of classical liberal thinking may then locate him as a 'modernising voice' in Irish society and place him among the ranks of late twentieth-century Irish revisionist historians. Yet his work from the 1960s and early 1970s is generally regarded as distinct from 'revisionism' in Ireland. As Gearóid Ó Tuathaigh observed, 'despite the fact that, technically, he [Lee] is relentlessly revisionist in his assessments of a broad range of issues and themes in the history of modern Ireland, he is not considered a "revisionist" by the main critics of revisionism'.[74] Indeed, Bradshaw's intervention on revisionism praised *Modernisation* (along with Ó Tuathaigh's work) as an example of the 'feasibility of combining a fully critical methodology in the analysis of the evidence with a more sensitive response to its content'.[75]

How is Lee different? His embrace of social history and statistical approaches might mark him out from those Irish revisionists who adopted a primarily political focus in their historical work. But statistical analysis and a strong focus on social history was also a feature of some of the better revisionist histories of the late twentieth century.[76] He is perhaps more sympathetic to, and comfortable with, the idea of the Catholic Church as a positive and potentially modernising force in Irish society than some revisionists. His attempts, throughout *Modernisation,* to downplay the power and influence of the Catholic Church are, indeed, striking and jar considerably with the view of post-Famine society as one where the writ of the Church ran through the cultural and social life of the country, shaping the lives of ordinary men and women in ways they barely understood. Perhaps as liberalism and Catholicism came increasingly to be perceived, within key areas of Irish intellectual life, as antithetical rather than complementary forces, Lee's work stood distinct from this development and from the mainstream of revisionist writing. Yet, this too would be to create something of a false opposition between revisionism and religion, in particular Catholicism. Much Irish revisionist history was by no means inconsistent with a sympathetic reading of the contribution of religion and the churches. Even among some prominent members of a later generation of historians, working from the 1970s onwards, there was no real inconsistency between a revisionist take on Irish history and a relatively sympathetic reading of the modernising impetus provided by the Catholic Church.[77]

In the end, what perhaps marks Lee out as different is his approach to republicanism. He was not slow, when necessary, to be critical of the intellectual limitations of nationalists and republicans. Unlike many Irish historians in the late twentieth century, however, he was far more open to the progressive potential of republicanism. He was also quicker than many Irish historians at the time to point out the faults and foibles of British thought on Ireland and the inadequacy of state interventions. He generally succeeded in this by drawing on continental comparisons and not indulging in Anglophobia, although, arguably

---

74 Ó Tuathaigh, 'Irish Historical "Revisionism"', p. 321.
75 Bradshaw, 'Nationalism and historical scholarship'. As Ó Tuathaigh pointed out, Lee's *Ireland 1912–1985* was criticised by some as a revisionist work and yet it was 'recognizably the same Lee in both works'. Ó Tuathaigh, 'Irish Historical "Revisionism"', p. 321.
76 See, for instance, W. E. Vaughan, *Landlords and Tenants in mid-Victorian Ireland* (Oxford, 1994).
77 See, for instance, R. V. Comerford, *Ireland (Inventing the Nation)* (London, 2003), p. 113.

a mild form of Ulster-phobia occasionally raised its head. This sympathetic reading of republicanism and, at times, critical approach to the British state in Ireland was, in the context of armed conflict in the early 1970s, somewhat unusual within Irish historical studies (although perhaps in tune with a sizeable section of the wider population). Few within Irish academic history circles were keen to offer a sympathetic reading of Irish republicanism or to align such sympathies with liberalism and a positive take on Catholicism in Irish society. For Lee, in 1973, the modernisation of Irish society was consistent with and, to some extent, driven by republicanism and Catholicism, whereas in the ensuing decades concepts of Irish 'modernity' became increasingly detached from both. Such a reading of republicanism was, of course, not rooted in a kind of ideological purity but remained pragmatic and critical. This would famously shine through in later work, where the treatment of Irish republicanism was aligned with a supportive analysis of the pro-Treaty position in the civil war, allowing for a sympathetic approach without aligning with more uncompromising forms of republicanism. But even this distinguishes him from many Irish revisionist historians of the time. It is difficult, if not impossible, to think of any other figure who achieved the rank of professor in an Irish history department in the 1970s and 1980s who adopted a similar perspective on modern Irish history.

******

Joe Lee's scholarship in the late 1960s and early 1970s reveals a deep engagement with the historical development of modern Ireland. His work was critical, iconoclastic and robust in its assessments of the forces and personalities at the heart of Irish economic, social and political life in the nineteenth and early twentieth centuries. It drew on the finer qualities of the 'technical history' that dominated historical studies in the mid-twentieth century and combined these with key developments in European and American historiography from the 1960s and 1970s, particularly the development of new forms of comparative economic and social history. This allowed for a distinctive reinterpretation of modern Irish history at a time when Irish society was setting out on the path to greater European integration while still having to confront the continuing conflicts at the heart of its relationship with Britain. In response, Lee asserted the fundamental 'modernity' of key aspects of Irish society, seeing them as part of wider European patterns of political, economic and social development and not, forever, shaped by and tied to the machinations of its nearest neighbour. For Lee, Irish 'modernity' was fundamentally European and incorporated central elements of European thought and culture, including liberalism, Catholicism and republicanism.

TRÍOCHA BLIAIN AG FÁS: SOME REFLECTIONS ON A CLASSIC

Cormac Ó Gráda

If *The Modernisation of Irish Society*, in 1973, was the young Joe Lee's *Communist Manifesto*, then *Ireland 1912–1985: Politics and Society*, from 1989, was the mature Lee's *Das Kapital*. The analogy is not that farfetched.[1] Both the *Communist Manifesto* and *Modernisation* were written (in one case, it is said, partly dictated) at speed. Both were brilliant. Lee was just 30 when *Modernisation* appeared, as Karl Marx was in 1848. Both the young Lee and the young Marx promised and delivered much. Like *Das Kapital*, *Ireland 1912–1985* was long in the making, commissioned soon after the publication of *Modernisation* as a 200-page introduction to modern Ireland, it ended up as an 800-page doorstopper. It was launched in Dublin on 15 January 1990, a decade and a half later than planned.

Ireland 1912–1985 was (and is) a heavily footnoted academic book with powerful crossover appeal. It won the prestigious *Irish Times* Irish Literature Prize in 1990 and caught the public imagination. It sold like proverbial hot cakes, catching its publisher, Cambridge University Press, and booksellers like Easons in Dublin completely off guard. A friend at Cambridge University Press recalls Bill Davies, the book's editor, telling him that they were completely caught out by its success.[2] By early 2019 *Ireland 1912–1985* had sold over 33,000 copies and it is still widely read. Of the 18 copies purchased by UCD Library, by mid-2019 two had disappeared. Between July 2012 and mid-2019 the remaining copies were checked out 628 times – and there was doubtless a lot of in-library use. In an era when many undergraduates do not bother with books at all that is pretty impressive.

Part of Joe Lee's success is that nobody writes quite like him. No other Irish historian invokes humour – and I mean laughter-inducing fun, not just learned witticisms – to the same effect. With Lee humour and wit are a rhetorical or stylistic device. Perhaps the closest to him in the broader humanities is Terry Eagleton, whose new book *Humour* (2019) is the culmination of a career steeped in humour. Where Eagleton and Lee differ is that with the historian humour was there virtually from the start, but with the critic it came later and was more a self-conscious thing. Eagleton would later describe one of his first major successes, *Criticism and Ideology* (1976), as 'a young man's book – tight lipped,

---

1 Revised version of a contribution to the conference marking the 30th anniversary of the publication of *Ireland 1912–1985: Politics and Society*, Royal Irish Academy, 24 April 2019. Thanks to Frank Barry, Deirdre McCloskey, Breandán Mac Suibhne, Joel Mokyr, Antoin Murphy, Peter Solar, and Paul Sweeney for comments on a previous draft. *Tríocha bliain ag fás* means '30 years a-growing', although something is lost in the translation.
2 Email from Michael Watson, Cambridge University Press, 10 January 2019.

rather puristic, a touch high-minded, a little too sure of itself here and there' and would go on to suggest that '[t]oday the idea of writing a book without any jokes in it would strike me as decidedly eccentric'.[3]

True, humour was not a feature of those devastating early articles that Lee published in the mid- and late-1960s in the *Economic History Review* and elsewhere; it is in his contributions to *The Formation of the Irish Economy* (1969) and in *Modernisation* that he really let go. *Ireland 1912–1985* has more gravitas than *Modernisation*, but it is also full of examples of Lee's humour. To mention just a few, there is his gentle put-down of the claim that General Eoin O'Duffy's followers were fascists: 'Fascism was far too intellectually demanding for the bulk of the Blueshirts'.[4] And there is Lee on Eamon de Valera's famous 'The Ireland that we have dreamed of' speech of St Patrick's Day 1943: 'As the Fianna Fáil nag trotted up to the starting tape for the 1944 election, "comely maiden" was unceremoniously dumped out of the saddle, and "rural electrification" plonked in her place as a better bet to brighten up the countryside'.[5] While conceding that James Craig's successor, J. M. Andrews, was 'not a total non-entity', Lee could not resist adding that Andrews 'is best remembered for his remark that he had counted the number of Catholics among the porters at Stormont' – an 'exercise [that] did not require a command of higher mathematics'.[6] And, of course, there is wit too: Lee ends a very serious discussion of how the Irish would have reacted to a Nazi occupation during World War Two with a quip worthy of Samuel Johnson or Oscar Wilde: 'it is sometimes happier for a country, as for an individual, not to have to learn too much about itself'.[7]

IRISH ENTREPRENEURSHIP

Moving on to more serious matters, one of the themes that sustains both *Modernisation* and *Ireland 1912–1985* is that indigenous Irish business, both before and after independence, was second-rate.

> Few businesses of international calibre emerged in post-famine Ireland ... [T]he fact that no investment banks emerged in Ireland partly reflects the timidity of the business community ... The public interest required an industrialization drive ... the private interest simply required to be left in quiet possession of one's patrimony'.[8]

Or, to quote *Ireland 1912–1985*, 'It was risk capital and entrepreneurship that Ireland lacked. Rentiers did not know what to do with their money, except to export it'.[9]

---

3   Quoted in Ola Sigurdson, 'Emancipation as a matter of style: Humour and eschatology in Eagleton and Žižek', in *Political Theology*, 14:2 (2013), p. 238; Terry Eagleton, Introduction to *Criticism and Ideology: A Study in Marxist Literary Theory* (new edn, London, 2006), n.p. See also James Smith, 'The Humour of Terry Eagleton', in *Literature & Aesthetics* 13:2 (2003), pp. 73–81.
4   J. J. Lee, *Ireland 1912–1985: Politics and Society* (Cambridge, 1989), p. 181.
5   Ibid., p. 241.
6   Ibid., p. 257.
7   Ibid., p. 268.
8   Joseph Lee, *The Modernisation of Irish Society, 1848–1918* (Dublin, 1973), p. 19, 20.
9   Lee, *Ireland 1912–1985*, pp. 109–110.

Lee's point was that Irish business both before and after independence was about rent-seeking or 'possessing', not about creativity or thinking outside the box or 'performing'. For Ireland to succeed, he wrote in the *Irish Times* on 13 January 1990, just before the book's launch in UCD's Newman House, 'a performer ethic must escape the suffocating grip of a possessor ethic'. It might be noted that this core theme in Lee's research predates both *Modernisation* and *Ireland 1912–1985*. The 'marked tendency of Irish investors to avoid risk' that he inferred in 1968 from his analysis of investment patterns in the early Irish railway system anticipated a recurrent pattern: 'Companies come and companies go, but the rentier goes on forever.'[10] In the jargon of economics, the claim here is that Ireland lacked the kind of unconventional Schumpeterian entrepreneur who works outside the box, creating something new and, of course, profiting from the result.

Modernisation was about the pre-independence period, *Ireland 1912–1985* about what followed. But the new state did nothing to change the role of rent-seeking; arguably it made things worse. That is because whereas in the pre-independence period foreign entrepreneurs had value added, in the post-independence period they were, for the most part, rent-seekers like their Irish counterparts. Those allowed in as 'tariff-hoppers' were expected to cater mostly to the domestic market, at least until the 1950s, when Minister for Industry and Commerce Seán Lemass became somewhat disillusioned with them and with Irish business in general.

In *Modernisation* Lee recognised that importing entrepreneurs could substitute for the lack of native talent. Indeed, it might be argued that in nineteenth-century Ireland such outsiders were almost too eager to try their hand; several got their fingers burnt, particularly in mining ventures. But probably as a whole they made up for any risk aversion and lack of imagination or ruthlessness in Irish entrepreneurs.[11]

The British market was crucial for most Irish producers of any size. Most linen was exported, so were nearly all the ships built. Arthur Guinness is another case in point: by 1840, at a time when the black stuff was still an exotic and virtually unknown drink in the west of Ireland, the Dublin brewery was exporting more than half its output. Indeed, for much of the nineteenth century its product was more familiar in the north of England than in Connemara or Erris. In response to an Irish Folklore Commission questionnaire, Mayoman Michael Corduff, one of the commission's greatest collectors, noted in the 1950s: 'It is only within the last half-century that porter made its appearance in this area. I remember being at a wedding feast about 50 years ago at which there was a jar of porter, by way of a novelty from the potheen, which was in abundant supply. Guests merely tasted the porter for the first time, but would not drink it. They said it was like a soot and water mixture, nauseous in the last degree and revolting as a drink, but the mountain dew was the elixir of life or 'uisce beatha' with all and sundry.'[12] Talk about the invention of a tradition!

---

10   Joseph Lee, 'The provision of capital for early Irish railways, 1830–53', *Irish Historical Studies* 16:61 (1968), p. 50.

11   For more on this point, see Cormac Ó Gráda, *Ireland: A New Economic History 1780–1939* (Oxford, 1995) pp. 324–30; Andy Bielenberg, 'The industrial elite in Ireland from the industrial revolution to the First World War', in Fintan Lane (ed.) *Politics, Society, and the Middle Class in Modern Ireland* (London, 2010), pp. 151–2.

12   This, with more evidence along the same lines, is cited in Cormac Ó Gráda, 'Real story of 250-year quest for the perfect pint', *Irish Times*, 25 Sep. 2009.

Ironically, this quintessentially 'Irish' brew would not have made it big but for its success on the British market before the Great Famine. Guinness survived and thrived by specialising and by exploiting a niche market.[13]

The industrial policies pursued by successive post-1932 administrations ignored two lessons of the pre-independence period. First, in order to thrive, Irish industry required the British market, or else some other foreign market as a – distant – second best. Second, given the chance, foreign capital will fill holes neglected by local entrepreneurs. However, allowing in foreign capital under the restricted conditions, discussed by Lee in *Ireland 1912–1985*, only added to the list of 'possessors' or rent-seekers. They were known as tariff-jumpers, and a subset of them were dubbed 'tariff Jews' in the Dublin Jewish community.[14] Probably the biggest policy mistake made after 1932 was the failure to quickly recognise that no economy is an island, not even an island economy. That lesson should have been learned by the late 1930s and rammed home by the hardships of the Emergency, but it was not.

In *Modernisation*, Lee highlighted the success of a few successful and mould-breaking entrepreneurs in the pre-independence era. He used the early history of shipbuilding in Belfast to rebut an argument popular among 'new economic historians' in the 1970s, that entrepreneurship 'does not matter':

> Had Edward Harland not received Hickson's offer [of £5,000 for his ailing shipyard] before finalizing his plans to transfer to the Mersey in 1858, it seems highly unlikely that shipbuilding and its subsidiary industries would ever have grown to dominate the Belfast economy, and later historians would doubtless dismiss Hickson's yard as a brave but futile venture predestined to collapse by 'lack of opportunity' due to the shortage of raw materials and markets.[15]

Touché! But where were the other Harlands? Lee referred to William Dargan as 'one of the most remarkable figures in Irish business history'. Dargan's claim that he employed a labour force of 50,000 in 1848 is only what the late Austin Bourke would have called an 'honest exaggeration'. Dargan did not just build the backbone of the railway network; he also had his entrepreneurial fingers in many other pies.[16] But for Lee, Dargan, Harland, the second Arthur Guinness and his son Benjamin Lee, linen magnates Andrew Mulholland and his son John, and a few others were the Irish swallows that didn't make a summer.

Who is there to compare to Dargan or Guinness or Harland in the post-1922 period? Strikingly, none is mentioned in *Ireland 1912–1985*, where the heroes (and villains)

---

13   For Lee's assessments of Guinness's brewery, see his 'Money and beer in Ireland, 1790–1875', in *Economic History Review*, 19:1 (1966), pp. 183–90; and 'The Guinnesses and beyond', in Eugenio Biagini and Daniel Mulhall (eds), *The Shaping of Modern Ireland: A Centenary Assessment* (Cambridge, 2016), pp. 210–220.

14   Frank Barry, Linda Barry, and Aisling Menton. 'Tariff-Jumping foreign direct investment in protectionist era Ireland', in *Economic History Review*, 69:4 (2016), pp. 1285–1308; Cormac Ó Gráda, *Jewish Ireland in the Age of Joyce* (Princeton, 2006), p. 211; Nick Harris, *Dublin's Little Jerusalem* (Dublin, 2002), p. 148.

15   Lee, *Modernisation*, p. 15.

16   For a comprehensive account of Dargan's career, see Fergus Mulligan, *William Dargan: An Honourable Life 1799–1867* (Dublin, 2013).

are politicians or administrators.[17] If we are prepared to accept that 'few businessmen of international calibre emerged in post-famine Ireland,' then this was all the more so during the decades covered in *Ireland 1912–1985*, when 'indigenous industry consisted overwhelmingly of small firms enjoying a captive domestic market and enduring few competitive pressures'.[18] One exceptional entrepreneur spawned by Ireland's semi-state sector, operating under very different constraints and pressures, deserves to be remembered: T. A. McLaughlin of the ESB.[19]

In more recent times, Ireland has produced its share of high-flying entrepreneurs in the likes of Michael Smurfit, Martin Naughton, Lochlann Quinn, Jim Flavin, Denis O'Brien, Tony O'Reilly, Tony Ryan, Larry Goodman, and Michael O'Leary. Note the difference that nearly all of them achieved their greatest successes abroad; most of the employment they created is abroad and, indeed, a few were or are tax exiles. Such is the way with global capitalism; whether Ireland's entrepreneurs are Irish or not, hardly matters. That is a measure of how the economy described in *Ireland 1912–1985* has changed since the 1980s.

Before the arrival on the scene of Michael O'Leary of Ryanair, Aer Lingus, noted for its high fares and the Shannon stopover, reflected perfectly the possessor ethic described by Lee. True, neither O'Leary – nor Stelios Haji-Ioannou of easyJet – were out-and-out originals. Both found their inspiration in Herb Kelleher's budget travel model for Southwest Airlines, but the abrasive O'Leary imposed his own stamp on the model, and his choice of using out-of-the-way airports with misleading names was inspired.[20] What Ryanair under O'Leary produced was new to Europe and badly needed in Ireland. Figure 1, comparing passenger numbers in Ireland and in Europe's biggest economies, is a measure of O'Leary's success. Figure 2, which compares Ryanair and its rivals, is a reminder of the Schumpeterian prediction that others will eventually copy.

The contrast between Irish banking before and since the 1990s also captures the changes post-*Ireland 1912–1985*. For decades, Irish banks epitomised the problem of risk aversion highlighted by Lee. That risk aversion was facilitated by the lack of competition sanctioned by the Central Bank and its predecessor, the Currency Commission.[21] Ironically, in less than two decades after *Ireland 1912–1985* appeared, the problem with the banks would not be risk aversion but its polar opposite. The shift was associated with increasing competition, changes in banking worldwide, and a new kid on the block in the form of Anglo-Irish Bank – and with even more disastrous consequences than the boring risk aversion of old.

17 Compare Frank Barry, 'Politics and fiscal policy under Lemass: A theoretical appraisal', in *Economic and Social Review*, 40:4 (2009), pp. 393–406.

18 Lee, *Modernisation*, p. 19; Lee, *Ireland 1912–1985*, p. 577.

19 Maurice Manning and Moore McDowell, *Electricity Supply in Ireland: The History of the ESB* (Dublin, 1984), pp. 18–21, 80–88, 123–125; Brendan Delany, 'McLaughlin, the genesis of the Shannon scheme and the ESB', in Andy Bielenberg (ed.), *The Shannon Scheme and the Electrification of the Irish Free State* (Dublin, 2002) pp. 11–27.

20 *New York Times*, 'Herb Kelleher, whose Southwest Airlines reshaped the industry, dies at 87', 3 Jan. 2019.

21 Cormac Ó Gráda, *A Rocky Road: The Irish Economy since the 1920s* (Manchester, 1997), pp. 175–8.

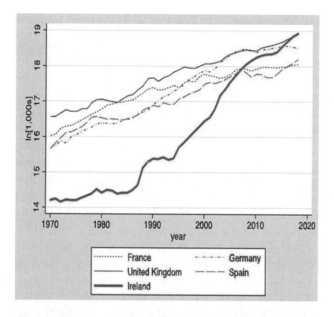

Figure 1. The Ryanair effect: passenger numbers 1970–2019

Source: World Bank, 'Air transport, passengers carried', https://data.worldbank.org/indicator/IS.AIR. PSGR, accessed 4 Oct. 2021.

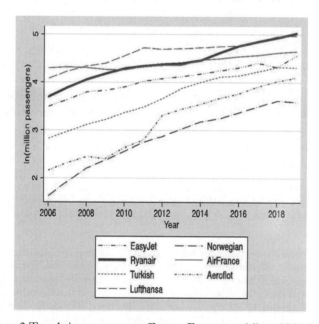

Figure 2. Trends in passenger traffic: top European airlines 2006–2019

Source: Wikipedia, 'List of largest airlines in Europe', https://en.wikipedia.org/wiki/List_of_largest_ airlines_in_Europe#ref_1, accessed 4 Oct. 2021.

HISTORY AS PROPHECY: THE CELTIC TIGER IN PERSPECTIVE

When *Ireland 1912–1985* was published, the 26 counties of the Irish Republic contained nearly one-fifth more people than in the 1920s, yet between the 1920s and the 1980s population grew less than in any comparable state, numbers at work in the formal labour force were fewer and emigration was higher. In economic terms the 1980s had been, like the 1950s, a wasted decade. Then quite suddenly and quite unexpectedly, just around the time *Ireland 1912–1985* appeared, it all changed utterly.

So successful was the Irish economy for a decade or so that policymakers from far and near came to learn about rapid sustained economic growth from Ireland. It was no longer a case of Sir Horace Plunkett's dairy cooperative-inspired mantra of 'Ireland another Denmark', but 'Denmark (and other places too) another Ireland'. The Danish embassy was one of several represented at the seminar held to mark the launch of Frank Barry's *Understanding Ireland's Economic Growth* in May 1999. Officials from Poland, Hungary, Estonia, Israel, Mexico, and Finland were also in attendance. It was an era of media-savvy and business-friendly commentators such as Colin Hunt (then a stockbroker, now chief executive of AIB), Brendan Keenan (*Irish Independent*), and Dan McLaughlin (Bank of Ireland) predicting growth without limit. Their bullish, Panglossian predictions were harmless enough at the outset. But in the new millennium, when some contrarian observers were already beginning to express doubts, their seductive 'feel good' groupthink was disastrous.[22]

A more historical and comparative perspective from commentators on the 1990s and the early 2000s would have suggested a positive but less dramatic spin. In corroboration of *Ireland 1912–1985*, measuring the performance of the Irish economy against that of the OECD 'convergence club' from the 1920s and the mid-1980s reveals serious Irish underachievement. However, applying the same simple convergence framework to 1950–2000 as a unit suggests that Ireland was 'on track', in the sense that over the half-century it grew as fast as an economy like it might be expected to grow. In other words, the growth of the Celtic Tiger years compensated for the earlier underperformance. That is not to imply that all was bound to right itself in the end. Lee's reference to Robert Hickson's shipyard applies here. We would be telling a very different but equally plausible (and very Lee-like) story if the Celtic Tiger episode, which at the time was a big surprise rather than an inevitability, had never happened.[23]

Delayed catch-up was by no means automatic, but it was an important part of the story. This change, and signs that the economy in the early 2000s was returning to more modest growth rates, might have suggested that one of the Tiger's main achievements was making

---

22 Morgan Kelly, 'How the housing corner stones of our economy could go into a rapid freefall', *Irish Times*, 28 Dec. 2006. Alan Ahearne and David McWilliams also warned of a disaster in the making. Compare Ciarán Michael Casey, *Policy Failures and the Irish Crisis* (London, 2018).

23 For competing and complementary discussions of the factors, exogenous and internal, which *allowed* late convergence to take place, see Paul Sweeney, *The Celtic Tiger: Ireland's Economic Miracle Explained* (Dublin, 1998); Patrick Honohan and B. M. Walsh, 'Catching up with the leaders: the Irish hare', in *Brookings Papers on Economic Activity* (2002), pp. 1–57; D. Donovan and A. E. Murphy, *The Fall of the Celtic Tiger: Ireland & the Euro Debt Crisis* (Oxford, 2013), pp. 15–30; Seán Ó Riain, *The Rise and Fall of Ireland's Celtic Tiger: Liberalism, Boom and Bust* (Cambridge, 2014).

up for lost ground. Seen from this perspective, the signs that growth was slackening in the early 2000s should have been nothing to be concerned about: reaching a new steady state of lower growth at an income level rivalling all but the richest economies in the world should have been deemed a huge achievement.

Press and political commentary evoked a sense of disappointment, however, and public policy, with its focus on the need for more imported capital and, in the new millennium, more imported labour was hell-bent on the pursuit of continued rapid growth. For a time, Ireland ranked globally very close to the top in terms of GDP per capita. However, given that Irish GNP was 15–20 per cent less than GDP, the situation seemed less rosy – for those who bothered to look. Nowadays the Central Statistics Office recommends measures of consumption as a clearer guide to relative well-being (in the spirit of Adam Smith's mantra that 'consumption is the sole end and purpose of all production'[24]), whether over time or in cross section.

The graphs in Figure 3 describe Irish household consumption rather than GDP or GNP per head in comparative European perspective. This offers a more balanced view of achievement during the Tiger years. Although the gap between Ireland and the rest had been eroded by the turn of the millennium, Ireland was by no means near the top as GDP data would imply. Then the surge in consumption in the mid-2000s placed Ireland near the top of the league, but the post-2008 reckoning left her no better off in 2017 than she had been a decade earlier, overtaken again by Finland, Germany, Denmark, and Sweden. The first quadrant shows how those economies worst affected by the crash have fared since. In the second quadrant, Ireland still lies behind all the Nordic countries. Overall, Ireland is far from being the leader of the pack as claimed by *The Economist* in 2004.[25]

Table 1 takes a longer view, beginning with the data taken by Lee from Nick Crafts.[26] The online Maddison Database (MDB 1910) suggests that Ireland was a bit poorer than those data show, whereas Ireland was behind everybody in 1985 and ahead of everybody except Norway in 2016. But those data refer to GDP per capita. Figures 3a–3e show that using World Bank consumption data as an alternative measure of economic well-being, Ireland does not shine so brightly. First, even in the late 2010s Irish consumption levels had barely reached the heights scaled before the crash, although in this respect it has fared better than Greece and Italy (Figure 3a) but still lags considerably behind Scandinavia (Figure 3b). Third, placed in a broader European context, Ireland's performance since both 1995 and 1970 is not so bad (Figures 3c and 3d). Moreover, comparing living standards in the two Irelands in 2016-2017, the latest year for which a comparison is available, the South now slightly shades it: €34,000 versus €29,4000 for household disposable income, €15,6000 versus €15,2000 for household final consumption.[27]

---

24 Adam Smith, *The Wealth of Nations*, Edwin Cannan (ed.) (New York: 1937 [1776]), p. 625. A caveat here: this measure fails to capture the consumption of public goods such as air quality and safety, which would also add to well-being.
25 *The Economist*, 'The luck of the Irish', 16 Oct. 2004.
26 N. F. R. Crafts, 'Gross national product in Europe 1870–1910: Some new estimates', in *Explorations in Economic History* 18 (1983), pp. 387–401.
27 Adel Bergin and Seamus McGuinness, 'Who is Better off? Measuring cross-border differences in living standards, opportunities and quality of life on the island of Ireland', *Irish Studies in International Affairs*, 32[2] (2021), p. 149.

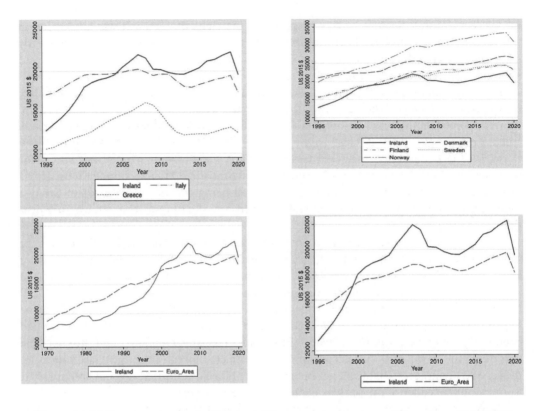

Figures 3a–3d. Consumption per head, selected European economies and Euro Area, 1970–2020 [constant 2015 $US]

Source: Word Bank, https://data.worldbank.org/indicator/NE.CON.PRVT.PC.KD?locations=IE-XC, accessed 4 Oct. 2021.

Table 1. Irish Income per Capita in Comparative Perspective

Country	Crafts 1910	MDB 1910	MDB 1985	MDB 2016	C 2017
Belgium	121.9	189.8	145.3	71.4	98.5
Germany	113.4	146.5	166.0	84.2	107.1
France	112.3	123.8	161.8	69.6	97.3
Denmark	109.0	146.5	171.6	81.1	119.6
Ireland	100	100*	100	100	100
Norway	97.4	130.0	223.1	137.3	169.6
Sweden	97.3	121.7	177.0	79.7	108.7
Italy	65.3	72.2	161.8	62.9	88.4
Finland	55.8	56.3	156.7	68.9	109.4

Sources: Lee, *Ireland 1912–1985*, p. 513 [after Crafts 1987]; Maddison database, https://www.rug.nl/ggdc/historicaldevelopment/maddison/releases/maddison-project-database-2020; World Bank, https://data.worldbank.org/indicator/NE.CON.PRVT.CD. [*] = 1913

Is Fearr an tSláinte[28]

In *Ireland 1912–1985* Lee refers more than once to infant mortality as a sensitive measure of living standards, castigating Cumann na nGaedheal for its lack of concern with the high levels in Dublin in the 1920s and noting how the infant mortality rate in Northern Ireland dipped below that in the South in 1943 and would remain below it for a few decades.[29] Life expectancy at birth $[e_0]$ in Ireland was, and still remains, low by northwest European standards (Figure 4). But for reasons that are poorly understood e_0 began to converge as the Celtic Tiger was fading. Was this due to increased spending on public health, was it due to rising incomes, or did changes in lifestyle play a role? For now, there is no obvious answer. Still, Ireland has more catching up to do in the life expectancy stakes.

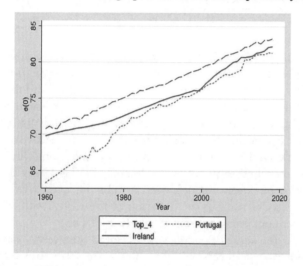

Figure 4. Life expectancy at birth $[e_0]$ in comparative perspective

Source: C. Ó Gráda and K. H. O'Rourke, 'The Irish economy during the century after partition', *Economic History Review* 75 (forthcoming, 2022), Figure 3. Top_4 is an average of the four western European economies with the highest e_0 in 2018. I'CF

Happiness

How unhappy were Irish people between the 1920s and the 1980s? Debates about trends in living standards are an attempt at addressing this question, in the sense that more is better; that is why we compare GDP per head across economies and over time, as Lee was the first to do for Ireland on the eve of independence. But it works only up to a point, because happiness is far from synonymous with material wealth. Lee refers to how crime, fear, and loneliness became much more widespread in Dublin between the 1950s and the

---

28   The proverb *Is fearr an tsláinte ná na táinte* means that health is worth more than great cattle herds.
29   Lee, *Ireland 1912–1985*, pp. 124, 256.

1980s, and elsewhere he cites the poet John Montague's take on 'creatures crazed with loneliness'.[30]

Insofar as the dreary decades – so they seem to us – covered by Lee are concerned, the temptation to invoke Patrick Kavanagh's poem *The Great Hunger* (1942), and to see everything that happened since as progress, is hard to resist. Whence critic Terence Brown's claim that 'if there is a case for viewing a major work of art as an antenna that sensitively detects the shifts and consciousness that determine a people's future, *The Great Hunger* is that work'.[31] Or how about:

> But the peasant in his little acres is tied
> To a mother's womb by the wind-toughened navel-cord
> Like a goat tethered to the stump of a tree –
> He circles around and around wondering why it should be.[32]

Peig Sayers, that much-maligned woman from Joe Lee's native county, never sounded quite so depressing! And Lee also cites a few lines from *The Great Hunger* about 'The grey and grief and unlove, / The bones in the backs of their hands, / And the chapel pressing its low ceiling over them'. But the fact that those of us alive today would be very miserable as latter-day Patrick Maguires does not mean that everybody in the 1940s was as miserable as Kavanagh's Maguire or, indeed, Kavanagh himself. There is no easy way of telling.

The relatively new field of happiness studies may offer some limited guidance here. Although evidence on whether people were happier in the 1980s than in the 1920s is lacking, *Eurobarometer* has been tracking what it dubs 'life satisfaction' since 1974 and it certainly captures episodes such as the deflation of the early 1980s, the crash of the late 2000s, and the subsequent recovery from the early 2010s on.

Figure 5 describes the share of people who declared themselves 'happy' in Ireland and in a selection of other west European economies since 1973. Ireland tracks the United Kingdom quite well; it is tempting to infer that it is 'happier' throughout than Italy, whereas Denmark emerges as consistently 'happier'. It is very important to note, however, that data like these are almost certainly more reliable as time series than in cross section.[33] For example, the implication from *Eurobarometer* that the typical Dane has bordered on the blissful since the 1970s while the average Italian has been miserable over the same period is hard to reconcile with the very similar rates of depressive and anxiety disorders in both countries and the much higher suicide rate in Denmark. In 2015 the recorded prevalence of depressive and anxiety disorders in Italy were 5.1 and 5.0 per cent per 1,000 population respectively; in Denmark they were 5.0 and 4.9 per cent; and in Ireland 4.8 and 6.3 per

---

30   Lee, *Ireland 1912–1985*, p. 649; John Montague, *Selected Poems* (Toronto, 1991), p. 126.

31   Terence Browne, *Ireland: A Social and Cultural History, 1922 to the Present* (London, 1981), p. 187; Roy Foster, *Modern Ireland* (London, 1988), p. 539.

32   Kavanagh, *Collected Poems* (London, 1964), p. 53. This passage from *The Great Hunger* has been much recycled: see Catherine Kilcoyne, 'Patrick Kavanagh and the authentic "dispensation": Rereading the role of narrator in "The Great Hunger"', in *Irish University Review*, 42:1 (May 2012), p. 90; Tom Walker, 'Patrick Kavanagh', in Gerard Dawe (ed.), *The Cambridge Companion to Irish Poets* (Cambridge, 2017), p. 146.

33   Compare Deirdre McCloskey, 'Happyism: The creepy new economics of pleasure', in *The New Republic*, 8 Jun. 2012.

cent. The suicide rate in Denmark in 2015 was 9.2 per 100,000 inhabitants compared to 5.5 per 100,000 inhabitants for Italy; and in Ireland it was 10.9 per cent.[34]

Perhaps the most striking outcome for Ireland is the failure of the index to record any sustained rise in happiness over half a century or so. While the share of 'happy' people in Ireland plummeted in the 1980s and in the wake of the 2007–8 crisis, the overall pattern is one of stasis. Daniel Patrick Moynihan, sociologist and long-time senator of Joe Lee's adopted home of New York, remarked in the wake of John F. Kennedy's assassination that he didn't think 'there's any point in being Irish if you don't know that the world is going to break your heart eventually.'[35] That might help explain stasis in the Irish case, but the data would also seem offer a pretty strong affirmation of the so-called Easterlin Paradox: that economic growth does not lead to an increase in happiness that persists in the long run.[36] That is not to deny that at any point in time the rich are 'happier' than the poor.

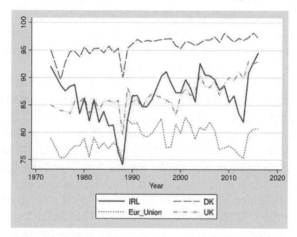

Figure 5. Irish 'happiness' in comparative perspective

Source: Derived from *Eurobarometer* from Our World in Data, https://ourworldindata.org/grapher/ share-of-people-who-say-they-are-happy-eurobarometer.

34   World Health Organisation, *Depression and Other Common Mental Disorders: Global Health Estimates* (Geneva, 2017); suicide rates from Wikipedia, reporting WHO data for 2016, https:// en.wikipedia.org/wiki/List_of_countries_by_suicide_rate, accessed 4 Oct 2021.

35   Quoted in Arthur M. Schlesinger, *A Thousand Days: John F. Kennedy in the White House* (Boston, 1965), p. 1028.

36   Richard Easterlin, 'Does economic growth improve the human lot? Some empirical evidence', in Paul A. David and Melvin W. Reder (eds), *Nations and Households in Economic Growth: Essays in Honor of Moses Abramovitz* (New York, 1974). By March 2020 this paper had been cited nearly 7,000 times according to Google Scholar. Compare Angus Deaton and Daniel Kahneman, 'High income improves evaluation of life but not emotional well-being', in *Proceedings of the National Academy of Sciences* 107:38 (21 Sep. 2010), 16489–93, https://doi.org/10.1073/ pnas.1011492107, accessed 4 Oct. 2021.

BACK TO THE FUTURE

Nowadays Joe Lee's classic is a measure of how radically Ireland and the Irish have changed in a generation. In *Ireland 1912–1985* Lee lamented Ireland's sluggish population growth since independence, but since 1990 population has grown by 40 per cent; where there were ten people there are now 14. Today the continuation of population growth at such a rapid pace might be regarded as a minus rather than a plus, given the accompanying environmental costs. It is no criticism of *Ireland 1912–1985* to state that the environment hardly features in it. But environmentally, we should be thinking a little about what an Ireland of eight or ten million people would entail – and the Central Statistics Office is threatening the republic alone with the possibility of 6.7 million by 2051.[37]

Again, Lee had much to say in *Ireland 1912–1985* about emigration but, not surprisingly, given there was virtually none, he was silent on immigration. The surge in immigration in the new millennium was fuelled in part by the hothouse or unwarranted economic growth that preceded 2007, but mass immigration was inevitable anyway in the wake of the European Union's opening to the east. For the most part, in Ireland immigration has been a win-win game: good for immigrants, good for the locals.

Opinion polls suggest that Irish people are no more enthusiastic about immigration than the average European: a long history of emigration has not made them particularly welcoming of immigrants. But – and this is crucial – immigration is not the headline issue in Ireland that it is almost everywhere else in Europe. Part of the reason for this difference, perhaps, is implicit in *Ireland 1912–1985*: the Irish had no golden industrial age to look back on. And perhaps that might also partly explain why Northern loyalists are markedly more anti-immigrant than their nationalist and republican neighbours.[38]

In the Irish general election campaign of 2020, the issue of immigration hardly featured, in marked contrast to the UK 'Brexit' election of 2019. That Ireland so far has not spawned a xenophobic populist party with mass electoral appeal is a cause for cheer – for now.[39] But the recent histories of Germany and Spain suggest that it is nothing to crow or be complacent about. And in that context, it bears noting that if the high migration/high fertility variant of the Central Statistics Office's latest population projections is met by mid-century, it will be met mainly through immigration, and that the immigrant share of the total population will be considerably higher than it is now.

All historical writing is a product of the time it is written. Lee's *Ireland 1912–1985* is no exception, and the same applies to the 'coolest' bestselling treatises of today. But Lee's book is also a book for the ages: if we are not careful and vigilant, in another three decades it will be just as relevant and as provocative as it is now.

---

37 Central Statistics Office, *Population and Labour Force Projections 2017–2051*, https://www.cso.ie/en/releasesandpublications/ep/p-plfp/populationandlabourforceprojections2017-2051/populationprojectionsresults, accessed 4 Oct. 2021.

38 Helen Grady, 'The complex rise in Northern Ireland racist hate crime', BBC News, 11 Sep. 2014, https://www.bbc.com/news/uk-northern-ireland-29141406, accessed 2 Nov. 2021; Julian O'Neill, 'Racism high in unionist areas, Lilian Seenoi-Barr claims', BBC News, 15 Sep. 2021, https://www.bbc.com/news/uk-northern-ireland-58572588, accessed 2 Nov. 2021.

39 Bryan Fanning, *Diverse Republic* (Dublin, 2021).

THE THEME OF EMIGRATION IN *IRELAND 1912–1985: POLITICS AND SOCIETY*

Andy Bielenberg

I

The appearance of *Ireland 1912–1985: Politics and Society* was undoubtedly Joe Lee's most significant academic intervention in Irish historiography. One of its many strengths was that it straddled the fields of political, social and economic history over a long time frame, while a strong comparative element contextualised the Irish story within a wider international framework. Published in the late 1980s, when unemployment in Ireland had risen to stellar levels by EU standards, the book was trenchantly critical of the state's relatively poor economic performance since independence.[1] Among the many issues the book confronted, emigration stood out as a core theme.

Lee continued to research and write on emigration subsequently. In particular, the introductory chapter to a jointly-edited collection, *Making the Irish American*, was an eloquent and searching critique of the historiography of Irish America,[2] bringing further depth to his reflections on emigration and diaspora some years after he left Cork for New York in 2002, so that he could take up a new position as the Glucksman Professor of Irish History at NYU. If this marked a decisive shift in focus of his work on emigration, there had already been a high degree of reflexivity in his handling of the topic in *Ireland 1912– 1985*, probably influenced by the re-emergence of exceedingly high levels of emigration in the 1980s as an outcome of the deep economic crisis. By the mid-1980s, he informs us, the minds of policymakers in the social and economic spheres 'were once more turning to the escape hatch of emigration.'[3] These observations were part of an expanding focus on the long history of mass emigration from Ireland, which identified a number of continuities from the early twentieth century right through to the 1980s.

---

1   Joe Lee was appointed professor and chair of the Department of Modern History at UCC in 1974, and in 1992, when three separate departments (Medieval, Irish and Modern) were amalgamated, he became chair of the new combined department (now the School of History). Despite many leadership responsibilities during a dynamic period of expansion, he continued to research and publish extensively, also serving as dean of arts and vice president of UCC, and for a spell as a member of the NUI Senate and Seanad Éireann.

2   J. J. Lee, 'The Irish diaspora in the nineteenth century', in Laurence M. Geary and Margaret Kelleher (eds), *Nineteenth-Century Ireland: A Guide to Recent Research* (Dublin, 2005); J. J. Lee and Marion R. Casey (eds), *Making the Irish American: History and Heritage in the United States* (New York, 2006).

3   J. J. Lee, *Ireland 1912–1985: Politics and Society* (Cambridge, 1989), p. 539.

The central significance of emigration in *Ireland 1912–1985* is emphatically stated in the following passage: 'In no other European country was emigration so essential a prerequisite for the preservation of the nature of the society. The interests of the possessing classes came to pivot crucially around emigration.'[4] In the century or more after the Great Famine he notes, population was ruthlessly controlled by relatively few marriages, a late average age of marriage and through emigration.[5] These collectively helped Ireland achieve a relatively higher standard of living than in a number of European countries where population growth was significantly greater. This strategy of ruthless population control to maintain the interests of the status quo became firmly established, with the emigrants drawn largely from the offspring of the poorer sections of the rural population, in addition to non-inheriting members of the farm population who were channelled out of the country in droves.[6]

Lee describes this process of widespread emigration as one of 'the social scars that disfigured the face of Ireland'. Farm labourers and their families in particular were disappearing from the landscape, and the new state in the interwar years took no measures 'to prevent the continuing dispersal of families ravaged by the cancer of emigration.' Ireland, he noted:

> continued to be characterised by a high incidence of mental disease, by hideous family living conditions in its urban slums, and by a demoralised casual working class, urban as well as rural. Few voices were raised in protest. The clergy, strong farmers in cassocks, largely voiced the concern of their most influential constituents, whose values they instinctively shared and universalised as "Christian". The sanctity of property, the unflinching materialism of farmer calculations, the defence of professional status, depending on continuing high emigration and high celibacy.[7]

In short, the central role of emigration in Irish society between the mid-nineteenth century and the 1950s he argued, was to preserve the social order and the material interests of the possessing class.[8] Indeed, unemployment and emigration remained major problems in de Valera's Ireland.[9] It was only in the 1960s and 1970s when a greater degree of economic growth got underway and there was an improvement in access to education, that emigration slowed down. The long-term incidence of net emigration from southern Ireland (26 counties) is best discerned from census returns set out in Table 1.

Table 1 illustrates the dramatically higher levels of net emigration witnessed in the last third of the nineteenth century compared to what followed (leaving aside the more stellar levels experienced during and after the Great Famine). Though net departures in the 1980s did not remotely approach the high levels witnessed in the 1950s, during the second half of the decade (when *Ireland 1912–1985* was published) emigration levels were certainly moving upwards, hitting levels not seen since before the 1960s. The curse of emigration had not gone away and was back on the agenda.

---

4   Lee, *Ireland 1912–1985*, p. 374.
5   Ibid., p. 374.
6   Ibid., p. 384.
7   Ibid., p. 159.
8   Ibid., pp. 651, 664.
9   Ibid. pp. 323, 333, 359, 365.

Table 1 reveals the relatively lower net outflow recorded between the mid-1920s and the end of the Second World War, which had much to do with the diminishing prospects of migration to the United States. If there was significant migration to Great Britain in the war there were restrictions on this; moreover, there was also movement from Great Britain to Eire which contained net emigration to levels only marginally higher than the preceding decades.

Table 1. Average annual net migration from southern Ireland, 1871–1991	
1871–81	50,000
1881–91	60,000
1891–1901	40,000
1901–11	26,000
1911–26	27,000
1926–36	17,000
1936–46	19,000
1946–51	24,000
1951–56	39,000
1956–61	42,000
1961–66	16,000
1966–71	11,000
1971–79	plus 14,000
1979–81	3,000
1981–86	14,000
1986–91	27,000

Source: derived from R. E. Kennedy, *The Irish: Emigration, Marriage and Fertility* (Berkeley, 1973), Statistical Appendix, Table 1, p. 212; Central Statistics Office, *Census 1991*, vol. 1 (Dublin, 1993) p. 16. Figures have been rounded. The plus figure for 1971–79 is due to the fact that the 1970s witnessed net immigration into Ireland, in contrast to the net emigration in all other periods in the table.

The figures also reveal a general reduction in emigration in the 1960s as living standards rose and employment opportunities in industry and services increased in Ireland. The 1970s, in contrast to preceding decades, witnessed a net inflow, which was surely linked to improved employment prospects in industry and services, rising living standards, state investment, and the economic, social and cultural benefits of improved educational access. Likewise, industrial development, public investment and improved incomes in agriculture resulting from EEC entry in 1973 temporally altered the long-term cycle of net emigration into net immigration. The economic recession which got underway from 1979, following on from the second oil crisis, witnessed a return to the familiar pattern of net emigration in the 1980s, by the end of which *Ireland 1912–1985* arrived on the bookshelves.

Even those graduating from universities were leaving Ireland in droves in the second half of the 1980s. Jim McLaughlin reminds us that the familiar pattern of unskilled departees continued nonetheless, but with a far stronger urban element compared to the 1950s.[10] The net outflow in the second half of the 1980s was particularly high, but it's worth noting the average net annual figures at this time were broadly matched over the entire first quarter of the twentieth century, the period with which this chapter is predominantly concerned. While Ireland had been consistently posting the highest levels of emigration from Europe in the second half of the nineteenth century, in the first decades of the twentieth century it had fallen to levels relatively lower than those experienced in Scotland and Italy, and fairly similar to those in England, Spain, Portugal, Norway, Finland and Austria-Hungary. So, Ireland at this stage was no longer an outlier when it came to emigration.[11]

Ireland 1912–1985 dealt with emigration from the period prior to the First World War, up through the Irish revolution and onwards, in contrast to much of the historiography which either ends before the war or begins with the birth of the new state. While the latter approach makes sense in terms of the implications of regime change, partition, and the changing statistical coverage of emigration, this periodisation has left many unanswered questions around a major hiatus in departures from 1914 to 1923, when the traditional pattern of emigration was significantly disrupted. These issues have become more pertinent with the recent turn in the historiography towards the so-called 'decade of commemorations', notably the extent of conflict migration during the Irish revolution and its aftermath. This chapter will focus on this transitional window in Irish emigration history.

II

One of the key arguments made in *Ireland 1912–1985* was that the Irish revolution brought no major change to the general pattern of emigration in terms of which strata were departing. Lee argued, 'Emigration remained as central to both the viability and value system of de Valera's Ireland as of Cosgrave's or Redmond's.'[12] This invites closer scrutiny.

For those destined for the United States, there was a fall in the unskilled component for both men and women between the pre-war years and the second half of the 1920s, which was not evident in the figures for British imperial destinations. This marked rise in the skilled minority destined for the USA contained a progressively growing share of former anti-treaty IRA veterans, whose occupational profile would have been of a slightly higher social status on average than the typical pre-war economic emigrant bound for the US. Protestants would have added to this shift. Recession in Ireland and boom conditions in the USA down to 1929 at least, additionally provided stronger push and pull incentives for those with skills. Nonetheless, Table 2 reveals that before, during and after the Irish revolution the major emigrant strata were (as Lee suggested) predominantly made up of those defined as relatively unskilled.

---

10 Jim Mac Laughlin, *Ireland: The Emigrant Nursery and the World Economy* (Cork, 1994).
11 Dudley Baines, *Emigration from Europe 1815–1930* (Cambridge, 1995) p. 4.
12 Lee, *Ireland 1912–1985*, p. 390.

Table 2. Percentage share of Irish male emigrants stating they were in agricultural or labouring occupations 1912–30

	1912–13	1921–4	1925–30
USA	82%	76%	62%
Canada	69%	78%	73%
Australasia	69%	65%	70%
South Africa	19%	18%	19%

Percentage share of occupied Irish female emigrants stating they were in domestic, hotel etc., service 1912–30

	1912–13	1921–4	1925–1930
USA	87%	90%	74%
Canada	80%	81%	85%
Australasia	73%	67%	78%
South Africa	31%	22%	22%

Source: N. H. Carrier and J. R. Jeffery, *External Migration: A Study of the Available Statistics, 1815–1950* (London, 1953), pp 116–123.

The smaller share of artisans and middle-class migrants travelling to the United States, Canada or Australasia still constituted sizable outflows of this group to the receiving countries. While Lee focused more on the poorer majority of migrants from the Irish countryside, who provided raw labour much in demand in the more industrial and urban American and British economies in particular, it's worth noting that Irish skilled and professional males destined for the United States, who accounted for merely 18% of male emigrants in 1912–13 had grown to a sizable 38% by 1925–30 (see Table 2). This reveals that economic recession in Ireland for much of the 1920s, while conversely the American economy was performing well, provided greater incentives for people higher up the social scale to emigrate there.

Rough indications of the extent of Irish-born settlement globally are available in the census of England and Wales in 1911, which returned natives of the United Kingdom who lived abroad, and in most locations the Irish share was identified. The significance of the United States stands out with nearly 1.4 million Irish born living there in 1911; Great Britain comes next with over 0.5 million, while over 0.3 million were recorded in a multiplicity of locations throughout the British empire and elsewhere, which understates the true figure, as the Irish share was not recorded in all locations.[13] They nonetheless

---

13 *Census of England and Wales, 1911: Summary Tables* (London 1915), Table 96, 'Summary of returns relating to natives of the UK living in foreign countries at or about the date of the census, 1911', pp. 420–422; Table 99, 'British Empire area and population of the UK and British colonies, dependencies, etc. distinguishing the natives of the UK', p. 423; *Census of England and Wales, 1911: General Report* (London, 1917), Appendix D, pp. 352–61.

reveal the scale and geographical extent of Irish emigration in the preceding half century or more, most notably to more urbanised locations in Britain and North America, where poorer migrants were more likely to find work and higher wages then they might expect in Ireland.

III

The First World War disrupted transatlantic emigration. By November 1915 many intending Irish emigrants to the United States were turned back at Liverpool. In early December 1915 drastic regulations regarding emigration were announced by the British government and no one could leave Ireland without a passport, so effectively thereafter no man of military age was allowed to leave without good reason.[14] Kevin O'Shiel noted the arrest of transatlantic emigration in the war years, in addition to the restriction on seasonal migration to England and Scotland for harvest work; he observed the country was teaming with young men and women who had money and work because of wartime prosperity. This combined with the inflation of land prices and Sinn Féin propaganda, considerably animated land agitation and the independence movement in the west of Ireland in particular by 1920.[15] This effective ban on overseas departures was also identified by Lord Lieutenant French to a reporter in early 1920 as a major factor in the independence movement. In his view, 'The principal cause of the trouble is that for the last five years emigration has been practically stopped. There are here 100,000 or 200,000 young men from 15 to 25 years of age who normally would have emigrated'.[16] On this at least, French had a point.

As overseas destinations became difficult or impossible to reach during the war, Britain assumed relatively greater significance. Although anything up to 50,000 may have emigrated from Ireland to Britain for war work, much of this was of a fairly temporary nature and following the armistice, demobilisation and the closure of munitions works, many returned home.[17] If Britain was the dominant destination for a number of the war years (excluding 1914–15), this appears to have been only temporary.

The annual figures for overseas emigration provide us with a clearer picture of variances in departures over these years. The quality of the overseas data for Irish emigration to the United States (by far the most important destination for all Irish emigrants) and to other overseas destinations (largely within the British Empire) are reasonably well covered by the Board of Trade returns.[18] Nonetheless, these returns for the war years for the United States appear to be too low when compared to those for immigrants entering the United States from Ireland. To correct this, UK Board of Trade data for the United States between 1914 and 1918 have accordingly been replaced with data on Irish immigrants entering

---

14   Military Archive, Dublin, Bureau of Military History, 1916–1921, WS 1530, Christopher O'Connell, p. 1; WS 1698, Liam De Roiste, p. 247.
15   Bureau of Military History, WS 1770, part 7, Kevin O'Sheil, p. 940.
16   Bureau of Military History, WS 687, section 1, Monsignor Curran, p. 425.
17   F. Walsh, '"We work with shells all day and night": Irish female munitions workers during the First World War', in *Saothar* 42 (2017), pp 19–30. D; David Fitzpatrick, 'The Irish in Britain, 1871–1921', in W. E. Vaughan (ed.), *A New History of Ireland, vol. VI: Ireland under the Union 1870–1921* (Oxford, 1996), pp. 653–702.
18   *Commission on Emigration*, pp. 316, 331.

the United States. Table 5 reveals net overseas emigration was particularly low during the war and its immediate aftermath. More people returned to Ireland in 1919 than left for overseas destinations, and regular emigration only began to get going again in 1920.

Total overseas emigration during the Irish revolution at large was not spectacular. Qualitative evidence from emigration agents encouraging Irish departures to Canada, confirm that emigration was curtailed in the years between 1916 and 1922, notably in the south, where there was significant hostility to those promoting emigration. Moreover, the republican government in waiting forbade emigration, and both agents and their clients were threatened. Interest in Canada only began to recover from 1923 when the Civil War ended, and applications in that year were greater than for many seasons.[19] In June 1920, the IRA had issued a general order forbidding volunteers to leave the country or apply for a passport without written authority from GHQ, viewing ordinary emigration as 'desertion in the face of the enemy'. It also forbade the advertising or promotion of emigration by agents.[20] More significantly, this was followed by a Dáil decree in July 1920 prohibiting the emigration of any citizens to settle abroad without the written permission of the republican government.[21] While this was difficult to enforce, ad hoc efforts were made to check intending emigrants and British passports were confiscated. If it remains difficult to assess the precise impact of this prohibition, since documentation could be quickly replaced by the British emigrant authorities, it still appears to have deterred a number from travelling. Two assigned the task of controlling emigration (volunteers Simon Donnelly and Sean Healy) gave the impression that they viewed it as only applying to men, possibly due to the fact that they were following army orders as opposed to the Dáil.[22] It may have acted as more of a deterrence to men, thus contributing to the female preponderance in these years (see Table 6). The general disruption to travel and transport in these years are also likely to have reduced the migrant flow. A group of intending emigrants to America, largely women, in October 1922 who left Dingle, Co Kerry, took five days to get to Cobh by sea in bad weather in order to avoid the hazards of road and rail.[23] It appears likely that such disruptions, along with republican limitations on emigration (both pro- and anti-Treaty) during the Civil War, and the potential dangers would-be emigrants faced, contributed to the relatively restrained levels of departures in these years.[24]

Net outward movement during the revolution was somewhat lower than the average before the First World War and after the revolution, but higher than during the war years. This revolutionary share of 28 per cent was lower than the gross share, which constituted 30 per cent of total gross movement between 1911 and 1925 (see Table 3). This reveals that the share of net departures during the Irish revolution out of total net departures

---

19 Marjory Harper, 'Enticing the emigrant: Canadian agents in Ireland and Scotland, c. 1870–c. 1920', in *Scottish Historical Review* 83:215 (2004), pp. 50–4.

20 Bureau of Military History, WS 883, John MacCarthy.

21 Dáil Eireann, *Minutes of the Proceedings the First Parliament of the Republic of Ireland, 1919–1921* (Dublin, 1921), pp. 206–7.

22 Bureau of Military History, WS 814, Patrick Daly, p. 37; WS 1535, Hugh Early, p. 6; WS 1643, Sean Healy, 6–8; WS 481, Simon Donnelly, p. 36.

23 Síobhra Aiken, 'Sick on the Irish Sea, dancing across the Atlantic: Anti-nostalgia in women's remembrance of the Irish revolution', in Oona Frawley (ed.), *Women and the Decades of Commemoration* (Bloomington, 2021), p. 95.

24 Tom Doyle, *The Civil War in Kerry* (Cork, 2008), p. 206.

between 1911 and 1925 were not radically different from the share of gross departures in these years.

Table 3. Estimated emigration from the 26 counties overseas 1911–25 (excluding Great Britain and Europe).

Years	% Irish emigrants from south	Gross emigration	Gross share	Net emigration	Net share	Average annual net
1911–13	71	97,346	35%	84,301	37%	28,100
1914–18	78	50,652	18%	36,658	16%	7,331
1919–20	72	25,044	9%	14,951	7%	7,476
1921–23	72	58,100	21%	48,397	21%	16,132
1924–25		49,613	18%	43,430	19%	21,715
Total		280,755	100%	227,737	100%	15,182

Sources: Southern Irish annual figures for 1911–23 are estimated from 32 counties figure in *Commission on Emigration*, p. 316, except war years (1914–18), which are estimated from 32 counties figure in Susan B. Carter et al., *Historical Statistics of the United States: Earliest Times to the Present*, vol. 1 (Cambridge, 2006), 562. Southern Irish per cent share of total Irish gross emigration from these sources from 1911–21 is estimated from 26 county annual share in Irish emigration statistics in *Annual Report of the Registrar-General*, except war years, which are assumed to be the same throughout as average for 1914–16. Per cent share of net emigration relative to gross estimated share from figures for 32 counties in Carrier and Jeffery, *External Migration*, Table C/1, p. 93, with net share in 1911 and 1912 (when emigration data was reported differently) assumed to be same as for 1913, when it was 86.6% of gross. Figures for 1922–1925 taken from Registrar General's *Annual Report*. Southern Irish share of total Irish gross emigration for 1922 and 1923 interpolated from 1921 and 1924.

Movement to the six counties which became Northern Ireland from the 26 counties which became the Irish Free State between 1911 and 1926 was estimated in the General Report of the Census of Northern Ireland (1926) to have been in the region of 24,000, with about 10,000 moving in the other direction, implying a total net inflow to Northern Ireland of about 14,000 between 1911 and 1926.[25]

Net movement to Great Britain is more difficult to capture. In the absence of complete annual statistical coverage of the movement from Ireland to Great Britain, one option is to work off the census coverage of the Irish-born in Great Britain in the census returns for 1911, 1921 and 1931. The death rates, within this group are assumed to be roughly 18 per 1,000 per annum, and the assumption is made that new migrants from Ireland were required to maintain population to an annual level which has been interpolated between census years, thus providing a rough indication of the immigrant inflow (see Appendices a, b and c). Those originating from the 26 counties are estimated based on the results of the 1911 and 1931 censuses. The outcome implies there were roughly 79,000 Irish-born immigrants into Great Britain from the 26 counties between 1911 and 1926, and the levels

25   *Census of Population of Northern Ireland, 1926: General Report* (Belfast, 1929), xxv, l–li.

of emigration were slightly higher from 1921 onwards. With this data, it is possible to compare net emigration to Britain with the far larger number going overseas (see Table 4).

Table 4. Net emigration from the 26 counties, 1911–26	
Emigration overseas	228,000
Emigration to Great Britain	79,000
Emigration to Northern Ireland	14,000
Total	321,000

This can be compared to the inter-census estimate of net emigration of 405,000, indicating a balance of 84,000, which has not been accounted for. This, the Irish Free State census general report of 1926 points out, would have included Irish First World War dead, British withdrawal from Ireland (including army, navy and their dependents), and Irish-born persons who joined the British Army during the First World War and survived the war but did not return to Ireland.[26] It would also cover those destined for Europe who were not recorded among those going overseas.

IV

The United States experienced something of a resurgence in the 1920s, briefly reasserting its status as the premier destination for Irish emigration; recessionary conditions in north-western Europe and the relatively more buoyant economic experience of North America, down to the Great Crash animated this westward population movement. The statistical coverage for US immigrants arriving from Europe in the 1920s provides an alternative to those of the Board of Trade. These returns (which end mid-year) indicate that the year ending June 1921 was a peak year for the 1920s for immigrants not only from Ireland, but also from Scandinavia, Poland, Greece, Italy, Portugal, Spain, and other regions in north-western, central and eastern Europe. Wider transcontinental factors were at work in 1921 in Ireland, other than simply a flight from revolution; recessionary conditions in Europe, paralleled by an increase in demand for labour in America are likely explanations here. More remarkable than this sharp peak in American arrivals in 1921, from a European comparative perspective, was a second peak at a similar level from Ireland in 1927. But this was not shared with other parts of Europe, though Ireland shared the increased level of arrivals with Europe in 1921, as Lee observed,[27] American quotas denied many eastern Europeans from participating in this second outflow to the United States between 1925 and 1928, with levels steadily declining thereafter, becoming inconsequential in 1931 (see Table 5).[28] At this stage deep recession had finally terminated the great American exodus which had dominated Irish departures since the years of the Great Famine, making this an important turning point.

British imperial destinations also continued to attract emigrants from the Irish Free State in the 1920s, providing options for some southern Irish loyalists who wished to leave

---

26   Irish Free State, *Census of Population 1926: General Report* (Dublin, 1934), pp. 11–12.
27   Lee, *Ireland 1912–1985*, p. 71.
28   Carter et al., *Historical Statistics of the United States*, p. 562.

the new state, including some of those forced out. Irish recruitment for the British colonial service, for example, was not diminished by independence.[29] Great Britain and Northern Ireland provided a wider spectrum of employment for departing southern loyalists. Table 5 reveals that in most years (the notable exception being 1924) Great Britain was still far behind the United States. The Canadian government's emigration agent in Dublin reported that emigration only began again on a major scale following the end of the Civil War; he noted the bulk of these were largely from poorer farming areas and holdings in the south and west.[30]

Table 5. Number of gross outward emigrants from Irish Free State, 1922–1931

Year	USA	Colonies	Total	Great Britain	Total	Great Britain %
1922	12,180	2,820	15,000			
1923	16,700	3,870	20,570	7,608	28,178	27%
1924	12,234	7,077	19,311	18,000	37,311	48%
1925	26,546	3,756	30,302	8,800	39,102	23%
1926	26,367	3,992	30,359	11,400	41,759	27%
1927	23,947	3,362	27,309	7,500	34,809	22%
1928	21,775	3,025	24,800	5,500	30,300	22%
1929	18,119	2,763	20,882	7,900	28,782	27%
1930	14,295	1,907	16,202	8,600	24,802	35%
1931	890	667	1,557	9,800	11,357	86%

Source: Figures for the United States and colonies taken from *Annual Report of the Registrar-General*, 1932, p. ix; 1922 and 1923 taken from *Annual Report of the Registrar-General*, 1923, p. viii. Figures for Great Britain taken from R. S. Walshaw, *Migration to and from the British Isles* (London, 1941), p. 72. The Great Britain figure for 1923 is based on Walsaw, p. 78, who estimates that 27% in that year were going to United Kingdom and 73% to all extra-European destinations. United Kingdom is assumed to mean Great Britain, as no record was kept of land crossing to Northern Ireland.

The Irish government lifted the emigration ban in October 1923. Following defeat in the Civil War, the anti-Treaty IRA retained this ban until 1925.[31] Nonetheless, Gavin Foster asserts that republicans were already leaving the country in droves in 1924, which accelerated in 1925 and continued in the following years. He concludes persuasively that post-Civil War IRA migrants 'were simultaneously political refugees and economic migrants', as recession

---

29 Sean William Gannon, *The Irish Imperial Services: Policing Palestine and Administering the Empire, 1922-1966* (London, 2019).

30 K. Fedorowich, 'Reconstruction and resettlement; the politicization of Irish migration to Australia and Canada 1919-1929', in *English Historical Review* 114:459 (Nov. 1999), pp. 1164–65.

31 Jennifer Redmond, *Moving Histories: Irish Women's Emigration to Britain from Independence* (Dublin, 2018), p. 25.

deepened in the mid-1920s.[32] Brian Hanley specifically mentions the impact this had along the western seaboard, from west Cork to Donegal, with Connaught and Munster featuring more strongly. His work on IRA pension files suggests the majority of these emigrants went to the United States, but Britain accounted for something in the order of 50 per cent of the US level.[33] An examination of pension data carried out in Co. Cork, revealed that while Britain featured to a limited extent in east Cork and the city, as one moved westward in the county, America progressively dominated the relatively higher level of departures registered on IRA company lists, which largely reflected significant outward movement throughout the 1920s. In the worst hit districts on the Beara peninsula about half the original IRA companies had emigrated predominantly to the USA.

V

The 'gender' balance of Irish emigrants (see Table 6) reveals the south tended to have a higher female share while the North posted higher male emigration, at least until 1919–21, a period which witnessed a higher female outflow across all Ireland, underlining a reduction in employment opportunities for women in these years, corroborated by personal testimony.[34]

Table 6. Female share of emigration, 1904–28

Years	Female emigration from 26 counties			Female emigration from 6 counties		
	female	total	share	female	total	Share
1904–08	62,901	123,020	51.1%	18,317	42,279	43.3%
1909–13	52,329	106,296	49.2%	18,587	45,721	40.7%
1914–18	15,719	30,399	51.7%	5,397	10,967	49.2%
1919–21	14,580	22,950	63.5%	5,072	9,191	55.2%
1922–23	-	-	-			
1924–28	63,800	131,137	48.7%			

Source: *Commission on Emigration.*

Male emigration appears to have been disrupted to a greater extent between 1916 and 1921. While overseas departures slowed down in 1914 and 1915, these years still accounted for much of the wartime outflow overseas. Munitions work in Britain during the war provided a stronger alternative focus for female migrants in particular.[35] The female share

---

32   Gavin Foster, 'No "wild geese" this time?: IRA emigration after the Irish Civil War', in *Eire-Ireland* 47 (2012), pp. 94–122.
33   Brian Hanley, *The IRA, 1926–1936* (Dublin, 2002).
34   Síobhra Aiken, '"Sinn Féin permits…in the heels of their shoes": Cumann na mBan emigrants and Transatlantic revolutionary exchange', *Irish Historical Studies*, 44 (2020), p. 110.
35   Walsh, 'We work with shells', pp. 19–30.

rose even more dramatically in the War of Independence, with the greater prohibition on males departures providing a potential explanation here.[36]

While at this point there was likely some conflict migration out of Northern Ireland, economic recession and unemployment were probably a more significant cause of departures. By late 1921, unemployment in Belfast was running at three times the level as Dublin, an indication of the depth of recessionary conditions in Northern industry.[37] The annual reports of the Provincial Bank noted that 1922 was a disappointing year for the linen industry, which was the major source of female employment in the north-east. While the 1923 report noted there was an improvement in orders at the beginning of the year, the spinning end of the trade was still in depression due to foreign competition. Despite continued unemployment and a series of labour disputes, economic conditions in the Irish Free State were reported to be improving in 1923, despite the fact that it was a poor year for farmers.[38] In the south at least a more even balance between male and female migrants had been restored by 1924–8, with slightly higher male departures, as in the five years before the First World War.

The age profile of Irish emigrants set out in Table 7 also reveals that between 1912 and 1927 a higher share of female emigrants were likely to leave at a younger age (12–17). Conversely, males tended to have a higher share in the 18–45 cohorts. Table 7 reveals that the great bulk of emigrants, male and female, throughout this period, were aged between 18 and 30 (this cohort provided a far higher share of the Irish outflow than the corresponding cohort emigrating from England and Wales).

Table 7. Proportion of Irish male and female emigrants from all Ireland in specific age groups, per 10,000 persons, 1912–27

Males	under 12	12-17	18-30	31-45	46 and over	all ages
1912–13	864	413	6983	1385	354	10000
1920	850	456	6406	1758	530	10000
1921–23	810	406	6566	1666	552	10000
1924–27	696	472	6860	1546	426	10000
1924–27★	411	384	7360	1476	369	10000
Females	under 12	12-17	18-30	31-45	46 and over	all ages
1912–13	832	770	6885	1140	374	10000
1920	602	578	6626	1578	616	10000
1921–23	752	657	6456	1484	652	10000
1924–27	797	957	6395	1297	554	10000
1925–27★	444	1018	6948	1120	470	10000

★Southern Ireland only. Source: *Carrier and Jeffery*, External Migration; a study of the available statistics 1815-1950 (London, 1953), p. 106.

---

36 *Commission on Emigration*, statistical appendix table 28, p. 319.
37 Doyle, *Civil War in Kerry*, p. 79, citing *Cork Examiner*, 29 Dec. 1921.
38 *Freeman's Journal*, 25 Jan. 1923; *Irish Independent*, 24 Jan. 1924.

VI

Since *Ireland 1912–1985* was published in 1989, one of the more animated debates on emigration in the historiography has revolved around the cause and timing of Protestant departures between 1911 and 1926. Peter Hart attributed greater significance to revolutionary violence and intimidation in driving the Protestant exodus than earlier interpretations.[39] Although he did not put precise numbers on this, he stated that an 'unintended effect of political violence in the south was the flight of Protestants and other "enemies" of the Republic out of Ireland. Tens of thousands of people were lost who might have stayed.'[40] The late David Fitzpatrick, in contrast, argued that demographic factors other than emigration played an important role in this decline, based on an analysis of the Methodist membership records which he believed provided a good microcosm of the wider southern Protestant experience. The main source of decline, he argued, was not emigration (though this contributed), but sluggish recruitment due to age structure, falling nuptiality and fertility, and mixed marriages and conversions. IRA violence in contrast was of limited consequence in departures he argued, so the malaise was largely self-inflicted.[41] The main problem with Fitzpatrick's argument is that falling nuptiality and fertility and failure to enrol new members were all strong symptoms of excessive emigration of the most fertile and marriageable cohorts in the Protestant population between 1911 and 1926.[42] Revolutionary turmoil and regime change certainly accelerated departures, but the big question is by how much? The Methodist emigration data used by Fitzpatrick undoubtedly provide the most sensitive barometer of annual Protestant emigration in these years since they are based on actual movement out of Ireland.[43]

In a recent contribution, the late Donald Wood has extracted more evidence on the Protestant element of population change between 1911 and 1926, deducing that they accounted for almost 19 per cent of the civilian emigration component (though only accounting for roughly 10 per cent of the population of the 26 counties). Wood's numerical formulation of total net Protestant emigration in 1911–26 at 67,517 has been derived from a more careful assessment of the census data than previous efforts. However, his conclusions on the timing of departures are less convincing, as they ignore the advances made by Fitzpatrick on this front. Wood concludes that 40,000 of these departing emigrants (over 59 per cent of the total between 1911 and 1926) might be deemed 'excessive emigration', (i.e., above the equivalent level of Catholic emigration). Implicit in this assumption is that Protestant and Catholic economic emigration followed similar patterns throughout this period; this is highly questionable. Moreover, he concludes, this excess 'represents the number who migrated for reasons ranging from dissatisfaction with regime change through to fear of violence and actual violence against their person or property'. This implies the

---

39   Peter Hart, 'The Protestant experience of revolution in Southern Ireland', in Richard English and Graham Walker (eds), *Unionism in Modern Ireland: New Perspectives on Politics and Culture*, (London, 1996), pp. 93–4.
40   Peter Hart 'On the necessity of violence in the Irish revolution', in Danine Farquharson and Sean Farrell (eds), *Shadow of the Gunmen: Violence and Culture in Modern Ireland* (Cork, 2008), p. 32.
41   David Fitzpatrick, *Descendancy: Irish Protestant Histories Since 1795* (Cambridge, 2014).
42   Andy Bielenberg, 'Exodus: The emigration of southern Irish Protestants during the Irish War of Independence and the Civil War', in *Past and Present* 219. (2013), pp. 199–233.
43   Fitzpatrick, *Descendancy*.

excess was from 1919 onwards.[44] The only evidence he advances on the timing of this outflow is the significant fall in Protestant marriage numbers. The problem with marriage numbers is they don't provide an accurate indication of emigration levels prior to 1920. Methodist emigration figures from the south of Ireland provides more sensitive data on the timing of southern Protestant departures between 1911 and 1926, since it is based on observed levels of emigration; these reveal a more dispersed pattern of emigration across these years than Wood assumes, with emigration between 1911 and 1914 actually exceeding that during the revolutionary years 1920–3.[45] Wood has opted to disregard the Methodist data, since he argued they merely measure gross departures, when overall movement requires figures for net departures. However, Table 3 reveals that the distribution of gross and net departures of the bulk of Irish emigrants, annually between 1911 to 1926 broadly followed a similar pattern. It is argued here that the overall net volume of Protestant emigrants between 1911 and 1926, as revealed by Wood's advance in this area, can be reconciled with an estimate of the timing of departures, based on the southern Methodist outflow (Appendices Table D). From this estimate of total net Protestant departures between 1911 and 1926, net Protestant movement to Northern Ireland between 1911 and 1926 needs to be deducted. Digital manipulation of census returns has revealed that the majority of southern-born living in the six northern counties in 1911 were Catholic, with a female excess reflecting the traditional pattern of economic migration northwards. Although we have no data yet on changes to the confessional balance of southern-born in Northern Ireland by 1926, Fitzpatrick's assumption that this changed little in the interim[46] is hard to sustain given the increase of the Protestant population in Northern Ireland by 1926 (notably among the Church of Ireland congregation, presumably the largest group of southern Protestant migrants) and a fall in the Catholic population. It seems likely the Protestant share of cross-border migrants increased between 1911 and 1926 due to the revolution and regime change, which, it has been assumed here, constituted net northward emigration of 7,500 people (i.e., slightly more than half the net departures northwards between 1911 and 1926). If this amount is deducted, it leaves a figure of total net Protestant emigration out of Ireland from the south of 60,000. This is distributed across the years between 1911 and 1926 using the share of Methodists leaving in each year (see Appendices Table D), following Fitzpatrick's assumption that the timing of Methodist departures mirrored those of the wider Protestant community.

Table 8 implies that over 55 per cent of Protestant departures from the 26 counties between 1911 and 1926 took place before 1919. Adding departures for 1924 and 1925 raises this figure to 63 per cent, revealing that considerable emigration was taking place in the years other than those of the revolution. Moreover, an additional share of the 21,600 emigrants who left during the revolution were also economic emigrants, and many departed who were not forced to leave. So, those who left Ireland out of fear of violence, actual violence against themselves or their property, expulsion or the articulated or written

---

44   Donald Wood, 'Protestant population decline in southern Ireland', in Brian Hughes and Conor Morrissey (eds), *Southern Irish Loyalism, 1912–1949* (Liverpool, 2020), pp. 39-46.

45   Fitzpatrick, *Descendancy*, p. 256.

46   Ibid., pp. 167, 180.

threat of violence during the revolutionary years would have been somewhat lower than this figure.

Table 8. Estimated Protestant share of total net emigration from southern Ireland, 1911–26

	Overseas	Great Britain	Total	Protestants	Protestant share
1911–13	84,300	15,700	100,000	17,900	18%
1914–18	36,700	25,700	62,400	15,500	25%
1919–20	15,000	10,100	25,100	9,300	37%
1921–3	48,400	16,700	65,100	12,300	19%
1924–5	43,400	11,100	54,500	4,800	9%

Source: See Table 3 and Appendices table d. This excludes Northern Ireland.

These findings do not support Wood's contention that excessive Protestant migration was a primarily associated with the Irish revolution. Raised levels were already apparent before this, when the Protestant emigration rate was evidently higher than that among Catholics.[47] Wood's assumption that normal Protestant emigration simply mirrored the Catholic pattern prior to the revolution is erroneous; the pattern of excessive Protestant emigration noted by demographers for decades after 1926 was evidently already there between 1911 and 1926. This new finding indicates there were significant differences in Catholic and Protestant emigration patterns already between 1911 and 1919, just as there was in the decades thereafter. Push and pull factors in encouraging emigration played out differently for Protestants, who were more responsive to the pull factors of employment opportunities outside Ireland, particularly in Britain and its empire, before, during, and after the revolution. In the revolution, push factors provided additional incentives to leave: fear, intimidation, forced departures and terror undoubtedly all combined with a less optimistic view of a future in a new Catholic nationalist state to increase departures, but not to the extent suggested by Wood.

The figures on Table 8 imply that up to 27,000 Protestants left the south of Ireland between 1919 and 1923 (including those going to the six northern counties), and since many who left in this window were not forced to leave, these statistics are consistent with my earlier conclusion that there was a relatively lower number of forced or involuntary departures (something under 16,000).[48]

Niamh Dillon notes in a comparison of the independence transition in Ireland and India (based on oral testimony) that while violence was a factor for both the southern Irish Protestant community and the British community in India, it did not constitute the primary motive for emigration. Many departures in both groups were due to the fact that

---

47   For relative emigration levels from 1926, see J. J. Sexton and Richard O'Leary, 'Factors affecting population decline in minority religious communities in the Republic of Ireland', in *Building Trust in Ireland: Studies Commissioned by the Forum for Peace and Reconciliation* (Belfast, 1996) p. 302.
48   Andy Bielenberg, 'Exodus'.

'their role had fundamentally altered in both countries.'[49] Wood has somewhat simplified my position suggesting I have argued 'it was an exodus primarily fuelled by harsh economic conditions' when in fact I have demonstrated a range of factors at work, across all the years between 1911 and 1926. Moreover, in the light of Table 8 my original estimation of relatively higher Protestant economic emigration does not appear to be misplaced. While the *Church of Ireland Gazette* in 1929 lamented the economic pressure which forced such a large number of our young men and women to seek careers abroad if they wished to be upwardly mobile,[50] this chapter has revealed that this reality was already evident before the Irish revolution and even before the First World War.

In further analysis Leigh-Ann Coffey perceptively warns there is a danger that southern Protestants in the 1920s are being considered solely in terms of their conflict with the nationalist majority, when emigration was not a new phenomenon for the Church of Ireland. Although the *Church of Ireland Gazette* in the 1920s revealed the extent to which emigration posed a threat, she notes it also reinforced its influence within the wider Anglican community, increasing (rather than reducing) interest in wider imperial links in the 1920s.[51] This chapter suggests that an intensification of links to Britain and its empire for southern Protestants was already very apparent in relatively higher emigration levels to these destinations even before the revolution, though intensifying during its course. An important difference for Protestant departees was that they were on average drawn from higher social strata than the great bulk of Catholic emigrants identified by Lee. These important differences, it is argued here, also contributed to differences in the timing and the ultimate destination of Protestant departees for whom a different set of opportunities existed in imperial and British contexts relative to Catholics, adding further complexities to the 1911–26 exodus, over and above those specifically connected with revolution and regime change, significant as these undoubtedly were.

CONCLUSION

During and after the Irish revolution, the United States quickly reasserted its dominant position as a destination for Irish migrants, as its economy was more buoyant (at least until the Great Crash). Irish unskilled labour continued to flow westward, despite new American immigration restriction acts in 1921, 1924, and 1929, which were imposed variably on sending countries, thus affecting eastern and southern European countries more than Ireland. But the 1929 economic recession in the United States, which deepened in the 1930s, was particularly damaging to the Irish-American employment networks built

---

49 Niamh Dillon, '"We're Irish, but not that kind of Irish": British Imperial identity in transition in Ireland and India in the early twentieth century', in Ian d'Alton & Ida Milne (eds), *Protestant and Irish; the Minority's Search for Place in Independent Ireland* (Cork, 2018), p. 218.

50 Enda Delaney, *Demography, State and Society: Irish Migration to Britain, 1921–1971* (Liverpool, 2000), pp. 79–80.

51 Leigh-Ann Coffey, 'Drawing strength from past migratory experiences: *The Church of Ireland Gazette* and southern Protestant migration in the post-independence period', in Colin Barr and Hilary Carey (eds), *Religion and Greater Ireland: Christianity and Irish Global Networks* (Montreal, 2015), pp. 55–61.

up around manufacturing and urban patronage.[52] The flow of emigrants to Britain only slightly increased in the 1920s over the previous decade. Gross outward movement to Great Britain from the Irish Free State between 1923 and 1928 (see Table 5) constituted far less than half of the flow to the United States, and it was only in 1931 that Britain surpassed it, largely due to the complete collapse of transatlantic departures.

Lee has noted that in the 26 counties the number of agricultural labourers fell dramatically, from 300,000 in 1911 to merely 150,000 by 1936.[53] The sisters of these men also left in droves. This chapter has demonstrated that war, revolution, and regime change temporarily disrupted the traditional pattern of emigration, stemming the outflow of this underprivileged group of men and women, who contributed to the revolutionary opposition to the old order, which was evident in similar movements across Europe during and after the First World War. As republican expectations rose, those of southern unionists simultaneously fell, accelerating Protestant departures, which were already running at higher levels, even before 1919, due to the superior employment opportunities they could exploit in both British and colonial contexts. With economic recession and diminishing expectations of the new social order among anti-Treaty republicans, many of this group joined the post-revolutionary exodus, contributing to the final swansong of mass transatlantic emigration in the 1920s, when the United States briefly regained its traditional dominance as a destination for Irish emigrants after the wartime hiatus. This transatlantic movement was particularly apparent in the poorer districts of the south and west of the country, where republican pension claims registered dramatically higher levels of emigration, to the United States, in particular.[54] They joined a wider group of emigrants in the second half of the 1920s, in which the share engaged in labouring, agricultural work or domestic service was certainly still in a substantial majority, but falling somewhat since 1911, reflecting a growing share of emigrants higher up the social scale. Ranging widely across the social spectrum, all these departees left a very different social landscape in independent Ireland by the end of the 1920s. These decades had a narrowing impact on the population.

Emigration was certainly the most volatile component of population change throughout the twentieth century,[55] but between 1911 and 1926, excess deaths resulting from the First World War, the flu epidemic, and to a far lesser extent the Irish revolution collectively added to this volatility. But, war and revolution only temporarily altered and disrupted traditional patterns of emigration. If the focus of Irish emigration in terms of destination predominantly shifted to Great Britain in the 1930s,[56] occupational data collected during the Second World War indicate that the familiar profile of the emigrant strata identified by Lee was still quite apparent: unskilled workers dominated the wartime male outflow, while

---

52 Matthew O'Brien, 'Transatlantic connections and the sharp edge of the Great Depression', in *Eire-Ireland* 37 (2002).

53 Lee, *Ireland 1912–1985*, p. 159.

54 While this assessment is based on my own examination of the First Cork Brigade and West Cork Brigade IRA pension claims Military Service Pension Collection, Bureau of Military History, Dublin. See also Aiken, 'Sick on the Irish Sea', p. 94.

55 Liam Kennedy, *People and Population Change: A Comparative Study of Population Change in Northern Ireland and the Republic of Ireland* (Dublin, 1994), p. 23.

56 Delaney, *Demography, State and Society*.

domestic service and nursing dominated the female share.[57] Lee's identification of the fundamental continuity in emigration of this underprivileged strata of rural migrants from the late-nineteenth century through to the 1960s was a particularly important insight.[58] When emigration numbers climbed again to high levels in the 1980s, this was seen by Lee as the single greatest failure of the Irish status quo, consigning another generation to be departees.

APPENDICES

Table A; estimated net Irish emigration (32 counties) to Great Britain, 1911–20

	Irish-born in Great Britain	Estimated annual deaths	Population reduction	Estimated net Irish immigrants
1911	[550,040]	9,901	540,139	7274
1912	547,413	9853	537,560	7226
1913	544,786	9806	534,980	7179
1914	542,159	9759	523,400	7132
1915	539,532	9712	529,820	7085
1916	536,905	9,664	527,241	7037
1917	534,278	9617	524,661	6990
1918	531,651	9570	522,081	6943
1919	529,024	9522	519,502	6895
1920	526,397	9475	516,922	6845
1921	[523,767]			
Total net emigration to Great Britain: 70,606				

Sources: 1911 and 1921 are from census returns of Irish-born living in Great Britain in D. Akenson, *The Irish Diaspora,* (Toronto, 1996), p. 198. Annual deaths of Irish in Britain estimated to be 18 per 1,000, (slightly higher than death rate in Ireland). Estimate of net immigrants required following population reduction each year from deaths to bring the population number back up to interpolated estimate of Irish-born in following year, between 1911 and 1921.

---

57   Tracey Connolly, 'Emigration from Ireland to Britain during the Second World War', in Andy Bielenberg (ed.), *The Irish Diaspora* (Harlow, 2000), pp. 58–59.
58   Ibid., 390.

Table B; estimated net Irish emigration (32 counties) to Great Britain, 1921–1925

	Irish-born in Great Britain	Estimated annual deaths	Population reduction	Estimated net Irish immigrants
1921	[523,767]	9,428	514,339	7590
1922	521,929	9395	512,534	7557
1923	520,091	9362	510,729	7523
1924	518,252	9329	508,923	7492
1925	516,415	9295	507,120	7457
1926	514,577	9,263	505,314	7425
1927	512,739	9229	503,510	7391
1928	510,901	9196	501,705	7358
1929	509,063	9163	499,900	7325
1930	507,225	9130	498,095	7290
1931	[505,385]			
Total net emigration to Great Britain 1921–25: 37,619				

Sources: 1921 and 1931 Irish-born in Great Britain derived from census returns given in D. Akenson, *The Irish Diaspora,* (Toronto, 1996), p. 198. Annual deaths of Irish in Britain estimated to be 18 per 1,000, (slightly higher than death rate in Ireland). Estimate of net immigrants required following population reduction each year from deaths to bring the population number back up to interpolated estimate of Irish-born between census years.

Table C; estimated number of net immigrants of Irish birth to Great Britain, from the south of Ireland (26 counties) 1911–25

	Net immigrants from 32 counties	Estimated share 26 counties (%)	Net estimate immigrants from 26 counties
1911	7,274	72	5,266
1912	7,226	72.52	5,240
1913	7,179	72.64	5,215
1914	7,132	72.76	5,189
1915	7,085	72.88	5,164
1916	7,037	73	5,137
1917	6,990	73.12	5,111
1918	6,943	73.24	5,085
1919	6,895	73.36	5,058
1920	6,845	73.48	5,030
1921	7,590	73.6	5,586
1922	7,557	73.72	5,571
1923	7,523	73.84	5,555
1924	7,492	73.96	5,541
1925	7,457	74.08	5,524
Total	108,225		79,272

Note: The annual immigrant estimate from all Ireland into GB (left hand column) is based on appendices tables a and b. The Irish-born share in Great Britain from 26 counties is estimated by linear interpolation between 1911 and 1931 based on census returns for those years. There is no return for Scotland in 1911, but it is assumed percentage share of 26 counties in Scotland in 1911 was the same as in 1931. Data taken from Akenson, *The Irish Diaspora*, (Toronto, 1998), pp. 198, 206.

Table D; estimate of annual Protestant emigration from the south of Ireland (26 counties) 1911–26

	% of annual Methodist emigration	Estimated annual Protestant emigration
1911	11.1	6,600
1912	9.2	5,500
1913	9.7	5,800
1914	7.8	4,700
1915	4.9	2,900
1916	4.8	2,900
1917	4.6	2,800
1918	3.6	2,200
1919	7.2	4,300
1920	8.3	5,000
1921	8.4	5,000
1922	7.9	4,700
1923	4.3	2,600
1924	4	2,400
1925	4	2,400

Source: Methodist Historical Society of Ireland Archive, Edgehill College, Belfast. I would like to thank Revd Robin Roddie, archivist, for providing the annual Methodist membership information, from which the annual data for the south of Ireland has been extracted. The percentage in the left-hand column is % share of each year of total Methodist emigration from the south of Ireland between 1911 and 1925. This % share is utilised to distribute total Protestant emigration between 1911 and 1925 on an annual basis.

'The Lash of the Liberators': *Ireland 1912–1985* on Independence

Anne Dolan

Some time ago I was asked to present a paper at a conference on the history of happiness.[1] After two very enjoyable days discussing all sorts of shapes and sizes and species of happiness in nineteenth-century Ireland, I was to bring up the rear with an experiment, an indulgence if you will, to see if a historian of the twentieth century could even manage to uncover anything amounting to pleasure and contentment at all. In trying to find something, anything, to fill my allotted 50 minutes, I very quickly found that twentieth-century Ireland has no history, no obvious historian of happiness, nor for that matter many other emotions either. While we can certainly capture anger, hate, fury, scorn, while we're good at spite, rage, wrath, and irritation, that's tone rather than intention, object rather than subject; that's the unhappiness we have made for ourselves out of our seemingly unhappy lot. But to a century that presents its historians with famine, death, emigration, just as an obvious start, and yet so many of them could still seek happiness out, we in the twentieth century must seem a cross and sore, a sour and cantankerous lot.

As part of my search for happiness, I set upon *Ireland 1912–1985* because I remembered the preface promised 'occasional meditations on *mentalité*'.[2] I didn't even need to get to the 'flint-minded men and women whose grandparents had done well out of the Famine', or to the bit about our begrudgers' hearts to recognise that I had probably come to the wrong place.[3] As far as the fourth page of the preface was all it took to know: 'the modern Irish, contrary to popular impression, have little sense of history. What they have is a sense of grievance, which they choose to dignify by christening it history.'[4] And, God help me, after just four pages, I knew that I was home. I made the conference's sole and sorry reference to the happiness of gossip and one-upmanship, to the devilment in malice, to the sanctimony of scaling your own social heights along with the satisfaction of watching others tumble and fall. I made the case for the study of many of the less reputable along with the all too obvious joys.

I suppose I can say without meaning to be pretentious or glib that I grew up with this book and, given the type of history of happiness I sought out, I have clearly been

1   'Happiness in nineteenth-century Ireland', The Society for the Study of Nineteenth-Century Ireland Annual Conference, Trinity College Dublin, 28–29 June 2018.
2   J. J. Lee, *Ireland 1912–1985: Politics and Society* (Cambridge, 1989), p. xii.
3   Ibid., p. 158, p. 646.
4   Ibid., p. xiv.

shaped by it to the core. I was among the first classes of undergraduate history students to grapple with the intent and the ambition and the consequences of it, to tussle with its rage and its anger and its scorn. Up until this book I had been largely used to much more sombre tomes. Someone in secondary school thought I should read *Ireland Since The Famine*; it was measured and mellifluent, sensible and sophisticated, almost smoothly austere, but then came this.[5] It was as if I'd gone from a Noel Coward drawing room to the fury of a John Osborne flat, and nothing had really readied me for the wrench. But it wasn't just the tone that had changed, although of course the tone mattered. Indeed, you can see just how much it mattered in some of the disparate reviews the book provoked. While there were those who clearly welcomed it as a 'revisionist history', albeit one all the more valuable because it boldly thumbed its nose at 'the value-free caution' of its many contemporaries, others baulked at its use of irony and sarcasm, and pettifogged over too many 'Americanisms' and split infinitives and its 'welter of exclamation marks'.[6] There was a wariness, as one reviewer put it, of the 'driven rage' that 'suffuses the book with an Old Testament intolerance … shifting between the stark and brutal afflations of Isaiah and the equally bitter … lamentations of Jeremiah'.[7] If *The Modernisation Of Irish Society* was a 'rapier', the same reviewer adjudged, then this was a nuclear bomb launched from a 'Cork Los Alamos'.[8] For those more inclined to hurl on the ditch it was 'iconoclastic', it was 'history as critique', it was 'innovative', and 'energetic' and 'challenging' and other such words that don't commit themselves to too much more than that.[9]

The reviewers seemed slightly taken aback by the 'incisive – not to say lacerating – tone', by the 'invective [that] courses volcanically through the whole book'.[10] Although some cautioned 'readers wanting judicious and balanced accounts of recent Irish history' to stick with Lyons and Fanning and Harkness, and while others saw it as a welcome fall from the 'Olympian' heights of Foster's *Modern Ireland, 1600-1972*, the ambition of the book seemed to be made of more than the revisionist debate many of these reviewers tried to contain it within.[11] It was clear from the earliest pages that it was trying to engage with debates much

---

5   F. S. L. Lyons, *Ireland Since the Famine* (2nd edn, London, 1973).

6   'This is "revisionist" history, certainly, but without the value-free caution sometimes charged against modern Irish historians.' Owen Dudley Edwards, 'Brilliant jeremiad', in *New Statesman and Society*, 2 Feb. 1990, p. 37. Hugh Kearney, 'The Irish and their history', in *History Workshop* 31 (Spring 1991), p. 149. On language, irony, Americanisms, exclamation marks, and split infinitives, see D. W. Harkness, 'Review of *Ireland 1912–1985*', in *The English Historical Review* 106:420 (July 1991), p. 680; M. A. G. Ó Tuathaigh, 'Review of *Ireland 1912–1985: Politics and Society*', in *The Canadian Journal of Irish Studies* 17:1 (July 1991), p. 109; Raymond Crotty, 'Review of *Ireland 1912–1985*', in *Studies: An Irish Quarterly Review* 79:315 (Autumn 1990), p. 319; David Fitzpatrick, 'A record of failure', in *Times Literary Supplement*, 8–14 June 1990, p. 604.

7   K. Theodore Hoppen, 'Review: Ireland, Britain, and Europe: Twentieth-century nationalism and its spoils', in *The Historical Journal* 34:2 (June 1991), p. 508.

8   Ibid.

9   Paul Bew, 'An iconoclastic history, yet partly it's dated', in *Fortnight* 283 (Apr. 1990), pp. 23–4; Charles Townshend, 'History as critique', in *The Irish Review* 8 (Spring 1990), pp. 117–18; Tom Garvin, 'Review of *Ireland 1912–1985*', in *Irish Historical Studies* 27:105 (May 1990), p. 87; Ó Tuathaigh, 'Review of *Ireland 1912–1985*', p. 109.

10   Townshend, 'History as critique', p. 117.

11   Paul Canning, 'Review of *Ireland 1912–1985*', in *Albion: A Quarterly Journal Concerned with British Studies* 23:2 (Summer 1991), p. 375; Fitzpatrick, 'A record of failure', p. 604; Garvin, 'Review of *Ireland 1912–1985*', p. 86.

more ambitious than that. Fearghal McGarry looked back at it with the hindsight of 2007 and described it as 'a trenchant, even scathing, critique of the shortcomings of the politics, administration and society of independent Ireland under the guise of a traditional survey history', but that gets at only part of what I mean.[12] I'm not sure *Ireland 1912–85* was ever working under the pretext that it was a survey in any 'traditional' sense, even though it may have been 'originally commissioned as a 200-page introduction to modern Ireland'.[13] But the uneasiness of those early reviews that did not seem to know what to do with the book's irony and 'bitter sarcasm' and 'contempt' seems to spring from the assumption that it should be a survey in the traditional sense, that it should aspire to 'the detachment of tone' of the 'invariably polite' Lyons, and that it should be content to dance, yet another angel on the head of the revisionist pin.[14]

But *Ireland 1912–85* was never as insular or straightforward as that. Even the preface sets it out as a much more wayward thing. The aspiration to 'total history', announced three paragraphs in, 'not in the futile sense of trying to write everything about everything', but in seeking out 'linkages between the varieties of activity', gives the book its sweeping Braudelian ambition.[15] In the fourth paragraph come Bloch's *mentalités*; in the footnotes German and American scholars dominate.[16] The closing chapter, 'Perspectives', sees the book 'probing the layers of the popular psyche' as the preface promised, just as Theodore Zeldin tried to capture the manners and passions and character of the French.[17] In 1982 Zeldin wrote about how historians 'still generally keep a distance between themselves and their publications', about 'the great difference between learned and imaginative literature', and that 'the distinction or barrier between these two forms of writing has been raised in the name of professionalism, but it has become constricting, and is due for demolition'.[18] In an interview in the *Irish Times* in 1991 Lee remarked: 'I think we have tended too rigidly in the past to isolate work of this type from creative literature....We badly need imagination in our historical writings.... I wanted to explain my country to myself.'[19] His book may have been 'conceived in the tranquil atmosphere of Peterhouse ... and completed on the serene slopes of Fiesole', it may have sharpened its teeth during 'more turbulent times in Cork', but there were French and German ideas flowing through this Ireland's veins.[20]

And this showed in other fundamental ways. There is a very telling use of the word 'however' in the fourth paragraph of the book:

> The nature of Anglo-Irish relations has traditionally constituted the main organising principle

---

12 Fearghal McGarry, 'Twentieth-century Ireland revisited', in *Journal of Contemporary History* 42:1 (Jan. 2007), p. 137.
13 'I wanted to explain my country to myself', *Irish Times*, 26 Oct. 1991.
14 Townshend, 'History as critique', p. 117; Terence de Vere White on Lyons, *Irish Times*, 20 Apr. 2019.
15 Lee, *Ireland 1912–1985*, p. xii.
16 Ibid., pp. xi–xii.
17 Ibid., p. xii. For example, Theodore Zeldin, *France 1848-1945*, Vol. 1: *Ambition, Love and Politics* (Oxford, 1973); Theodore Zeldin, *France 1848-1945*, Vol. 2: *Volume Two Intellect, Taste and Anxiety* (Oxford, 1977).
18 Theodore Zeldin, 'Personal history and the history of emotions', in *Journal of Social History* 15:3 (Spring 1982), p. 339.
19 *Irish Times*, 26 Oct. 1991.
20 Lee, *Ireland 1912–1985*, p. xi.

of Irish historiography. The historian of independent Ireland, however, and to some extent even of Northern Ireland, must focus more on the relationship between the potential and the performance of sovereignty, however much that relationship may be moulded by external influences.[21]

That shift in the register of analysis away from the relationship which had been at the heart of the revisionist debate towards a reckoning of how this place had fared, may well have come from a frustration with the scant analysis of 'the period after 1921' ('it was as if Irish history culminated with independence'), but the instinct was more ambitious than, not as parochial as, that.[22] 'Performance', 'potential', while 'elusive, complex and, in certain respects, subjective concepts', do demand scale, demand measurement, demand comparison, and *Ireland 1912–1985* had a broad comparative framework at its core.[23] Whether in the running or left fading badly as an also-ran, the myopic Anglo-Irish race was run. Czechoslovakia, Hungary, Austria, Finland, Poland, Denmark were now amongst others in the field, and although this turning outwards, this shift beyond the familiar was in the first order to 'illuminate our understanding of the Irish condition', these comparisons were always undertaken with the type of brio that knew the Irish case would 'enrich wider historical perspectives' in turn.[24] Comparison was to point again and again to Ireland's poor performance, but comparison was also a means to put manners on those instincts that Liam Kennedy would later identify in the context of nineteenth-century Ireland as 'M. O. P. E. – the Most Oppressed People Ever – the Irish'.[25] In the interwar period, the part of the book I am most concerned with here, comparisons come as sobering rebukes to those who would play the poor mouth or use history as a means to stir up 'old grievances to keep them on the boil'.[26] The civil war was a 'more modest inheritance' compared to Finland's tearing of itself apart; agrarianism yielded 'few pickings for an Irish Stamboliski', and we might do well to remember that the Bulgarian premier's head ended up sent to Sofia in a biscuit box.[27] Party politics was remarkably stable compared to the fragmentation of Czechoslovakia, Yugoslavia and Poland.[28] Literacy rates were close to 100 per cent, far from the 50 per cent of Yugoslavia or the 20 per cent of Albania.[29] And the Free State had no 'predatory' neighbour, it had 'no Banat, no Bessarabia, no Bukovina, no Dobruja, no Macedonia, no Salonica, no Silesia, no Slovakia, no Teschen, no Thrace, no Transylvania'.[30] This is just a small sample across ten pages of the book and there were more. While the Irish Free State was found wanting on so many scales by *Ireland 1912–1985*, these were sharp reminders that some races were better not to win.

Comparative approaches may well have been trumped in recent years by the transnational and the global turn within Irish history, but one of the most striking points of comparison

21 Ibid., p. xii.
22 *Irish Times*, 26 Oct. 1991.
23 Lee, *Ireland 1912–1985*, p. xii.
24 Ibid., p. xiii.
25 Liam Kennedy, *Unhappy the Land: The Most Oppressed People Ever, the Irish?* (Sallins, 2016).
26 Quoting Dick Walsh, Lee, *Ireland 1912–1985*, p. xiv.
27 Lee, *Ireland 1912–1985*, p. 69, p. 73.
28 Ibid., p. 80.
29 Ibid., p. 76.
30 Ibid., p. 79.

the preface asked historians of Ireland to pursue was 'a truly comparative history of North and South'.[31] Despite David Fitzpatrick's *The Two Irelands* and Peter Martin's study of censorship, amongst others, that work, as Lee wrote, 'has yet to be adequately conceived, much less completed'.[32] But *Ireland 1912–1985* itself might explain some reasons why. The book had rather testy relations with its Northern Ireland; it was on Ulster Unionism that Gearóid Ó Tuathaigh said the irony 'hardens into something more severely sardonic', and with 'less than a dozen of the 200-odd pages devoted to the period 1922–45' dealing directly with Northern Ireland by Theodore Hoppen's count, it seemed that sense of being 'ambivalent towards the North' expressed at the outset of the book was tussling it out with something much more strident and altogether certain instead.[33] But for all the ease with which the book had slipped into the use of '*Herrenvolk*' by page four, there was also much to unsettle any easy nationalist reading of Northern Ireland or of partition even more.[34] While Lee admits openly that 'my own preferences are not concealed' on Northern Ireland, that does not mean we should assume they are so easy to pigeonhole and pin down as that.[35] Those who might hear echoes of their own sentiments in the 'trenchant comments on the "*Herrenvolk* democracy" established in the North', might well be stung by these appraisals of partition: 'partition, in particular, saved the Free State from many of the problems of new nations'; 'partition now saved the South from the most explosive internal problems subverting new states, race and religion, by the simple device of exporting them to the North'.[36] To be saved once, Professor Lee, may be regarded a misfortune; to be saved twice looks like waywardness.[37] If the Northern Irish state was to be exposed to scorn, then 'the veil of delusion concerning the North in which the South cocooned itself' was just as robustly cast aside.[38] 'Sacred cows' were going to be shown for the scrawny beasts they were, never mind the 'intense resentment among the guardians of the bovine faith'.[39]

That 'duty' to tell not just the Emperor but 'all his Irish readers' that they were not just politely '*déshabillé*', but a downright naked disgrace was certainly not shied away from as the book measured 'the performance of a sovereign people'.[40] But across this process of holding to account, two words kept cropping up: 'illusion' and 'delusion' appear again and again. While historians were the first to be warned about succumbing 'to delusions of grandeur', the illusions ran rampant.[41] Eoin MacNeill's 'The North Began' was 'a combination of insight and illusion'; the 'essential assumption … that Ulster Protestant attitudes were basically the consequence of British duplicity' was 'the illusion implicit'

31 Ibid., p. xiv.
32 David Fitzpatrick, *The Two Irelands: 1912–1939* (Oxford, 1996); Peter Martin, *Censorship in the Two Irelands 1922–1939* (Dublin, 2006); Lee, *Ireland 1912–1985*, p. xiv.
33 Hoppen, 'Review: Ireland, Britain, and Europe', p. 512; Ó Tuathaigh, 'Review of *Ireland 1912–1985*', p. 109; Lee *Ireland 1912–1985*, p. xiv.
34 Lee, *Ireland 1912–1985*, p. 4.
35 Ibid., p. xiv.
36 Harkness, 'Review of *Ireland 1912–1985*', p. 679; Lee, *Ireland 1912–1985*, p. 93, p. 77.
37 With apologies to Lady Bracknell and Oscar Wilde.
38 Lee, *Ireland 1912–1985*, p. 250. In the course of an interview in the *Irish Times*, Lee was quoted: 'We lived a lie about partition, that we were actually deeply concerned about abolishing partition.' *Irish Times*, 26 Oct. 1991.
39 Lee, *Ireland 1912–1985*, p. xiii.
40 Ibid.
41 Ibid.

in the Irish Volunteers' approach that 'would continue to bedevil Irish nationalism for generations'.[42] 'Constitutional nationalists had garbed the 1914 Home Rule Act' in a 'veil of illusion'; in turn they failed 'to effectively expose the illusions in Sinn Féin's proclaimed policy'.[43] At the Treaty negotiations Griffith 'reflected the immaturity of nationalist thinking about Ulster in allowing himself to be deluded' by Lloyd George; all sides of the Treaty divide 'would predictably complain in due course when nobody came to rescue them for the consequences of their own proclivity for self-deception' about what the Boundary Commission would bring.[44] It was another 'illusion to assume that had the Treaty not been signed, everything could have continued simply as before, irrespective of the validity of Lloyd George's threat', and 'contrary to a comforting Irish illusion, civil wars were not normal events in the new state of the time'.[45]

After independence there were more. Patrick Hogan's 'assumptions' about agricultural policy 'were either illusory, or, at the very least, debatable, even within his own terms of reference'; the '"agricultural community" was a convenient cosmetic concept used to foster the illusion that what was good for the strong farmer was good for the country.'[46] Indeed, Hogan and his department were left to 'indulge their illusions throughout the twenties', while Kevin O'Higgins was prone to illusions of his own.[47] Although censorship 'served the materialistic values of the propertied classes by fostering the illusion that Ireland was a haven of virtue surrounded by a sea of vice', the 'mere existence of the Dáil fostered the illusion that a new society was being shaped'.[48] Cumann na nGaedheal had rather prosaic 'illusions' about Fianna Fáil's inability to govern, but de Valera trumped them with something more grandiose, with 'historical illusion', with grander 'rhetorical illusions' instead.[49] The Constitution was exposed as fostering the illusion 'that Irish society placed a special value on motherhood' though 'social values prevented a higher proportion of women from becoming mothers than in any other European country'.[50] There are more illusions than those noted, and I have only got as far as 1937 here. By the book's final chapter illusions have given way to 'fantasy' and to something more grindingly insidious – 'self-deception', and it was 'a capacity for self-deception on a heroic scale'.[51] There was nothing worse than making a virtue out of settling for less.

One of the consequences of this weighing up and being found wanting was the type of people this book began to bring within the ambit of twentieth-century Irish history, those same 'flint-minded men and women whose grandparents had done well out of the Famine'.[52] While one reviewer complained that the book made no single reference to Countess Markievicz, I saw very little wrong with such a gap.[53] History didn't have to

42 Ibid., pp. 18–19.
43 Ibid., p. 37, pp. 41–2.
44 Ibid., pp. 52–3.
45 Ibid., p. 53, p. 68.
46 Ibid., pp. 115–16.
47 Ibid., p. 118.
48 Ibid., p. 158, p. 172.
49 Ibid., p. 178, p. 185, p. 201, p. 214.
50 Ibid., p. 207.
51 Ibid., p. 513, p. 652.
52 Ibid., p. 158.
53 Canning, 'Review of Ireland 1912–1985', p. 374.

be about the Countess Markieviczes anymore. (Indeed, in light of all the sound and fury about commemorations past and still to come, it is rather intriguing to see that the dispute over the Mayo librarian got more room in the book than the War of Independence.) Plenty of ink, it seemed, had already been spent on the exceptions, the cranks, the elites, the glorious failures, and the faded grandeur of those who might, or should, or wanted to be in charge of independent Ireland. The disgruntled and the disaffected had been heard often and heard well, and there was certainly time for the George Russells and the Sean O'Faolains and the like to rest on their cantankerous and eloquent laurels for a while. And although *Ireland 1912–1985* spoke of them only in their broadest terms, and held them nonetheless ruthlessly to account, it was a history of their twentieth century, those who had the bad taste to be middling and to aspire to middling things, those who voted and kept voting for de Valera and Fianna Fáil, those who went to mass and maybe even liked it, those who didn't protest, those who turned a blind eye, those who craved respectability above and beyond the achievement of most other things.[54] We may well know them, bland and inanimate, as the people, the public, the electorate in most of the other twentieth-century Irelands up to this point, but here they were its dark and beating heart, they were the possessors who wanted nothing more out of independence than to increase what they possessed; they produced the civil servants in the Department of Finance who saw it as their purpose to stymie and to thwart, and in the pages of this book they seemed worth the passion and the fury and the spirit of approach that had, up to this, only really been spent on the obviously great and the notoriously good. I suppose I saw in it for the first time a history of independent Ireland that dealt with the people I knew and recognised. And maybe for some of the same reasons I understood but was also troubled by some of the anger these people had provoked.

The comfort of some of the other histories of independent Ireland was partly their propensity to blame those in charge for what went wrong. If independent Ireland was the history of a disappointment it was due to the conservatism and narrow vision of its politicians not to the natural propensity to narrowness on its own people's part. Lyons began his discussion of independent Ireland thus: 'That the revolutionary of today is the conservative of tomorrow is a truism of politics in no way contradicted by the recent history of modern Ireland.'[55] Within a few pages the state slinks away to the flickering shadows of Plato's cave. By the time of Roy Foster's *Modern Ireland* conservatism was a given. A chapter on the Irish Free State could begin with the phrase 'the rigorous conservatism of the Irish Free State has become a cliché', and like most clichés it was found to have more than its share of truth.[56] Theodore Hoppen went further still. Independent Ireland was not just conservative. It had, as he put it, a 'singular capacity … for standing still'.[57] An Ireland going nowhere was his last word. But all of this – even John Regan's later classification of the first leaders of the Free State as counter-revolutionaries intent on undoing that which

---

54 See Charles Townshend on how the book holds 'the Irish' as a whole to account. Townshend, 'History as critique', pp. 117–18.
55 Lyons, *Ireland Since the Famine*, p. 471.
56 R. F. Foster, *Modern Ireland 1600–1972* (2nd edn, London, 1989), p. 516.
57 K. T. Hoppen, *Ireland Since 1800: Conflict and Conformity* (London, 1989), p. 256.

may have been revolutionary in the first place – put the locus of blame firmly on those in charge.[58]

Somewhere in all these disappointments and missed opportunities was a people who wanted and deserved and aspired to better and more; they were let down by a limited and an insular ruling class. Don't worry, Joe Lee gives us that from the start to withering effect, but the book gives us far more than that: the challenge that it was all our own fault, that it always had been, right from the start, and not fixing it, whatever *it* may be, was always down not just to a cohort of politicians, but to ourselves. In every period since independence we have been lucky enough to get the governments we have wanted and maybe even deserved. And we have been independent long enough now to only have ourselves to blame for all the things we are prepared to admit we need to fix. And that's a far harder one to dole out as well as take. While imagining if we had been overrun by the Nazis in the 1940s, Lee asks, 'how many torturers and sadists, racy of the soil, as well as opportunists and careerists, would have seized their chance in the New Order?' He concludes that 'it is sometimes happier for a country, as for an individual, not to have to learn too much about itself.'[59] In most other contexts he was not so inclined to hold back. If 'the poor, the aged, and the unemployed must all feel the lash of the liberators', the middling sorts of twentieth-century Ireland would all feel the lash of Joe Lee.[60]

One of the most scathing passages in the whole book is reserved for these plain people of Ireland. He writes:

> Few peoples anywhere have been so prepared to scatter their children around the world in order to preserve their own living standards. And the children themselves left the country to improve their material prospects. Their letters home are full of references to their material progress, preferably confirmed by the inclusion of notes and money orders. Those who remained at home further exhibited their own worship of the golden calf in their devotion to the primacy of the pocket in marriage arrangements calculated to the last avaricious farthing, in the milking of bovine TB eradication schemes, in the finessing of government grants, subsidies and loans, of medical certificates and insurance claims, in the scrounging for petty advantage among protected businessmen, in the opportunistic cynicism with which wage and salary claims, not to mention professional fees, were rapaciously pursued. The Irish may have been inefficient materialists. That was not due to any lack of concern with material gain. If their values be deemed spiritual, then spirituality must be defined as covetousness tempered only by sloth.[61]

And this is well over 100 pages before we get to our begrudgers' hearts. When we do get to that blistering and short section on 'Character' towards the end of the book, with footnotes drawing on a telling and potentially combustible combination of sources, such as John Healy and Theodore Zeldin, there seems to be a wholesale indictment of the many and not the few.[62] 'Status depended not only on rising oneself, but on preventing others from rising'; 'envy of the thrusting neighbour frequently lurked beneath the cloak of ridicule'; 'nothing could sweeten the rancid pill of a rival's success'; 'the Irish begrudgers must return again and again to the same obsessive resentment, like a circle of Invidias eternally gnawing

---

58   John M. Regan, *The Irish Counter-Revolution 1921–1936* (Dublin, 1999).
59   Lee, *Ireland 1912–1985*, p. 268.
60   Ibid., p. 124.
61   Ibid., p. 522.
62   Ibid., pp. 643–57.

at the same heart. The cancer of begrudgery probably drove many to drink, for spite and drink were often children of the same frustration.'[63] Across that section, there appears the 'mercenarily married', the 'shrivelled personalities', the 'families pursuing ancestral feuds', 'the half-indulged, [the] half-despised', those who just 'lingered through life', 'a legion of stunted personalities', and all through it we are reminded that our capacity for hypocrisy is matched only by our hunger for 'self-deception' – and think on just what might have followed if that section had gone on.[64]

While some reviewers questioned whether 'the Irish', each and every one, did indeed beat time to a begrudger's rather than a fanatic's heart, I knew and understood well what a begrudger's heart might be.[65] I come from a long line of them, and I have huge sympathy for the anger that comes from the pages of this book, because it prods where prodding hurts, because it still cuts closer than I would like to the bone. I had sat through enough Sunday dinners that invariably ended up marching out every acre of land that should have gone one way in a will rather than another, on who was and wasn't getting ideas above their station, on who you should vote for because, like their father before them, they'd always do you a good turn. What I learned about right and wrong was less about good and bad and more about respectability and disgrace, and to be seen to be respectable mattered above all else. And 1920s, 1930s, 1970s, 1980s, no matter – another generation with their own twist on the same 'thwarted ambition ... frustrated hopes, shattered ideals'.[66] I knew all of this and much more that went with it was part of what was meant by a begrudger's heart. It's fundamental to what we might try to understand as class in twentieth-century Ireland, to what thwarts and what prohibits, to how what changed did change, and much more to what never changed at all. And I have been struck by the challenge that *Ireland 1912–1985* laid down and also by how loath as historians of independent Ireland we have been to actually take that challenge up. Padraic Colum captured some of it in his *Road Round Ireland* back in 1926; there are threads of it everywhere before and since, more benignly perhaps in John Waters's characterisation of the 'people with straw in their hair, cow dung on their shoes and the taste of stale tea on their tongues', but their history largely remains unwritten for all of our attempts, for all the last 30 years of books.[67]

In some ways Padraic Colum's *Road Round Ireland* might be required reading alongside *Ireland 1912–1985*'s interwar years, alongside what David Fitzpatrick called the 'homily of 177 pages' at the end of the book.[68] Colum wrote with the same compassion Lee does for those who felt 'the lash of the liberators'. Towards the end of Colum's wanderings, he gives us Maureen at the age of 'fourteen, there or thereabouts', churning butter, waiting for something in Kerry. Apparently, she hasn't 'the type of good looks that would draw the young men to her' when the time comes, and her 'people are poor; they could hardly get together a dowry for her'.[69] But already she knows she'll go. Her aunt in America will send

---

63   Ibid., pp. 646–7.
64   Ibid., p. 645, pp. 648–9, p. 652.
65   Ibid., p. 646; Joy Rudd, 'Review: Innocence is bliss', in *Books Ireland* 139 (Mar. 1990), p. 30.
66   Lee, *Ireland 1912–1985*, p. 647.
67   Padraic Colum, *The Road Round Ireland* (New York, 1926); John Waters, 'Taste the difference', in Máirtín Breathnach (ed.), *Republican Days: 75 Years of Fianna Fáil* (Dublin, 2002), p. 73.
68   Fitzpatrick, 'A record of failure', p. 604.
69   Colum, *The Road Round Ireland*, p. 480.

the passage money and 'failing that, the Reverend Mother who was here lately, and who brought girls over to Texas to become postulants in a convent there, will be here again…. The prospect seemed a good one to her.' And like Lee, Colum drives it home: 'the children listen to her entranced as she says the wonderful name "Texas". Anyway, Maureen will go'.[70] Colum had the same rage with 'the shut-in, unlovely little town', that same sympathy with 'the girl behind the counter in a little shop [who] gets dissatisfied with her meagre wage, gets discontented with her employer's pettiness, gets filled up with the tedium of a place', and he had the same fury for the petty and the powerful as well.[71] James Covey and his mother from Colum's midlands had begrudgers' hearts. 'Left a widow with a bit of land … this woman's life has succeeded. Her son has shop and farm; he is on the County Council.'[72] He thwarted the forming of a cooperative credit society because it went against his interests and, as the local agent for a shipping company, he profited from the hurry to get away. '[A] young man with a bald forehead and blinking eyes', Covey is 'the richest man now in the place'.[73] Colum proves Lee was not the first to draw attention to these people, or to count the cost of what it took to keep their small ambitions satisfied, but 30 years on from *Ireland 1912–1985*, do they still prompt the same reply? The begrudgers made their own choices, took their own risks, chose which opportunities they wanted to escape as well as miss, and we might do well to remember that posterity will inevitably condescend to us in turn.[74]

What has been taken up with real verve since *Ireland 1912–1985* is the anger with the state and with the key institutions of Irish life, the anger with the Coveys and their kind 'who placed such value on inheritance and appearance' above all else.[75] What Diarmaid Ferriter calls the 'scandal-inspired lens', which 'we cannot now look at Ireland in the 20th century without', has brought to the surface so much more of what those begrudgers' hearts were capable of than *Ireland 1912–1985* ever could.[76] The groundbreaking histories that have been written since of institutionalisation, infanticide, child abuse, sexual abuse, the urgency to uncover the 'hidden histories' of those who have suffered the most and harmed the most have let us see how many of the most vulnerable in our society were treated at the hands of institutions in this state, and how willingly we put from us those deemed to have transgressed.[77] We have learned the hard way how in the kingdom of the Coveys respectability was a cruel and an exacting king. But re-reading *Ireland 1912–1985* in the light of this work, are there things that we can now come with more impetus to pursue? The broadest and most comprehensive sense of social responsibility may well be coming back into our accounts of Irish life, but it poses the hardest challenge, because it implicates us all; it leaves less room to be so certain or so shrill. What do we do with the tuppence ha'penny who looked down on tuppence, with the steady belittling drip of slights? How do

---

70   Ibid., pp. 480–1.
71   Ibid., pp. 43–4.
72   Ibid., p. 33.
73   Ibid., p. 32, p. 35.
74   E. P. Thompson, *The Making of the English Working Class* (London, 1963), p. 12.
75   Lee quoted in Diarmaid Ferriter, 'J. J. Lee's "total history" of modern Ireland: Still required reading 30 years on', *Irish Times*, 20 Apr. 2019.
76   Ferriter, 'J. J. Lee's "total history"'.
77   Ibid.

we tackle the many fathers and mothers who brought their daughters to the gates of those Magdalen laundries or those mother and baby homes because respectability trumped compassion and affection or at least what we assume those things meant? What do we do with all the many sins of omission, with all those who could have helped and didn't and just looked the other way? Lee's world of narrow begrudgery is central to this work but so too are the challenges he posed about the part religion played in twentieth-century Irish life. In some respects, he was calling for a clear distinction to be drawn between religious belief and the mobilisation of sin towards very certain ends. Acknowledging that it is 'the glory of authentic religious belief that it can never be reduced to mere expression of material interests', his take on sin is an altogether different one: 'sin was sculptured in a style appealing to the aesthetic interests of the possessing classes.... The precise manner in which the spiritual and the material interact ... reveals much about the nature of a society. In the case of "traditional" Ireland, it requires exploration of surgical delicacy.'[78] While few could argue, in the light of so much that has been revealed, that church and state and people can be separated as wheat from chaff, but that relationship between sin and material interest still awaits its surgeon and its knife.

But so do so many other things. Across that final chapter, across the book's other 'meditations on *mentalité*', there should have been the beginning of Ireland's history of emotions, but for some reason it did not quite transpire.[79] Apart from Breandán Ó hEithir's *Begrudger's Guide To Irish Politics* there is yet to be a history of begrudgery.[80] The disappointed, the thwarted and the envious go without their histories. '[T]he role of spite in individuals and institutions is a patent and potent fact of Irish life', Lee writes, but still we have no historians yet of Irish spite.[81] Of the 'inheritors and the disinherited "relatives assisting"... the losers who remained at home', he says, 'their history has yet to be written', and arguably remains so still.[82] These and many other aspects so central to the section on Irish character go without their books, because in this, as in so many other things the book identifies, those who bear most blame are the bones and stuff of us still and for that reason are the hardest to hold to some type of account.

If *Ireland 1912–1985* was laying the basis for a history of Irish emotions, it was redolent of Lucien Febvre's call for histories of hate, fear, pity, cruelty and love back in 1941.[83] The overwhelming darkness of Febvre's selection made sense given the France in which he wrote, just as Ireland of the 1980s readily suggested disappointment and envy and begrudgery and spite.[84] Some of the surprise in the contemporary reviews of the book about the anger of its tone seem strangely removed from the resonant chord that same anger seemed to strike at the time. Diarmaid Ferriter refers to the 'huge influence' of 'its ferocity' on him, and 30 years ago, ferocity made sense.[85] Even as a teenager, I could see why. Part of the

---

78 Lee, *Ireland 1912–1985*, p. 650.
79 Ibid., p. xii.
80 Breandán Ó hEithir, *The Begrudger's Guide to Irish Politics* (Dublin, 1986).
81 Lee, *Ireland 1912–1985*, p. 647.
82 Ibid., p. 649.
83 Peter Burke (ed.), *A New Kind of History: From the Writings of Lucien Febvre* (London, 1973), p. 24.
84 Barbara Rosenwein, 'Worrying about emotions in history', in *American Historical Review* 107, 3 (June 2002), p. 822.
85 Ferriter, 'J. J. Lee's "total history"'.

point of going to university was to postpone what seemed to be the inevitable decision to leave. And I would be leaving in much the same way that my father (albeit briefly) and all the rest of his siblings had left a generation before – the macroeconomics of it might have been different, but explain that to my parents, to my older sister who had already left. There was plenty to be angry about as dole queues and queues for American visas grew and grew, as Northern Ireland tore itself more furiously apart. And as a great wealth of the state's earliest records were released, Brian Farrell and Pat Kenny reminded us just how bad it still was every bloody evening on *Today Tonight*. While Clifford Geertz gave a theoretical turn to the frustration with the recent past, and though the 'deflating experience' of living in, rather than imagining independence, clearly influenced *Ireland 1912–1985*'s seminal interpretation of the interwar years, the actual turn of living in another round of economic depression may well have shaped it more.[86] Interwar Ireland is presented as a disappointment, as Lee puts it, 'in the context of historical expectations'.[87] And it is a view that has been broadly echoed since. Nothing was as we would have liked it to have been, and as research has developed in the last 30 years, the 1920s and 1930s have found more and more ways to let us down. Although we have presumed to, it is too narrow to speak of the 'failures of Irish independence' alone.[88] How can we speak of failure, without a sense of what we mean by, what anyone at the time could have conceived of as, success?

But though I understand the anger, this is where I want to take a different view, because the begrudger is too complex and too pervasive a creature to be written off as easily as that. The more I look at the period, the less important and entitled my own sense of anger becomes. What people at the time defined as their own expectations and norms are, needless to say, far more interesting than that. We can, for example, rail against the nature of poverty in the Irish Free State, but poverty is relative to its own times, abject according to each period's ways of making ends meet. In 1923 Frank O'Connor got a job as a trainee librarian in Sligo's Carnegie Library on 30 shillings a week. 'I found lodgings near Sligo Cathedral at 27 and six pence a week and had a whole half-crown for laundry, cigarettes and drink. Mother had worked it out that it would be cheaper to post my laundry home than to get it done locally, and every week I posted home my shirt, my underpants, a pair of stockings and some handkerchiefs.'[89] While this tells us much of how he measured out his life down to his last pint and cigarette butt, while it tells us more about his mother who took on a job herself to add half-a-crown to his weekly wage, it gives us a scale, maybe not the GNPs and the GDPs, not the grand comparative scales of Finland or Denmark, but at least a scale in one man's head, not thriving, not sinking either, a sense of what it took just to get by.[90] And if one shirt on, one shirt off, was getting by in what was probably thought a decent respectable job, where O'Connor went back to his digs with no dirt, with no calluses on his hands, we have a far better sense of what poverty meant in 1923. His sympathy for the 'poor country girl', as he called her, found sleeping in the garden of his lodgings because she had been 'thrown out by her parents and had nowhere in the world to go' said

---

86   Clifford Geertz, *The Interpretation of Cultures* (New York, 1973), p. 235.
87   Lee, *Ireland 1912–1985*, p. 173.
88   Diarmaid Ferriter, *The Transformation of Ireland 1900-2000* (London, 2004), p. 759.
89   Frank O'Connor, *My Father's Son* (3rd edn, Belfast, 1994), p. 14.
90   Ibid., p. 13.

what he thought poverty amounted to.[91] We cannot chart the gap between 'potential and performance' without the arithmetic at work in O'Connor's head.[92]

Ireland 1912–1985 makes the case eloquently and acerbically that the 'cabinet pursued a particular economic policy from choice and from conviction, not from ignorance of possible alternatives.... It took the view that the poor were responsible for their poverty. They should pay for their lack of moral fibre.' But there is still room to explore such experiences and such perceptions of poverty as well.[93] The utterances and the policies of Ernest Blythe and Patrick McGilligan have made it straightforward to hold the new state to account, but the women in rural Kerry who 'put on their boots coming into the town, so that they will be respectable-looking at Mass' leave us a different and more difficult task. While they were respectful of their religion, perhaps, they were also determined not to give their 'betters' the satisfaction of sneering at their bare and dirty feet.[94] In the sneering and the slights, in the names called off the altar for what was not given, in the begging letters written and the cost of the help received, we begin to see what poverty meant and how some were never allowed to forget the help they got.[95] In the power of local charity over local need, of local credit over local debt, of local snobberies over local slights, the tyrannies of proprieties in a small place need still to be understood. We need to think more about who ordered out the everyday in society as a whole. And how thoroughly content many were to have it ordered in that way.

Behind so much of this, so much of what *Ireland 1912–1985* identified as envy, hypocrisy, spite, and driving those 'splenetic surges or jealousy', even the begrudgery, was perhaps something the book said far less about – overarching respectability.[96] If censorship can be understood as a mark of 'the risen bourgeoisie, touting for respectability', if the 'preoccupation with occasions of sin in dance halls ... amounted in practice to issuing a moral blank cheque to other types of behaviour that wouldn't be found out', if we have taken the measure of the cruelties respectability exacted at the door of mother and baby homes and Magdalen laundries, if we can see it writ large in the social tyrannies that kept people in their place and wearily convinced that it was their place to keep, then we know just how much respectability ordered out the measure of this place.[97] What we still need to understand is why. To be respectable by your own, or even more by someone else's reckoning, can be found too often in the striving and the trying; it's in the blind eyes turned, it's in the joy of scandal when someone else is caught, and it's the thing that hurts the hardest in any fall. Without it we cannot understand work and family and religion, or why another 1,000, another acre always counted for far more than just money and land. Respectability is just another way to measure, and in all of this Ireland was perhaps no different than any other place. If Lee shifted 'the main organising principle of Irish historiography' away from Anglo-Irish relations to those 'subjective concepts' of 'potential

---

91 Ibid., p. 14.
92 Lee, *Ireland 1912–1985*, p. xii.
93 Ibid., p. 124.
94 Colum, *The Road Round Ireland*, p. 31, p. 474.
95 See Lindsey Earner-Byrne, *Letters of the Catholic Poor: Poverty in Independent Ireland 1920–1940* (Cambridge, 2017).
96 Lee, *Ireland 1912–1985*, p. 646.
97 Ibid., p. 159.

and performance', perhaps the time has come to shift again, this time towards respectability in all its pleasures and its slights.[98]

And tangled up in all of this, is there more to be got from the intensity of fears that never came to pass, or the enthusiasms for ideas that have fallen out of fashion or favour in our times? Are we too readily taken with those who push and aspire to change when the instinct to stick, to hold, to risk nothing might be stronger for far more? So much that is now perceived as conservatism in the state often had overwhelming popular support, even had advocates prepared to push for what seems even greater control. And getting to grips with that takes far more than scorn. The voices that spoke up for women's rights went largely unheeded, the worry that the 'farmers' dole' might finally break the 'old fellow's' grip on his labouring sons, the pressure to put a child's labour or earnings ahead of their education when it came to raising the school-leaving age, these and so many other examples suggest people were not always thwarted: they just were not prepared to do as we hoped they should have done.[99] And maybe that's the quandary we forget they are absolutely entitled to pose. Across the interwar period, as across all of *Ireland 1912–1985*, there is more than the sum of our fury and our disenchantment looking back; the lives that were lived were more vivid than that.

It is clear from the sources that the begrudgers are contrary and contradictory in their passions and their views. They had hopes and aspirations, maybe born of what we might see as narrow ambition, but hopes and aspirations all the same. It might seem a step too far and too much of a nod back to where I started, but maybe we might even be ready to bear a history of some sort of happiness for these begrudgers in their own right. In the face of Lee's 'mercenarily married' I carried out a quick experiment in the matrimonial classifieds, and paid for by the word, each one was meant to count. Typical were 'Gentleman £350 age 36 R[oman] C[atholic], T[ee] T[otal] wishes to meet girl with farm of 20 acres or some means' or 'Young Lady (29), refined, domesticated, dowry £250, wishes to meet gentleman with business or income; must be R[oman] C[atholic], T[ee] T[otal]', so much so that 'Young west Cork farmer, comfortable circumstances, desires correspondence with nice, refined, intelligent young lady, view to matrimony, not wanted for mercenary ends' stood rather tellingly out.[100] In the many I read, there is a sense of what was meant to impress; there is the tangle of respectability and class and, maybe eventually, love. And while happiness in a cheap novelette might be content with love under the stars without 'acres' and 'means'; the 'respectable man' who wished to meet a 'respectable country girl' would not have been happy with her, or she with him, any other way.[101] Although there may be less urgency to find them happy in some kind of sterile courtship at the end of a novena, or eyes meeting across the sweaty mists of a Blueshirt dance, there was at least some pleasure taken, some happiness glimpsed, some spark at best in some of those begrudgers' hearts. Given the anger of *Ireland 1912–1985*, happiness, even brief and at best cheeseparing, might well seem a whitewash, a papering over the cracks, when there is still so much to be brought out into the light. But that depends on what we think our purpose with this past is: to be outraged,

98 Ibid., p. xii.
99 C. M. Arensberg & S. T. Kimball, *Family and Community in Ireland* (2nd edn, Cambridge Mass., 1968), pp. 53–5.
100 *Irish Independent*, 24 Feb. 1934; *Irish Independent*, 10 Jan. 1934; *Cork Examiner*, 18 Jan. 1928.
101 *Cork Examiner*, 23 Aug. 1934.

appalled, even defiant for the past, or to meet it on the measure of its own defiance rather than our own, to be confused by its wayward capacities for great hatreds, great cruelties and great joys just as we might hope to confound our successors in a century's time when they dare to reduce us to dull outlines of our much more muddled selves.

Ireland 1912–1985 indelibly shaped my understanding of independent Ireland, of the Irish Civil War, of the primacy of bread-and-butter politics when most other scholars seemed happy, and still do, to understand the 1920s and the 1930s along the simpler lines of pro- and anti-Treatyites. This book entirely shaped my thinking. It made de Valera something far more complex than the caricature he had already become, and not just because it described him as the one who gave 'the deprived a sense of dignity', but rather because this book, so caustic about so many others in so many ways, rather stubbornly suggested that we 'should speak his name with pride'.[102] But more than this, I admired the book because it gave the begrudgers their place in twentieth-century Irish history, and it is a place I have been worrying away at ever since. The book laid down the challenge of how to respond to the independence those begrudgers crafted, very much after their rather than our own lights. And that is a challenge we are getting to grips with still. Although George Bernard Shaw complained in the 1920s that the 'few million moral cowards' on that 'little grass patch' were slipping back into the Atlantic, into narrowness and irrelevance.[103] Whatever he or we might think, those few million imagined their futures with the same excitement and exhilaration as any of us here and now. What they did, what they hoped for their independence, what they tried and achieved, what they feared and how they failed, may not suit us, nor sit well with us, as Lee has gloriously shown, but they are still the mess and the makings of us all the same. I know that such begrudger's blood courses through my own veins – and maybe after 35 years it's time to make the best and not the worst of that. Maybe I should try and write that history of Irish spite and respectability after all.

---

102 Lee, *Ireland 1912–1985*, p. 541, p. 341.
103 G. B. Shaw, *The Irish Statesman*, 17 Nov. 1928, p. 207.

TOUTING FOR RESPECTABILITY: CHURCH AND STATE

Diarmaid Ferriter

When introducing his short history *Ireland in the Twentieth Century*, published in 1975, University College Cork's John A. Murphy noted that 'in the absence of both perspective and documentation, it is obvious that analysis and assessment can only be tentative', but also that 'no Irishman writing about his own time can honestly claim to be academically remote from it all: he must try to be fair but he cannot escape feeling involved'. There was, nonetheless, something worthwhile in 'combining contemporary observation with the analysis born of professional experience'.[1]

Fourteen years later, his colleague J. J. Lee published his *Ireland 1912–1985: Politics and Society*, considered a landmark publication. Lee's book caused a great stir precisely because of the mix of contemporary observation and historical analysis. It was also, at 700 pages, a much weightier affair than was possible in the 1970s, because of what Lee referred to as a 'massive expansion in the available archival material', though he warned that such expansion could 'obscure perspective beneath mounds of detail', and make the historian too complacent about 'the enduring quality of necessarily provisional conclusions'.[2]

While Roy Foster's sweeping and probing *Modern Ireland 1600–1972* appeared in 1988, prior to Lee's 1989 tome, the most comprehensive history of the period Lee focused on was F. S. L. Lyons's *Ireland Since the Famine* (1971) in which Lyons had noted the historian of modern Ireland was condemned to make bricks without straw. Lee had plenty more straw and a lot more attitude, even more striking given that when Terence de Vere White reviewed the Lyons book in 1971, he found the tone 'admirable … [H]e is invariably polite. So a scholar should be.'[3] Lee was much spikier and adamant about the need for the historian to rise above narrow specialisation to 'transcend the fragmentation of perspective characteristic of the contemporary mind'. He desired to craft a 'total history', not in the sense of covering everything, but by 'seeking to reveal the relevant linkages between the varieties of thinking' he was preoccupied with, and to engage in comparative perspectives, what he referred to as 'a shift in the angle of approach'[4].

What Lee described in 1989 as a 'massive expansion' in archival availability has, in the decades since, become gargantuan, including for the revolutionary period of 1913–23, to the extent that Peter Hart was able to refer in 1999 to Ireland as a great laboratory for the study of revolution: 'Ireland's is quite possibly the best documented revolution in modern

---

1 John A Murphy, *Ireland in the Twentieth Century* (Dublin, 1975), preface.
2 J. J. Lee, *Ireland 1912–1985: Politics and Society* (Cambridge, 1989), p. xi–xv.
3 Terence de Vere White, 'A pride of lions', *Irish Times*, 1 May 1971.
4 Lee, *Ireland 1912–1985*, p. xii.

history.[5] The National Archives Act of 1986, facilitating the availability of state papers under a 30-year rule, also came into operation after Lee's book was published. There was expanded physical research space in the National Archives building in Bishop Street, from 1992, in contrast to the 1970s when the State Paper Office in the Four Courts could only accommodate eight researchers sitting around one big table, and when there was a disturbing attitude on the part of some public bodies to the preservation of archives.[6]

Alongside archives legislation, and the opening of a multitude of private archival collections, various digitisation projects made possible in the era of the internet have also contributed to the transformation and expansion of the research horizon. One result, as pointed out by James Kelly in 2010, was a trend 'away from the traditionally rarefied narratives with high politics at their heart'.[7] One of the values of Lee's book, however, is that it stands as a monument to the ongoing importance of understanding elite governors and policymakers given the short- and long-term consequences of their ideologies and decisions and the need to look at their thought processes in a broader context.

While allowing for Ireland's distinctiveness, Lee insisted, 'comparative perspective can illuminate our understanding of the Irish condition'. He provided bountiful references to Finland, Denmark and Austria and was critical of the idea that Britain should be the main point of comparison for Ireland; this was just an excuse for failure (whether through blame or emulation) and an endurance of the 'serf-mentality'. He acknowledged, however, that he was writing from a southern Irish perspective and the partitionist mindset he shared with his peers: 'Southern Irish historians like myself are likely to be as ambivalent towards the North as are citizens of the Republic in general.'[8]

He also declared when introducing the book, 'my own preferences are not concealed'. That was quite an understatement. The final section of Lee's book, at 177 pages, was titled 'Perspectives', starting with the question 'How well has independent Ireland performed?' He did not hold back in relation to Irish institutions, intelligence, character and identity. Irish economic performance had been 'the least impressive in western Europe'; there had been 'long-term mediocrity'; and he maintained, 'patriotism proved powerless, except in brief and specific conjunctures, against the instincts of the possessing classes.' This was one of his towering themes: national adherence to a 'possessor' principle rather than a 'performance' principle with the concomitant rewarding of vested interests – property owners, public sector employees, comfortable farmers – rather than genuine effort, with many outside of these interest groups forced to emigrate[9].

Lee lacerated the 'incapacity of the Irish mind to think through the implications of independence for national development'. Consider, for example, his damning comment on Irish emigration: 'few people anywhere in the world have been so prepared to scatter their children around the world in order to preserve their own living standards'. In a similar vein, he concluded the state was controlled by 'the flint-minded men and women whose grandparents had done well out of the Famine and who intended to do better themselves

---

5   Peter Hart, 'The social structure of the IRA, 1916–23', *The Historical Journal*, 42:1, March 1999, pp. 207–231.
6   Diarmaid Ferriter, *Ambiguous Republic: Ireland in the 1970s* (London, 2012), pp. 249–50.
7   James Kelly, *Writing Irish History Today* (Dublin, 2010), p.17.
8   Lee, *Ireland 1912–1985*, p. xiv.
9   Ibid., p. 390.

out of the Free State'. He also admonished the Irish cardinal sin of begrudgery: 'The Irish carry from their mother's womb not so much a fanatic heart as a begrudger one.'[10]

Lee's book was deliberately provocative; evaluating 'the performance of a sovereign people,' he noted, was 'not destined to win [the historian] the affection of all his Irish readers'.[11] Nor did he spare historians for their failures: 'the historians, who were in a unique position to contribute deeper understanding, failed', chiefly due to an excessive concentration on political and diplomatic history.[12]

Published at the very end of a disenchanting decade ravaged by economic failure, emigration, and cultural civil wars, the book was discussed on *The Late Late Show* with Lee revelling in the spotlight, as comfortable as he was articulate, continuing in voice the same sharpness, humour and honesty that were characteristic of his disputatious, often acerbic prose. Lee's tone was so scalding and so driven by his personal perspectives and passions that the book generated both consternation and accolades. It was a bestseller and won numerous awards including an *Irish Times*/Aer Lingus Irish Literature Prize in 1991. Tom Garvin suggested the book's main achievement was its innovativeness, 'in part because of its own contradictions ... the product of an energetic, fertile and patriotic intelligence'.[13]

The book was published the year I entered UCD as a history undergraduate and was a big influence, not just because of its ferocity but because it highlighted areas that needed further excavation, which encouraged history students down various research paths. It was also lambasted by some feminist historians who were justifiably aghast that such a dense tome severely neglected the experiences of women. Margaret Ward, for example, was withering about 'a mere five substantive references to women' and the tendency to name women in masculine terms; Kathleen Clarke is 'Mrs Tom Clarke', while Maud Gonne is referred to by the men in her life: 'Seán MacBride, son of Major John MacBride, executed in 1916, and of Maud Gonne, of Yeats fame'. Ward concluded, 'Lee could hardly be more hostile to the notion of women's autonomy ... The male "gatekeepers" continue to do their job very effectively.'[14] Lee defended himself against this criticism in 1995: 'There was a lack of women in public policymaking ... It was overwhelmingly men who exercised that power at that time.'[15] It was an unconvincing defence given the inclusion of the word 'society' in the book's title. Responding to his alleged sins of omission and commission, Lee insisted, 'You can't please everybody, and you shouldn't try, because you will simply finish up in a morass of mediocrity.'[16]

The absence of more probing of 'society' by Lee meant that he completely omitted mention of the papal encyclical *Humanae Vitae* in 1968. While he could assert that 'by 1980 traditional church teaching on contraception was ignored by a substantial proportion, perhaps by a majority, of the relevant age group', we get little sense of how the expectations

10 Ibid., p. 646.
11 Ibid., p. xiii.
12 Ibid., pp. 632–8.
13 Tom Garvin, 'Review of *Ireland 1912–1985*', in *Irish Historical Studies* 27:105 (May 1990), pp. 85–87.
14 Margaret Ward, *The Missing Sex: Putting Women into Irish History* (Dublin, 1991), pp. 10–12.
15 Quoted in Gráinne Henry, 'Peripatetic professor', in *History Ireland*, Summer 1995, p. 46.
16 Ibid., p. 46.

of the late 1960s, especially for women, were dashed or the resultant defiance.[17] Former Taoiseach Garret FitzGerald, for example, who came to politics in the 1960s, has argued that a 'dam burst' coincided with *Humanae Vitae*. The encyclical, in his view, represented a position that was 'non-credible in rational terms ... and once the church took up a position which was non-credible in rational terms its authority over the whole sexual area disintegrated. At the worst moment for us, when pressure on the dam was great already, you suddenly put a hole in the dam ... everything fell.'[18]

As one of Ireland's best-known 'agony aunts', Angela Macnamara recalled:

> There were women with selfish husbands; women whose own needs for intimacy were great; couples who had very little other pleasure in life; men whose demands of their wives after excessive alcohol were unreasonable; couples who argued and fought about the meaning of the Encyclical ... I contacted a few priests for advice as to how to deal with all such queries from a compassionate but moral point of view. I received a variety of responses, from the tough line, the ultra-conservative, to the line that said 'encourage them to do their best' ... Even from the early stage, the public were not taking this 'lying down' (If I may pun on it).[19]

This is where, perhaps, the limitations of Lee's focus on the 'public sphere' are apparent; we now have much more of a sense of the private domain, of what things felt like, of the battles being fought personally, bringing to mind the observation of archivist Catríona Crowe:

> The private domain of personal experience has always been at odds with the official stories which were sanctioned, permitted and encouraged by the state and Catholic Church'; private experiences – in memoir, personal testimony, and correspondence – 'run like a parallel stream of information alongside the official documentary record and complement it with their personal immediacy and vibrancy. The official record can tell us what happened, but rarely what it felt like.'[20]

What these testimonies reveal is particularly significant given what Lindsey Earner Byrne identifies as a cultural tendency to 'see the family as a site of inviolate privacy about which no tales could be told'. That priority was also relevant to reliance on institutions and confinement, and as Catherine Cox notes, 'currently, academics seem to be as captivated by institutions as the contemporary advocates once were'.[21] Previously marginalised voices have begun to occupy a significant place, and that perhaps is also a reflection of the idea of a 'post-revisionist' phase of Irish history writing.[22]

---

17   Lee, *Ireland 1912–1985*, p. 656.
18   Finola Kennedy, *Cottage to Crèche: Family Change in Ireland* (Dublin, 2001), p. 164.
19   Angela Macnamara, *Yours Sincerely* (Dublin, 2003) p. 69.
20   Catríona Crowe, 'Our insatiable appetite for memoirs of Irish childhood', *Sunday Tribune*, 18 Jun. 2000.
21   Lindsey Earner Byrne, 'The family in Ireland, 1880–2015', in Thomas Bartlett (ed.), *The Cambridge History of Ireland*, vol. 4: *1880 to the Present* (Cambridge, 2018), p.666; Catherine Cox 'Institutional space and the geography of confinement in Ireland, 1750–2000', in Thomas Bartlett (ed.), *The Cambridge History of Ireland*, vol. 4: *1880 to the Present* (Cambridge, 2018), p. 676.
22   Fearghal McGarry, 'Twentieth century Ireland revisited', in *Journal of Contemporary History*, 42:1 (January 2007), pp. 137–48.

Lee's damnation of intellectual and cultural shortcomings was regarded by some as too sweeping, and the very range of work by economists, sociologists and anthropologists that he synthesised in the book did not suggest a cultural wasteland. He strangely neglected the media, and some queried his comparisons of international GNP and the appropriateness of the economic models he used. There was also ambiguity about what he termed 'a particular cast of Irish mind' or 'a certain type of Irish mind' and the frequency with which he referred to 'the Irish', 'the Irish insisted on living in a dreamland'.[23] As Charles Townshend saw it, these were 'casual indictments of the nation' and unsubstantiated. Another question that arose was whether his arguments were vitiated by his assertion that it was 'arguable that in the prevailing political circumstances, no alternative structure would have served the state as well as the inherited one.'[24]

Lee's various admonishments and indictments have led to calls for a more balanced assessment of preoccupations and lived experiences during the formative decades of the state. Anne Dolan, for example, has chided those who have narrated the history of the Free State between 1922 and 1939 as 'the history of disappointment' and a culture that 'saw and decried the devil at every turn'. Dolan does not wish to replace this with a 'blindly buoyant view', but 'poverty is relative to its own time' and more attention needs to be given to what Irish people did as opposed to what they were forbidden to do.[25]

Dolan took aim at Lee's sweeping assertion that 'the poor, the aged and the unemployed must all feel the lash of the liberators'.[26] It is undoubtedly true that perception, preoccupations, and expectations in the 1920s and 1930s need to be adequately acknowledged and that the historical narrative can be skewed by imposing early-twenty-first-century values on assessments of the infant state. And yet, while Lee's declaration that 'the cabinet waged a coherent campaign against the weaker elements in the community' might appear too strident, contemporary voices from the 1920s to the 1930s, now widely available through, for example, the files of the military service pension archive, detailing so many disillusioned and disappointed voices in relation to the post-revolutionary dispensation, give added weight to some of Lee's claims. Such testimonies reinforce the idea, apparent from the foundation of the state, that 'poverty was only a political virtue when it was respectable'. The 'most glaring omission from the Dáil's membership was unskilled workers', with TDs 'broadly representative of the upwardly mobile Catholic middle class but not of the mass of the population'.[27] De Valera had a genuine sympathy for the poor, but as Lee rightly pointed out, refused 'to invest this with ideological significance'.[28]

Dolan threw down a challenge based on the idea that Lee's interpretation of the 1920s and 1930s 'worked well with the anger of many of his conclusions written through the 1980s'. The Free State was a disappointment, Lee suggested, 'in the context of historical

---

23 Lee, *Ireland 1912–1985*, p. 489.
24 Charles Townshend, 'History as critique', in *The Irish Review* 8 (Spring 1990), pp. 116–18.
25 Anne Dolan, 'Politics, economy and society in the Irish Free State, 1922–1939' in Bartlett (ed.), *The Cambridge History of Ireland*, vol. 4: *1880 to the Present* (Cambridge, 2018), pp. 323–49.
26 Lee, *Ireland 1912–1985*, p. 124.
27 Peter Hart, *The IRA and Its Enemies: Violence and Community in Cork, 1916–1923* (London, 1998), p. 147; and Brian Hanley, '"Merely Tuppence Half-Penny Looking down on Tuppence?": Class, the Second Dáil and Irish republicanism', in Liam Weeks and Micheál Ó Fathartaigh (eds), *The Treaty: Debating and Establishing the Irish State* (Dublin, 2018), pp. 60–70.
28 Lee, *Ireland 1912–1985*, p. 331.

expectations', and as Dolan sees it, this 'view that has been broadly perpetuated since. More recent research has focused on how the most vulnerable were treated ... Nothing was as we would have liked it to have been, and as research has developed, the 1920s and 1930s have found more and more ways to let us down.'[29]

That is not quite the full picture either, however. Lee was also interested in the positive capacity to express and forge a vision. De Valera is thus assessed by him as a leader with 'superb tactical judgement', who used symbolism imaginatively and was a 'marvellous manipulator of private and public minds, of individual and collective mentalities'. Arguably more significantly, he insists:

> De Valera did not abuse his trust as leader throughout his long public life. He revelled in the cult of 'The Chief'. But he used it primarily for party and national purposes ... De Valera was, in a sense, greater than the sum of his parts. Behind the ceaseless political calculation and the labyrinthine deviousness, there reposed a character of rare nobility. His qualities would have made him a leader beyond compare in the pre-industrial world. It was in one sense his misfortune that his career should coincide with an age of accelerated economic change whose causes and consequences largely baffled him. But there are times in history when the stature of public men depends more on what they are no less than on what they do. That was arguably the case in Ireland for at least the first generation of independence. No modern state in Irish circumstances could flourish under a succession of de Valeras. But a small nation that 'could never be got to accept defeat and has never surrendered her soul', words that still held meaning when he spoke them in 1945, indeed held meaning largely because it was he who spoke them, should speak his name with pride.[30]

Subsequently, during the 'Celtic Tiger' era of the 1990s, Lee returned to this theme and provocatively suggested a re-examination of de Valera's 'Ireland that we dreamed of'' speech, broadcast on St Patrick's Day 1943. The most famous passage in the speech maintained, 'The Ireland which we dreamed of would be the home of a people who valued material wealth only as a basis of right living, of a people who were satisfied with frugal comfort and devoted their lives to things of the spirit – a land whose countryside would be bright with cosy homesteads, whose fields and villages would be joyous with the sounds of industry, with the romping of sturdy children, the contests of athletic youths and the laughter of comely maidens, whose firesides would be forums for the wisdom of serene old age.'[31]

Lee dismissed the modern derision of the speech and concluded that de Valera's words amounted to a desire to see a well-populated country, with full employment, good housing, healthy children, an interest in sport, respect for the elderly, and that 'de Valera's model emphasised the essential links between the generations as he identified his ideal for the dependent ages in society – childhood, youth, and old age. Giving was as important as taking, service as important as wealth. It was a society in which rights were balanced by responsibilities.'[32] This assessment chimed with others in the early-twenty-first century; in 2003, for example, Garret FitzGerald wrote about the decline of the influence of religion in

---

29 Dolan, 'Politics, economy and society', p.330.
30 Lee, *Ireland 1912–1985*, pp. 340–1. For the original context of de Valera quote, see Maurice Moynihan (ed.), *Speeches and Statements by Eamon de Valera, 1917–1973* (Dublin, 1980) p. 476.
31 De Valera, *Speeches and Statements*, p. 466.
32 J. J. Lee, 'A sense of place in the Celtic Tiger', in Harry Bohan and Gerard Kennedy (eds), *Are We Forgetting Something? Our Society in the New Millennium* (Dublin, 1999), pp. 71–94.

the republic and the 'inadequacy of any alternative lay or civic ethic, especially in the face of the double hazard of the siren call of individualist liberalism, on the one hand, and the off-putting face of fundamentalist Catholicism on the other.'[33] I suspect Lee would have concurred.

Crucially, Lee's book was written before the avalanche of revelations that engulfed Ireland from the 1990s; we cannot now look at Ireland in the twentieth century without that scandal-inspired lens and the exposure of the hidden histories and cruelties. Credibility was eroded to the point where, in 2000, historian James Donnelly suggested the need for an 'effective repositioning of the institutional Catholic Church in Ireland.'[34]

Just a few years after Lee's book was published the onslaught of information and testimonies about historic betrayals and systemic abuses of power came tumbling fast, cruelties that had often been met with 'denial, arrogance and cover-up'. As was underlined in the Murphy Report of 2009 that examined allegations of abuse in the Catholic Archdiocese of Dublin, there was a 'don't ask, don't tell' policy[35]. The report detailed cases involving 46 priests, and more than 320 children, most of them boys. Senior members of the Irish police force regarded the actions of priests as being outside their remit, and some of them reported complaints to the archdiocese instead of investigating them. The Murphy Report highlighted the determination to hide and deny rather than confront, noting that the main preoccupation was 'avoidance of public scandal'.[36]

That phrase is pertinent to many of the issues addressed by other reports, including the *Ryan Commission* (2009) which examined industrial schools, the *McAleese Report* (2013) that examined state involvement in the Magdalen laundries, and the Commission of Inquiry into Mother and Baby Homes (2021). When initially countenancing this new era of revelation, there was a focus by writers on what Roy Foster characterised as the 'coming to terms with cultural memory.'[37] This was underpinned by a strong sense of a 'duty to remember' and a 'duty to tell.'[38]

The scale of the reliance on institutionalisation, the network of alliances that kept the institutions full, and the implications for the vulnerable became more apparent as the reports accumulated. Accounts of abuse in relation to 216 institutions are contained in the Ryan Commission report, for example, and the total number of children committed to industrial schools between 1936 and 1970 was approximately 42,000. In the Magdalen laundries, run by congregations of nuns, that contained those deemed to be 'fallen women', there were 10,000 inmates between 1922 and 1996, and 26.5 per cent of those women were referred by the state. Many of the women who were sent to the laundries – not just by the state, but also by families or priests – were judged harshly due to the environment and values of the time. The attitudes towards them, underlined frequently in contemporary

---

33 Garret FitzGerald, *Reflections on the Irish State* (Dublin, 2003) p. x.
34 James S Donnelly, 'A Church in crisis: The Irish Catholic Church today', *History Ireland*, 8:3 (Autumn 2000), pp. 12–27.
35 Diarmaid Ferriter, *Occasions of Sin: Sex and Society in Modern Ireland* (paperback edn, London, 2012), p. xii.
36 Ibid.
37 R. F. Foster, *Luck and the Irish: A Brief History of Change 1970–2000* (London, 2007), p. 63.
38 James M. Smith, *Ireland's Magdalen Laundries and the Nation's Architecture of Containment* (Notre Dame, 2007) p. 89.

documents cited by the *McAleese Report*, generated descriptions of the women such as 'sub-normal', 'delinquent', and 'mentally deficient', and it was clear that they were seen as 'incarcerated', another word regularly used.[39]

Most recently, the mother and baby homes report found that there were 56,000 unmarried mothers and 57,000 children in the 18 mother and baby and county homes investigated; about 9,000 children died in the institutions. The report controversially asserted that responsibility for the harsh treatment of the women 'rests mainly with the fathers of their children and their own immediate families' and that treatment of the women by their families was 'contributed to and condoned by the institutions of church and state'.[40]

The collected revelations vindicate some of the claims Lee made in 1989 and even before that; consider, for example, his assertion in 1984 that one factor that had inhibited Ireland was 'an overbearing, destructive Catholicism which functioned as the most reliable lightning conductor for the repressed psychic tensions'.[41] In *Ireland 1912-1985* he referred to 'the cover-up techniques that came as second nature to a society that placed such value on inheritance and appearance'.[42] His withering assessment of censorship has also been validated: 'a convenient façade behind which a fabricated but reassuring self-image of moral probity' could flourish.[43] There was nothing unusual in this internationally, but it went especially deep in Ireland in relation to self-images of domestic purity. Lee argues that because it was impossible to sustain in practice there was a shrivelling of the domain of real morality 'to those teachings which happen to conveniently coincide with the objective material requirements' of socially dominant groups, and that 'a morbid preoccupation with occasions of sin' amounted in practice to issuing a 'moral blank cheque to other types of behaviour', which was also about the barrenness of mind of the rising bourgeoisie 'touting for respectability.'[44]

The use of the phrase 'occasions of sin' brings to mind Brian Moore's novel *Fergus* (1971) in which Fr Kinneally, who taught Fergus English when he was a student, is asked by Fergus many years later if it was true that he had once cut all the corset and brassiere advertisements out of magazines on the school dentist's waiting room table: '"There were young boys looking at those suggestive drawings", Fr Kinneally said. "I thought it wise. Remember, an occasion of sin is an occasion of sin, even if it is not intended to be."'[45]

The scale of what has been uncovered in recent years reminds us of the moral blank cheques issued to powerful prelates engaging in the same sins, and worse, that the church sought to denounce. Institutions were a solution to stigma – 'women contained meant

---

39   'Report of the Inter-Departmental Committee to Establish the Facts of State Involvement with the Magdalen Laundries', www.justice.ie/en/JELR/Pages/MagdalenRpt2013, accessed 17 Jul. 2018.
40   'Final report of the Commission of Investigation into Mother and Baby Homes', www.gov.ie/en/publication/d4b3d-final-report-of-the-commission-of-investigation-into-mother-and-baby-homes/, accessed 25 Feb. 2021.
41   J. J. Lee, 'Reflections on the study of Irish values', in M. P. Fogarty, L. Ryan, and J. J. Lee (eds), *Irish Values and Attitudes* (Dublin, 1984), p. 116.
42   Lee, *Ireland 1912–1985*, p. 158.
43   Ibid.
44   Ibid.
45   Ferriter, *Occasions of Sin*, p. 10.

shame contained' – but this was not solely about the Church; it was washing machines, and not public pressure, that closed the laundries, so 'what kind of society, people, allowed – wanted – this?[46] And what was the scale of the Church's manipulation of that society? Was Lee overly generous and conservative in depicting the Catholic Church as 'a bulwark, perhaps now the main bulwark of the civic culture?'[47] What is most striking about all we have learned since the 1990s is the ferocity of the misogyny directed towards those who supposedly compromised the official narrative of national and moral virtue. But it could also be argued that we have become too reductionist in apportioning blame and responsibility. Lee fairly argued that a superficial focus on the Church occluded too much else: 'If the nature of Irish Catholicism cannot be ignored in discussing any major question of significance in modern Ireland it is by no means the only factor requiring scrutiny.'[48] That remains a troubling issue relating to the historiography of the post-Famine Catholic Church. In 2018 the Catholic Archbishop of Dublin Diarmuid Martin asked, 'What was it in Irish Catholicism that led to such a level of harshness?'[49] The answers snake their way through the public and private archives of modern Irish history from the mid-nineteenth century, and much of it had to do with class: as Martin recognised, those who were victims of the Church's worst excesses were in the main 'poor and vulnerable'. The Church's approach to these people was a mix of charity and snobbery, and recent historiography has highlighted why that was and the consequences. One of the chief architects of modern Irish Catholicism was Cardinal Paul Cullen. An indefatigable reformer of the governance and practice of Irish Catholicism, he convened the Synod of Thurles in 1850, and the common factor in all his exertions was obedience to Rome rather than to Ireland.

While Cullen was appalled by the poverty of his era, which he frequently denounced, this, according to historian Ciaran O'Connell, was 'focused more on an appeal for compassion from the oppressors of the poor rather than a call for justice for them'. It was a crucial distinction. Cullen sought religious and class segregation in the education system and was obdurate about the need for denominationalism and a limited curriculum for poorer Catholics, as 'too high an education will make the poor oftentimes discontented and will unsuit them for following the plough or for using the spade ... The rich must have schools for themselves and learn many things not necessary for persons in a different state of life.'[50]

Cullen also created aspects of the governance and style of an Irish Catholicism that in the long-run appeared rigid, lacking sufficient humanity, and subservient to Rome, while at Maynooth College during that era, seminarians were imbued with a rigorist view of morality and Jansenism, emphasising the dark side of human nature. Nor was there much focus on interior spirituality: Cullen sought to build a disciplined, centralised, dominant Church but which in too many respects was about outward devotion rather than deep thinking. In 1895

---

46   Derek Scally, *The Best Catholics in the World: The Irish, the Church and the End of a Special Relationship* (London, 2021), pp. 117–23.
47   Lee, *Ireland 1912–1985*, p. 659.
48   Ibid., p. 621
49   'Archbishop Martin urges Pope Francis to tackle Clerical sexual abuse', *Irish Examiner*, 19 Aug. 2018.
50   Ciarán O'Carroll, 'The pastoral vision of Paul Cullen', in Dáire Keogh and Albert McDonnell (eds), *Cardinal Paul Cullen and his World* (Dublin, 2011), pp. 115–130.

Bishop John Healy of Clonfert boasted that St Patrick's College in Maynooth was not a place for reflective education but 'a machine for turning out … missionary men annually', with little emphasis on feelings about the faith.[51]

The social, political and military upheavals in the decades after Cullen's death in 1878 witnessed a church that was increasingly assertive and demanding, but also vulnerable because of the difficulties of retaining control during the land war and struggle for political independence. Brian Heffernan has outlined how, after these upheavals, 'for the conservatives, the foundation of the Irish Free State in 1922 was equivalent to the reaching of dry ground again'.[52] The Church made the most of this landing with an excessive number of priests, many ill-suited to religious life, and too much emphasis on communal outward devotion and obedience rather than interior and personal spirituality.

Lee had explored the impact of Cullen in his 1973 book *The Modernisation of Irish Society, 1848–1918*, labelling him 'the Pope's chief whip in Ireland', but argued he was more liberal than his domineering reputation and image suggested, an assessment some historians have recently returned to.[53] Lee did not mention Cardinal Cullen in the 1989 book, but his shadow loomed large. It suited the fledgling state, reeling from civil war, to allow the Church control over health and education. Unrelenting deference was expected and usually given; when elected a TD in October 1947, Seán MacBride, supposedly a radical republican, wrote to the Catholic Archbishop of Dublin John Charles McQuaid: 'as my first act, to pay my humble respects to Your Grace and to place myself at your Grace's disposal'. He later added he would welcome any advice 'which your Grace may be good enough to give me'. McQuaid replied, 'I will not hesitate to avail of your services'.[54]

Lee did not have access to the archive of McQuaid, which was opened to researchers in 1999. It is true, as pointed out by Deirdre McMahon, that McQuaid, who served as archbishop from 1940 until 1971, should not just be viewed through the lens of the late-twentieth century and revelations of abuse; McMahon warned against the 'crude caricatures of hidebound Catholic reaction with which McQuaid has become identified since his death in 1973'.[55] Many benefited from his public and private charity, and, she argued, his life and career 'cannot be understood without encompassing this context of change in the life of his church and his country'[56] McQuaid was a significant and often-enlightened educationalist in the 1930s and as archbishop coordinated many welfare activities in his diocese in relation to clothing, fuel and housing. He devoted much time to services for those with alcoholism, mental and physical disabilities, and the building of hospitals. The problem, however, as with the wider Church in Ireland, was that McQuaid wanted all on his terms and had too much power, which was abused, meaning 'McQuaid's Ireland' long

51   Scally, *The Best Catholics in the World*, p. 221.
52   Brian Heffernan, *Freedom and the Fifth Commandment: Catholic Priests and Political Violence in Ireland, 1919–21* (Manchester, 2014), pp. 240–7.
53   Colin P. Barr, '"An ambiguous awe": Paul Cullen and the historians', in Keogh and McDonnell (eds), *Cardinal Paul Cullen*, pp. 414–35.
54   John Cooney, *John Charles McQuaid: Ruler of Catholic Ireland* (Dublin, 1999), pp. 215–16.
55   Deirdre McMahon, 'John Charles McQuaid: Archbishop of Dublin, 1940–1972', in James Kelly and Daire Keogh (eds), *A History of the Catholic Diocese of Dublin* (Dublin, 2000) pp. 331–44.
56   Ibid., p. 333.

outlived the man himself, who died in 1973. To use some of Lee's terminology, McQuaid was also a possessor and a bully, and he failed victims of child abuse egregiously.[57]

Lee focused on McQuaid in the context of the mother and child controversy of 1951, highlighting his 'exalted sense of the dignity of the professions', and maintained the mother and child dispute was 'not a straight conflict between church and state.'[58] McQuaid's voluminous archive highlights the accuracy of Lee's claims about the exaltation of the professionals; McQuaid wrote in 1953 about 'a Catholic member of the judiciary, very highly placed, of the highest integrity and gifted with vision that has often amazed me'.[59] Lee also rightly identified class as knitted through these controversies: Fine Gael Taoiseach John A. Costello, he points out, had a 'piety absolutely genuine' which also 'happened to coincide with the material advantage of the interests he represented ... Only the unsporting would descend to wonder how professional fees came to be in the front line of spiritual fortification against materialism'.[60]

It is difficult at this juncture to construct a fair historical analysis of the nature of Church power and influence during those decades. It might be tempting to quote novelist John Banville about the 1950s in Ireland as a 'demilitarised totalitarian state in which lives were controlled not by coercive force and secret police but by a kind of applied spiritual paralysis maintained by an unofficial federation between church, civil service, judiciary and politicians.' Fellow novelist John McGahern suggested such were the class dynamics underpinning the power of the priests that 'in their hearts they despised their own people.'[61]

Some surely did, but many undoubtedly did not, and it was revealing that at a later stage, as an older man, McGahern came back to the subject with a dose of nuance:

> 'When a long abuse of power is corrected, it is generally replaced by an opposite violence. In the new dispensations, all that was good in what went before is tarred indiscriminately with the bad. That is to some extent what is happening in Ireland. The most dramatic change in my lifetime has been the collapse of the church's absolute power. This has brought freedom and sanity in certain areas of human behaviour after a long suppression – as well as a new intolerance ... It is easy to fall into the trap of looking back in judgement in the light of our own day rather than the more difficult realisation of the natural process of living which was the same then as it is now.'[62]

Finding a balanced path through the fog of abuse revelations is a difficult challenge for the historian. As James Smith observed when looking at the history of the Magdalen laundries, the dilemma is about 'how to separate academic detachment from personal indignation.

---

57 Diarmaid Ferriter, 'McQuaid's shadow hangs over mother and baby homes', *Irish Times*, 22 Jan. 2021.
58 Lee, *Ireland 1912–1985*, pp. 313–22.
59 Charles McQuaid to Rev. Ettore Felici, 17 Feb. 1953, in Clara Cullen and Margaret Ó hÓgartaigh (eds.), *His Grace is Displeased: The Selected Correspondence of John Charles McQuaid* (Dublin, 2013), p. 109.
60 Lee, *Ireland 1912–1985*, p. 317.
61 John Banville, 'The Ireland of de Valera and O'Faoláin', in *Irish Review*, 17–18 (Winter 1995), p. 47; John McGahern, 'The church and its spire', in Stanley Van Der Ziel (ed.), *Love of the World: Essays* (London, 2009), p. 139.
62 John McGahern, 'God and me' in *Love of the World*, pp. 150–1; John McGahern, 'Whatever you say, say nothing' in *Love of the World*, p.130.

Moral outrage and academic detachment do not sit easily on the same page.'[63] Lee asserted that the Church, despite increased secularisation, continued to provide 'psychic moorings for many who might otherwise have suffered a good deal more disturbance in the face of incomprehensible change', another version of McGahern's assertion that people drew solace from its 'authoritarian certainties'.[64]

In relation to the 1980s he was living and writing through, two things were noticeable about Lee: the acuity of his political analysis and his own conservativeness. He noted that with the passage of the Eighth Amendment to the Constitution in 1983 – giving 'equal right' to the life of the mother and the unborn – 'it is not clear what problem the result solved for the participants'; it diverted attention from other issues, opposing groups talked past each other, and it revealed the lack of a well-developed public sphere in Irish society. History has already vindicated those insights, and the extent to which 'the campaigns of the 1980s graphically highlighted the tendency in Ireland towards denial and a hypocrisy that saw Ireland's abortion issue dealt with in England'.[65] The Eight Amendment was eventually removed from the Irish constitution, in 2018, following a referendum, the culmination of over 30 years of confusion, rancorous debate and legal wrangling.

But Lee did not reflect on the reality that there were far too many male sermons in Ireland in 1983. While he lauded the administrative and managerial sophistication of the Church, he also, as a married, middle-aged, Catholic history Professor, sermonised about sexual mores: 'It seems clear that much of the general drift in terms of sexual morality was based on mere hedonism.'[66] Clear to whom exactly? And what of the hedonism of many of the denouncers of immorality? His crass generalisation about 'hedonism' might leave a bad taste in the mouth of a twenty-first-century reader, especially given the extent of fear, hypocrisy, and shame that enveloped sexual matters, a reminder that Lee could enlighten, stimulate, and infuriate. That is what gifted historians should do, and there is a strong contemporary relevance to Lee's pungent observation in 1995: 'There is always a danger of chasing the latest "politically correct" fashion, which would be to prostitute history to propaganda … I would have to examine my conscience if I found that everything I said was fashionable.'[67]

Lee's book is also relevant to the end of the recent decade of commemorations, given his focus on state building. Now that the orgy of reflection on the violence and divisions of 1913–23 is over, the issue of the state's 'performance' from the 1920s onwards will once again come under the spotlight and Lee's incisiveness will be appreciated because so few have matched the quality of his writing and the depth of his analytical probing of politics and policy formation in the formative decades of the Irish state. The claim made by Lee's publisher in 1990, that his book would 'become required reading for all who wish to deepen their understanding of the nature of modern Irish history',[68] was no empty boast; over three decades later the same assertion is valid.

---

63   Smith, *Ireland's Magdalen Laundries*, p. 2.
64   Lee, *Ireland 1912–1985*, p. 656; McGahern, 'The church and its spire', p. 36.
65   Diarmaid Ferriter, *The Transformation of Ireland 1900–2000* (London, 2004), p. 717.
66   Lee, *Ireland 1912–1985*, p. 656.
67   In Henry, 'Peripatetic professor', p.46.
68   Asserted on the back cover of Lee, *Ireland 1912–1985* (Paperback edn, Cambridge, 1990).

THE CONTRIBUTIONS OF *IRELAND 1912–1985* TO THE HISTORY OF THE IRISH LANGUAGE

Nicholas M. Wolf

Unless immersed in the historiography of the Irish language, the average researcher may not be aware that *Ireland 1912–1985* has had a significant influence on how researchers analyse the history of the language, in particular its status in the nineteenth century. Reviewing the state of the field in his 2005 contribution to an edited collection on the historiography of nineteenth-century Ireland, Niall Ó Ciosáin wrote that Lee had made 'the most informative, aware, and acute analysis by far of language shift in nineteenth-century Ireland', despite the focus of Lee's book on the twentieth century.[1] This appraisal has been echoed more recently by Margaret Kelleher, who writes of Lee's discussion of language shift as providing 'one of the most succinct yet in-depth analyses' of this topic for nineteenth-century Ireland.[2] The unexpected nature of this intercession is heightened by the fact that in addition to its concentration on the twentieth century, Lee's book – in an apt demonstration that excessive verbiage does not necessarily lead to better analysis – dedicates only a select few pages to the Irish language at all.

The fact that *Ireland 1912–1985* could be both brief and incisive in exploring the history of the language was very much a function of the state of scholarship at the time and of the changing currents of Irish-language advocacy that had emerged in the two decades prior to the book's publication. A work of summation and breadth, Lee's study was necessarily reliant on secondary sources to make its case, and at the time of its initial publication, in 1989, many key histories of the Irish language in the twentieth century had yet to be written. Pádraig Ó Riagáin's field work on Corca Dhuibhne (*Language Maintenance and Language Shift*, 1992) and language policy (*Language Policy and Social Reproduction*, 1997), Proinsias Mac Aonghusa's history of Conradh na Gaeilge (*Ar Son na Gaeilge*, 1993), Diarmait Mac Giolla Chríost's overview history (*The Irish Language in Ireland*, 2005), and Reg Hindley's more controversial investigation of Gaeltacht policy (*The Death of the Irish Language*, 1990) all appeared in ensuring years. Writing in the 1980s, Lee largely had to rely on Sean de Fréine's *The Great Silence* (1965) or the more heavily primary-sourced work of Brian Ó Cuív (especially his look at the Gaeltacht in lecture two of his *Irish Dialects and Irish-*

---

1   Niall Ó Ciosáin, 'Gaelic culture and language shift', in Laurence M. Geary and Margaret Kelleher (eds), *Nineteenth-Century Ireland: A Guide to Recent Research* (Dublin, 2005), p. 139.
2   Margaret Kelleher, *The Maamtrasna Murders: Language, Life, and Death in Nineteenth-Century Ireland* (Dublin, 2018), p. 56.

Speaking Districts, 1980).[3] Aside from some occasional scholarly studies, and of course the various Gaeltacht reports and government white papers produced over the years, the secondary material needed to readily flesh out the history of the Irish language for either the twentieth or nineteenth centuries, especially for exploring the administrative policies that so occupied Lee, simply were not at hand.

And yet the book appeared at a time of transition and uncertainty in the status of Irish language in Ireland, and Lee's conclusions should be placed within this context. The decades preceding publication had featured startling retreats by the state from previous approaches to supporting the language. The release of the report by An Coimisiún um Athbheochan na Gaeilge in 1963 and the growing criticism, by the 1970s, directed at state authorities, especially Gaeltarra Éireann, had drawn attention to the shortcomings of state-run economic and cultural programs for the language, including the lack of a robust Irish-language media and the reliance on top-down, even anglicising, industrial initiatives in the Gaeltachtaí. Further retreat ensued in the 1970s with the withdrawal of the Irish language as a compulsory subject for the Leaving Certificate in 1973, the failure to push for Irish as a working language at the time of Ireland's joining the European Union that same year, and the end to compulsory Irish for civil service entrance examinations in 1974 and the accompanying resultant decline in Irish-medium schools. Simultaneously, the 1970s had marked the beginning of a movement reconceptualising language rights as minority rights, built around protections for local dialects, locally-based media services (e.g., Raidió na Gaeltachta, founded 1972), and in general a demand that Irish deserved protection because of its threatened status, not because it might fulfil an often capricious national interest.[4] Against this backdrop, the reason for Lee's focus on the shortcomings of the state and the blow to Irish cultural heterogeneity that language loss would entail, central to his interpretation of both nineteenth- and twentieth-century linguistic trajectories, becomes clearer.

What follows is thus an effort to link the framework for interpreting the history of the Irish language presented in *Ireland 1912–1985* to the debate over language and identity that Lee himself foregrounded in the 'Perspectives' chapter in which his most extensive discussion of the language occurs. Furthermore, this essay seeks to summarise the ramifications of Lee's analysis for our interpretation of nineteenth-century Ireland in particular, highlighting his efforts to push for better comparative approaches, bring closer scrutiny to the role of the state, and question received assumptions about language shift that had been so prevalent in the field up until recent years.

3   Pádraig Ó Riagáin, *Language Maintenance and Language Shift as Strategies of Social Reproduction: Irish in the Corca Dhuibhne Gaeltacht, 1926–1986* (Dublin, 1992); Pádraig Ó Riagáin, *Language Policy and Social Reproduction: Ireland, 1893–1993* (Oxford, 1997); Proinsias Mac Aonghusa, *Ar Son na Gaeilge: Conradh na Gaeilge, 1893–1993* (Dublin, 1993); Diarmait Mac Giolla Chríost, *The Irish Language in Ireland: From Goídel to Globalisation* (New York, 2005); Reg Hindley, *The Death of the Irish Language: A Qualified Obituary* (London, 1990); Sean de Fréine, *The Great Silence: The Study of a Relationship between Language and Nationality* (Cork, 1965); Brian Ó Cuív, *Irish Dialects and Irish-Speaking Districts: Three Lectures* (Dublin, 1980).
4   Diarmait Mac Giolla Chríost, 'A question of national identity or minority rights? The changing status of the Irish language in Ireland since 1922', *Nations and Nationalism* 18:3 (2012), pp. 401–6; Jerry White, 'Place, dialect, and broadcasting in Irish: *Plus ça change . . .*', *Éire-Ireland* 50:1&2 (2015), pp. 114, 120–26.

Lee held back turning his attention to an extended discussion of the language until nearly the end of the book (the analysis begins on page 658 of 687) and chose to frame it as a critique of journalist Kevin O'Connor's appraisal of the youthfulness of 1980s Ireland that had appeared in the *Irish Independent* in July 1985. Reading O'Connor's essay today, one is struck by the prescience of many of his stances. He recognises the emergence of a multivalent, multi-ethnic Ireland, populated by a younger generation far more attuned to contemporary consumption, sport, and culture than the features of Irish identity that had been so dominant in the post-independence state. It is hard to argue, looking at twenty-first century Ireland, that O'Connor's predictions about the direction of the country have not come to pass. But as Lee shrewdly recognised, O'Connor also missed much about the vitality of the 'nationalistic skin ... being shaken off' and surely moved into shaky ground in asking whether 'we can afford to tote the blighted trinity of race, religion, and language into the rest of the functional 80s'.[5] Lee took issue in particular with O'Connor's dismissal of the relevance of the Irish language to this new emerging Ireland, shrewdly noting that far from a sign of hesitation in embracing a cosmopolitan (and specifically European) present, support for the Irish language aligned Ireland with 'defining characteristics of normal European states'.[6]

The argument Lee proffered here is subtle but profound, and was likely shaped in the emerging awareness of the reorientation of the language movement in Ireland around civil rights. Lee's close colleague Gearóid Ó Tuathaigh had noted this shift in a Thomas Davis lecture, which Lee as editor had included in *Ireland, 1945–70: The Thomas Davis Lectures* (1979), a source that appears in Lee's select bibliography to the 1989 book.[7] By the late 1980s, the movement known as Gluaiseacht (sometimes Coiste) Chearta Sibhialta na Gaeltachta was already two decades old and could point to the longevity of key local rights initiatives like Raidió na Gaeltachta as successes in framing language preservation around a new narrative of minority needs. Moreover, this shift away from a nationalist justification for Irish was on the verge of achieving key milestones that would mitigate some of the missed opportunities of the 1970s, including the commitment to the language under the republic's Education Act of 1998; in the North, protection of the language under the terms of Good Friday Agreement of 1998 via a template provided by the European Charter for Regional or Minority Rights; and the elevation of Irish to the status of official and working language by the European Union in 2005. The visibility of this same civil rights approach can be seen in Lee's rejection of O'Connor's scepticism toward bilingual road signs and governmental publications, for example. To O'Connor's question, 'Who reads road signs in Irish or the extensive duplication into Gaelic of official documents?', Lee answered that even if such readers were few, they were 'entitled' to have such services provided.[8]

The history of Irish through a minority rights lens extended to Lee's historical interpretation of the reasons for the ongoing shift from Irish to English. Here he appears to have been influenced by the frustrations with state actions on behalf of the language shared

---

5   Kevin D. O'Connor, 'Ireland – a nation caught in the middle of an identity crisis', *Irish Independent*, 20 Jul. 1985, p. 7.
6   J. J. Lee, *Ireland 1912–1985: Politics and Society* (Cambridge, 2012), p. 661.
7   Ó Tuathaigh's discussion of this changing focus of the Gaeltacht movement can be found in White, 'Place', p. 113.
8   Lee, *Ireland*, p. 660.

by many language advocates of the post-civil rights era. Supporters of *cearta sibhialta* had been inspired by writers Máirtín Ó Cadhain and Seosamh Mac Grianna, who had been strongly critical of the state-led publishing effort An Gúm and concerned that the initiative to create a standardised spelling for the language, An Caighdeán Oifigiúil, was effacing the local dialects central to Gaeltacht identity.[9] The limitations associated with the state's business- and industry-development projects in the Gaeltacht were also well known and compounded by a wider scepticism of the state's ability to promote growth more generally as emigration spiked again in the 1980s. Lee drew once again on Ó Tuathaigh, who had contributed a short history entitled 'The State and the Irish Language' to the *Irish Times* in 1977 as part of the series 'Watching Our Language', curated by journalist Brendán Ó hEithir. Ó Tuathaigh listed a series of missteps by the government in its language policy from the time of the creation of the independent Irish state, starting with its overreliance on the education system to counteract linguistic decline despite a severe shortage of qualified teachers. Initiatives such as An Gúm or grant support for Gaeltacht areas had been too modest in output or stingy in its financial outlay. In other cases, such as the push to increase Irish speaking in the civil service, or even the tendency to vest so much responsibility for language support in the state as opposed to non-governmental efforts – Ireland had experienced success in the early twentieth century with on-the-ground organising by Conradh na Gaeilge, for example – Ó Tuathaigh detected a slowness to correct course when efforts were failing.[10]

This critique of the state lay at the heart of the interpretation of the language in *Ireland 1912–85*, in which Lee contributed further details about the failed initiatives of early independence. Having doubled down on assigning much of the responsibility for preserving Irish to the Department of Education, the Cosgrave government balked at making the financial outlay needed to subsidise schools or set up commissions to successfully integrate use of Irish in the schools with international best practices in pedagogy. This was so even when its own commissions, such as the 1925 Coimisiún na Gaeltachta, had recommended that such support be made available. Worse, Lee argued, the state's ineffective efforts to press for Irish had simultaneously undermined the quality of education more generally, as in efforts to penalise teachers whose instruction in Irish was found to be below standards, even when they had proven successful in teaching other subjects.

Gaelicisation of the Irish civil service, a major goal from the inception of the state, had been likewise problematic. Lee memorably wrote:

> A knowledge of Irish was made compulsory for certain state posts, but no genuine attempt was made to Gaelicise either politics or the civil service prerequisites for the success of the revival. The result of all this fertilising was a luxuriant crop of weeds.[11]

The problem was not just one of a failure to preserve Irish through a Gaelicised state, but one of hypocrisy that shaded into cronyism. Like Ó Tuathaigh, who had complained of latter-day politicians professing to support Irish but knowing only a few words themselves, Lee asserted that 'the refusal of all governments since the foundation of the state to

---

9   White, 'Place', pp. 115–20.
10   Gearóid Ó Tuathaigh, 'The state and the Irish language', *Irish Times*, 19 Apr. 1977, p. 8.
11   Lee, *Ireland*, pp. 134–35.

practise what they preached alerted an observant populace to the fact that the revival was a sham.'[12] Even seemingly benign efforts like the requirement of knowledge of Irish for civil service posts, because of the otherwise anglicised nature of how the government conducted its business, could suffer from a perception that the entrance examination had become yet another tool of the nascent state to disburse offices to favoured applicants. Most significantly, Lee argued that the state's policy had been the most important factor behind language shift. Far from preserving Irish, the state had actually been an 'agency of Anglicisation' through its refusal to truly integrate the language into its daily conduct. The history of the Irish language, he wrote, was therefore 'intimately bound up with political history'.[13]

In other ways, however, Lee's analysis departed from the usual scholarship of the time, particularly in his consistently comparative approach. In retrospect his comparisons between Ireland's linguistic fortunes and those of Denmark, Finland, Switzerland, Austria and Wales, among others (including a look overseas to the Irish in the United States) seem essential given the abundance of examples of language maintenance and shift ready for placement next to the Irish case. But such comparisons were not widespread in the research of the time, which was instead viewed almost exclusively through the viewpoint of the Irish national struggle and English-Irish relations. As it happens, the comparative approach allowed Lee to make a double indictment: first of Ireland's twentieth-century economic record, and then of any attempts to link the causes of language shift to the country's industrialisation. Pointing to numerous examples of small counties who had remained bilingual even as they acquired the language of larger trading partners or (as in the Welsh case) neighbouring industrial giants, Lee emphasized that the evidence showed that there was no natural connection between economic advancement and language shift. This directly contradicted explanations for Irish language shift that had posited a causal relationship (however regrettable) between material advancement and the dominance of English. These also mistakenly discounted possible stable bilingual outcomes for the Irish case and the inconvenient fact that, as Lee observed, because 'the Irish have recorded the slowest rate of growth of gross national product in the western world since the mid-nineteenth century, it is difficult to believe that national economic performance could have been much more unsuccessful . . . had the country clung to the language.'[14]

Thus, sceptical of state efforts to preserve the Gaeltachtaí, wary of the track record of top-down language planning, and dismissive of purely economic explanations of language shift, Lee laid out an appraisal of the fortunes of the Irish language in the twentieth century that cut through what had been vague and assumption-laden scholarly writing on the subject for decades. What ramifications did Lee's interpretation of the twentieth century hold for understanding the history of the Irish language in the earlier decades? Here, too, Lee's assessment of the pre-independence years owed much to his take on the track record of the twentieth-century Irish state. At its heart was a posed counterfactual: would Ireland have found any different levels of economic success had it maintained Irish, even if only in a stable bilingual situation? The answer, Lee proposed, was yes, given the success

---

12 Ó Tuathaigh, 'The State', p. 8; Lee, *Ireland*, p. 135.
13 Lee, *Ireland*, pp. 204, 666, 671.
14 Ibid., p. 664.

of analogous cases such as Denmark, also a heavy dairy producer with an even smaller population of resilient speakers of Danish, which had nevertheless made significant moves into the English butter market by the end of the nineteenth century. At the very least, it was not evident that the usual reason posited for Irish language shift – proximity to English-speaking capitalism – held much sway.

Scholars had also repeatedly raised the role of emigration as a cause of language shift, but here again Lee sensed a more complicated situation. If Irish speakers in the nineteenth century had come to see acquiring English as a means of economic advancement, but also viewed imparting English to their children as a means to facilitate success in the future host country upon emigration, then economic development in Ireland (enabling commercial success) and its failure (leading to emigration) would both cause the same linguistic outcome (shift to English). Even if this paradoxical situation has not led scholars to seek alternate non-economic causes for nineteenth-century shift, one must further contend with Lee's observation that no other major emigrating group, among them Germans, Swedes, Norwegians, Italians, Poles or Jews, enacted a massive shift to a host country's language prior to arrival – and in some cases not for a generation or two afterward.[15]

Exploring this comparative record of Europeans who remained multilingual led Lee back to the culpability of the Irish state that had marked his analysis of the twentieth century:

> The main reason why the Irish did not remain satisfied, as did other trading partners of England, with acquiring the modicum of English required for economic intercourse while retaining their own language as the vernacular was the nature of the state.

And the nature of that state was one of growing presence in the lives of Irish individuals on an English-speaking basis. Lee wrote, 'When knowledge of English sufficed for all the transactions of public life, Irish became increasingly redundant.'[16] The language history of nineteenth-century Ireland was thus a political – we might also say colonial – one. Lee's contributions to the historiography of the nineteenth-century language shift in Ireland can therefore be summarised by two key concepts. The first is that because multilingualism was the norm in Europe, the central question is not why English was so widely acquired in the years prior to independence, but rather why a stable bilingualism did not persist in Ireland. The second is that we must trace the development of the state in the nineteenth century to understand its impact on Irish bilingualism. These two topics can be explored in turn.

If a shift to multilingualism is treated as one (more natural) process with its own set of characteristics, and the loss of multilingualism in Ireland as a separate (and not inevitable) one, then it follows that the historiography of nineteenth-century Ireland should better reflect the distinctiveness of these two developments. For one, they should not be treated as closely sequential chronological events. We know, for example, that it is likely that the Irish-speaking community was majority monolingual as early as the beginning of the nineteenth century. And yet acquisition of English was evidently widespread throughout the eighteenth century, as indicated by much recent scholarship on bilingual (or at least linguistically cross-fertilised) literature produced by Irish speakers and on the longer

---

15   Ibid., p. 665.
16   Ibid., p. 666.

trajectory of bilingual culture in the Gaeltacht as a whole.[17] Even if we posit that acquisition of English and the abandonment of bilingualism was a matter of a two- or three-generation transition at the individual household level, we should consider the likelihood that at a broader community or regional level, the two phenomena were not near-contemporary events. Timing also comes into play in terms of transition duration. We would expect that the acquisition of English by a community, a potentially difficult and extended process, would involve a longer transition (since it involves language acquisition) than a move away from bilingualism (involving language abandonment), a phenomenon that could more easily happen in a matter of years. Furthermore, we must be open to the possibility of different causes for each shift. Acquisition of English may be a matter of state presence, as Lee has suggested, but the collapse of bilingualism may turn out to have a more material basis – the long-standing question of the exact linguistic impact of the Great Famine being one such consideration.

Devoting greater attention to the role of the state in nineteenth-century language shift likewise requires a closer look at historical details because the size and characteristics of the Irish administration and its intersections with everyday life were in flux; we must be clear on the nature of governance in Ireland at any given time before assuming a particular impact on Irish-speaking communities. As Lee himself observed, the state was expanding in the nineteenth century, often in response to nationalist demands to address local concerns. But when did it expand, how visible was that expansion, and when did that governance most reveal itself in the regions that were heavily Irish speaking? Undoubtedly, the frequency and nature of interactions between state and individual changed over the course of the nineteenth century. At its outset, governance was decentralised and still largely in the hands of local magistrates and gentry. By mid-century, interactions with personnel of the state had grown to include members of the Royal Irish Constabulary (founded 1822), professionalised doctors through new state-established dispensaries (via the Medical Charities Act, 1851), lawyers and judges (especially owing to the establishment of petty sessions courts from the 1820s), water- and later coastguard personnel (from 1809), and most importantly, state-funded teachers from the founding of the national-school system (1831). It should be made clear that not all these officials were English monoglots. But there is no doubt that these personnel relied officially on English to conduct their business, even if Irish was used informally to help interactions along.

And yet, how impactful would such interactions be on the introduction of English into a community, or the abandonment of bilingualism? How often would the average Irish speaker have had recourse to doctors, the police, courtrooms or coastguards? We might argue that even if such encounters were infrequent, simply the presence of these officials on the fringes of a community would have made clear that knowing English was an advantage. On the other hand, the school system self-evidently would have existed in a different category of higher-frequency interactions. Unlike visits to a dispensary or participation in a court of law, attending school – even in the short duration primary-education focused system of the nineteenth century – involved more sustained contact with

---

17 Sarah McKibben, *Endangered Masculinities in Irish Poetry, 1540–1780* (Dublin, 2010); Liam Mac Mathúna, *Béarla sa Ghaeilge: Cabhair Choigríche, An Códmheascadh Gaeilge/Béarla i Litríocht na Gaeilge* (Baile Átha Cliath, 2017).

an English-language curriculum. But again, how sustained? Although 1831, the year of the Stanley letter outlining a vision for state-supported national schools, is sometimes treated by historians as a bright line dividing one educational regime from another, the shared-funding model at the heart of the system meant that its growth depended significantly on transferring pre-existing schools to the national school rolls and relying on local wealth to pay for the creation and upkeep of a schoolhouse. Up until the 1860s or, in the case of Connacht, the 1870s or later, that growth was initially concentrated in two of the already heavily English-only provinces of Ulster and Leinster. Ulster, for example, had some three or four times more schools per capita in the first decades of the national school system than Connacht.[18] National schools were not only latecomers to most Irish-speaking communities (County Cork being one exception), they were also more prone to periodic closure when local funds ran out and were more likely to see fluctuating or low enrolments.

This may explain why the state was able to deploy an English-only curriculum without finding evidence of inefficacy for some years before starting to see increased criticism of this approach. After all, while we would rightly question the willingness of the state under British rule to respond to Irish needs, it should be recognised – as Lee himself did – that the Dublin government in fact had a history of responding to pressure to reform to meet local demands. Lee's point that 'nationalist grievances' shaped the state's expansion reminds us that concession to the emergent strong farmer class on property rights after the 1877–79 period and the move toward local governance extended to Ireland by the Local Government Act of 1898 were also characteristic of British governance.[19] Notably, these concessions emerged on language and education too, albeit grudgingly. The complaints of schools inspector Patrick Keenan in his reports of the 1860s and 1870s – many centred on western schools, in places like Tory Island, where the national schools had by that time arrived – that English-only education was a failure where Irish speaking was still strong led, with the help of lobbying by new groups like the Society for the Preservation of the Irish Language, to concessions on using Irish on a limited basis to facilitate instruction in the primary and secondary schools. The expansion of the state in the nineteenth century was therefore not always a straightforward case of single-direction impact, with the new presence of the state shaping local communities in an unfettered manner. The state, too, had to compromise at times, even if in response to unrest, as in the case of the Land War.

Like Lee's counterfactual regarding a robust twentieth-century Irish economy built on a bilingual basis, it is interesting to consider a counterfactual in which the state, rather than

---

18   Kevin Lougheed, 'National education and empire: Ireland and the geography of national education system', in David Dickson, Justyna Pyz, and Christopher Shepard (eds), *Irish Classrooms and British Empire: Imperial Contexts in the Origins of Modern Education* (Dublin, 2012), pp. 12–14. See also Mary Daly, 'The development of the national school system, 1831–40', in Art Cosgrove and Donal McCartney (eds), *Studies in Irish History Presented to R. Dudley Edwards* (Dublin, 1979), pp. 150–63; Nicholas M. Wolf, 'The national-school system and the Irish language in the nineteenth century', in James Kelly and Susan Hegarty (eds), *Schools and Schooling, 1650–2000: New Perspectives on the History of Education*, Eighth Seamus Heaney Lectures (Dublin, 2017), 72–92. A further cause for the lag in arrival of national schools in some areas, beyond the lack of local financial support, was the opposition of certain religious figures, most notoriously the opposition of archbishop of Tuam John MacHale to the expansion of the state schools in his heavily Irish-speaking archdiocese.

19   Lee, *Ireland*, p. 666.

creeping slowly via national schools into Irish-speaking regions, had expanded everywhere quickly in the 1830s, 1840s and 1850s, forcing its administrators to reckon immediately with the limitations of an English-only curriculum in areas where little English was spoken or not spoken as a first language. Would the national system have responded by doubling down, ignoring local needs and preserving its English monoglot face? Or would it have sought Irish-speaking instructors, as many earlier Protestant missionary schools had done in the first three decades of the nineteenth century, in order to ensure the effectiveness of schools in exchange for encouraging bilingualism? The trends of the late-nineteenth century seemingly suggest an eventual openness to bilingual education, culminating in the 1904 Bilingual Programme, but those concessions also overlay shifting realities, as the number of Irish speakers declined precipitously in the post-Famine period. Allowing bilingual teaching in a few dozen schools, as happened in 1904, could be comfortably done without compromising on principles that held up reading and writing in English as central goals.

In the end, shifting the spotlight to the role of the colonial state in assisting, encouraging, or otherwise failing to stop the preservation of Irish in the nineteenth century makes it all the more disappointing, as Lee was quick to point out, to review the track record of post-independence Irish governments. 'It would, no doubt, be an exaggeration to suggest that sovereignty was the final death blow for Irish,' he wrote before ending on a somewhat optimistic note intimating that the epitaph for the Irish language, even at the nadir of the 1980s, had not yet been written.[20] In this assessment, Lee, like O'Connor, proved to be more or less predictive of twenty-first century directions. Many of the 'voluntary education effort in some middle-class urban circles' that Lee cited as showing signs of dynamism have in many ways come to the fore in leading language policy in the past 30 years. But just as there is much that needs to be done to protect all aspects of Irish-speaking life, most glaringly its native-speaking Gaeltacht communities, there is more work required to recover the pre-independence history of the Irish language in the nineteenth century and earlier. That history, helped by Lee's insistence that we move beyond received explanations to think harder about how culture operates, will only serve to enrich our perspective on Irish and its speakers.

---

20   Ibid., 674.

Leadership and Independent Ireland's Performance since 1922: A Historiographical Perspective on Lee's Assessment

Gearóid Ó Tuathaigh

The 1980s was not a comfortable time for reviewing with equanimity the performance of the Irish national state in the decades since 1921.[1] A contemporary commentator concluded, 'the economy is now in recession. Unemployment is rising, and the social problems that flowed from economic stagnation are growing.'[2] There was rancour in party politics, notably on issues pertaining to individual rights to make sexual and reproductive choices; the bloodshed continued in Northern Ireland, though nationalist opinion in the republic was edging close to consensus on the quest for an 'agreed' rather than a territorially-united Ireland.

It is not surprising, therefore, that a clutch of serious studies, conceived or written in the later 1980s, dealing with the Irish economic experience, and in Lee's case with wider historical experience, from the 1920s to the end of the 1980s had as a common preoccupation the troubling issue of 'failure'. In the case of the republic, the recurring nature of economic crises and the depressingly recurring social outcome – heavy emigration – was a central element in this verdict of failure. The 1950s seemed to be the appropriate historical reference.[3]

Thus, from 1982:

> Despondency seems to be on the increase, as though the intractability of our position has at last sapped our will to solve them [sic]. It is difficult to avoid recalling the grim fifties, the last severe economic depression. We survived the fifties to enjoy the boom of the sixties. What was accomplished once can presumably be accomplished again. External circumstances

---

1   The nature and constitutional status of Northern Ireland, with the limited competence of its administration, make direct comparison of its 'performance' with that of the republic extremely problematic. It would demand separate and more detailed consideration than is proposed in this essay.

2   Frank Litton, preface to Frank Litton (ed.), *Unequal Achievement: The Irish Experience 1957–1982* (Dublin, 1982), p. ix.

3   Kieran A. Kennedy, Thomas Giblin, and Deirdre McHugh, *The Economic Development of Ireland in the Twentieth Century* (London, 1988); Raymond Crotty, *Ireland in Crisis* (Dingle, 1986); Brian Girvin, *Between Two Worlds* (Dublin, 1989); Eoin O'Malley, *Industry and Economic Development: The Challenge for the Latecomer* (Dublin, 1989); Niamh Hardiman, *Pay, Politics and Economic Performance in Ireland 1970–1987* (Oxford, 1988); John Kurt Jacobsen, *Chasing Progress in the Irish Republic* (Cambridge, 1994).

undoubtedly played a part in our recovery then; equally, conditions in the world economy set limits in the chances of success today. But the important lesson of the fifties is not our dependence on the world economy. Things improved then because the administrative and political leadership searched out and responded to the opportunities which the improving world conditions brought. This responsiveness reflected not only a will to win; joined with it was a clear perception of reality and an understanding of the means required to transform it.[4]

Just as in the 1950s, failure to deal with economic and social crisis was accompanied by political volatility: five general elections in the 1980s, three within 20 months at the start of the decade.

Of the various analyses offered, Lee's was the most searing and, in its consideration of deep-seated cultural forces, the most ambitious. The main elements of Lee's socio-cultural exploration of the modern Irish *mentalité* are by now very familiar: the dominance of the 'possessor' principle over the 'performance' principle. This mentality – the fruit of a complex historical legacy – was exemplified by the 'begrudger', the prototype of the enemy of all who show an ambition to perform. Far from being reductive, this categorisation of the cultural predicament from which the failings of independent Ireland's 'performance' originated was quite protean and proved hospitable to an exceptionally wide-ranging commentary on the cultural and intellectual history of the first 60 years or so of post-Partition Ireland.

A central focus, obviously, in the battle between the possessor and performance principles was the quality of decision-making and the calibre of leadership, making the vital, strategic decisions determining the path and pace of Irish national development. What was the ideas market in which Irish leaders – decision-makers – sought and found the basis for public policy: what was their vision, their philosophy, their ideological moorings, their models for achieving 'the good life' for the citizens of the state?

The purpose of this essay is to consider, however selectively, Lee's assessment of leadership as a factor in independent Ireland's 'performance' to the mid-1980s; and to consider whether the historiography of the past 30 or so years – since Lee's major work was published – has challenged this assessment or caused it to be revised, and, if so, on what basis and to what extent. Leadership in this context is understood as the capacity for exerting, or persuading others to exert, demonstrably effective influence in shaping and driving crucial choices in public policy calculated to serve the national interest.

So far as political leadership is concerned – principally in government – the historian and broadcaster David McCullagh has revealed that when he finished his book on John A. Costello and was considering his next assignment, he mused that it would certainly not be 'another book' on de Valera.[5] Likewise, Bryce Evans, in the preface to his 2011 study of Lemass, confessed that he was met with 'not another book on Lemass', from colleagues, when he announced his intended project.[6] Happily, both writers proceeded, undaunted, to their reconsiderations of de Valera and Lemass. But compared to what had been published on Lemass and even on de Valera by the mid-1980s, when Lee was drafting his book, the surge of serious academic political biographical studies during the past 30 years is striking.

4   Litton, *Unequal Achievement*, p. ix.
5   David McCullagh, 'Not another book about Dev!', in *History Ireland*, 27:2 (2019), pp. 48–51.
6   Bryce Evans, *Seán Lemass. Democrat Dictator* (Cork, 2011), p. 1.

Nor is it only Lemass, de Valera, and Costello that have attracted attention, but a large cohort of prominent political actors. There have been substantial, largely archive-based biographical studies (by a single author or in edited collections) of W. T. Cosgrave, Seán McEntee, Frank Aiken, James Dillon, Kevin O'Higgins, Jack Lynch, Patrick Hillery.[7]

Nor is it only in biographical studies that there has been a bumper harvest: the crop has included academic studies of various political parties; of particular governments; of specific decades or periods ('long decades' such as 1958–73); of the 1920s, 1950s, 1960s and 1970s.[8] Additionally, there have been detailed political studies of particular episodes or themes: Partition; Second World War and Irish neutrality; Marshall aid; entry to the EEC; and, of course, Northern Ireland and the Troubles, from their origins to the present day, including the decades covered by Lee's 1989 study.[9]

The historiographical dividend from this powerful surge, during the past 30 years, of research and publications on political 'leadership' reflects the greatly enhanced access to primary historical source material, both state and private papers. It also, and understandably, reflects changing perspectives.

As a result, there is now a better understanding of the character, contacts, and personal views and preoccupations of leading political actors, as well as a richer sense of the 'inner history', as it were, of political decisions, as traced in communications between cabinet and different government departments. There are, to be sure, certain deficits. There is a dearth of contemporary diaries kept by politicians, a striking contrast with Britain.[10] Some exceptions to this include: Gemma Hussey in the 1980s and, for an earlier period, the invaluable memoir of Patrick Connolly.[11] The list of politicians who have published autobiographies has also lengthened in recent decades: including Garret Fitzgerald, Barry Desmond, Desmond O'Malley, Albert Reynolds, Brian Lenihan, Pádraig Faulkner, Pat Lindsay, Ruairí Quinn, Conor Cruise O'Brien, Mary O'Rourke, Bertie Ahern. It must be acknowledged that these are of variable quality and value for the serious researcher,

---

7   Anthony J. Jordan, *W. T. Cosgrave 1880–1965: Founder of Modern Ireland* (Dublin, 2006); Tom Feeney, *Seán McEntee: A Political Life* (Dublin, 2009); David McCullagh, *The Reluctant Taoiseach: A Biography of John A. Costello* (Dublin, 2010); John McCarthy, *Kevin O'Higgins: Builder of the Irish State* (Dublin, 2006); Bryce Evans and Stephen Kelly (eds), *Frank Aiken, Nationalist and Internationalist* (Dublin, 2014); Michael Laffan, *Judging W. T. Cosgrave* (Dublin, 2014); Maurice Manning, *James Dillon: A Biography* (Dublin, 2000); Dermot Keogh, *Jack Lynch: A Biography* (Dublin, 2008); John Walsh, *Patrick Hillery: The Official Biography* (Dublin. 2008).

8   For example, Mel Farrell, Jason Knirck, and Ciara Meehan (eds), *A Formative Decade: Ireland in the 1920s* (Sallins, 2015); Dermot Keogh, Finbarr O'Shea, and Carmel Quinlan (eds), *Ireland in the 1950s: The Lost Decade* (Cork. 2004); Mary E. Daly, *Sixties Ireland* (Cambridge, 2016); Diarmaid Ferriter, *Ambiguous Republic: Ireland in the 1970s* (London, 2012); David McCullagh, *A Makeshift Majority: The First Inter-Party Government, 1948–51* ((Dublin, 1998); Ciara Meehan, *Cosgrave's Party: A History of Cumann na nGaedheal, 1923–1933* (Dublin, 2010).

9   For example, Robert Lynch, *The Partition of Ireland 1918–1925* (Cambridge, 2019); Clair Wills, *That Neutral Island* (London. 2008); Bernadette Whelan, *Ireland and the Marshall Plan, 1947–1957* (Dublin, 2000); Marc Mulholland, *The Longest War* (Oxford. 2002); Michael Geary, *An Inconvenient Wait: Ireland's Quest for Membership of the EEC, 1957–1973* (Dublin, 2009); Brendan O'Leary, *A Treatise on Northern Ireland*, 3 Vols. (Oxford, 2019).

10 One thinks of the prolific diarists of Harold Wilson's Labour cabinets, such as Richard Crossman, Tony Benn, Barbara Castle.

11 Gemma Hussey, *At the Cutting Edge: Cabinet Diaries 1982–87* (Dublin, 1997); J. Anthony Gaughan (ed.) *Memoirs of Senator Joseph Connolly* (Dublin, 1996).

but several are clearly based on notes or other documents contemporary with the events described.[12]

The historiography of the past 30 years dealing with the period 1920–1988 reflects changing perspectives as well as expanding archival sources. Lee (and his fellow writers ruminating on the theme of 'failure' in the mid- to late-1980s) could not have anticipated that, after 1987 Ray McSharry would administer a sharp shock of austerity, followed by almost two decades of neo-corporatist 'social partnership' and economic growth. Ireland again skilfully surfed a favourable wave of international investment, aided by the decision to participate in a deepening EU integration project – from Maastricht to joining the euro – before ultimately creating its own domestic credit bubble in time for a seismic international shock from 2008. But throughout the years of partnership and prosperity, the leadership skills prized – and rewarded electorally – revolved around negotiation, mediating between and managing diverse, potentially competing, socio-economic interests and lobbies.[13]

And, of course, in the context of Northern Ireland, with moves towards ending violence and fabricating political accommodations conducive to mutual tolerance, which led in time to the GFA and St Andrews agreements, the leadership qualities demanded and lauded were also those rooted in consensus-building and compromise.[14] These pressing contemporary challenges might be expected to have coloured the perspectives on leadership that would feature in political analyses written in the decades after 1989. It is not suggested, of course, that a heavy, present-centred determinism informs all – or indeed any – of the serious historical writings of the past 30 years. On the other hand, it would be very strange indeed if the actual historical experience of Ireland during these recent decades had left no mark at all on the particular skills and accomplishments of leadership that have been valued, and at times valorised, by various commentators, including academics.

Allowing for all of that, in considering the fruits of this rich harvest of new archive-based history on political leadership, what is striking is how relatively stable during the past 30 years has been the academic assessment of the strictly political leadership cadres that featured in Lee's analysis of the 1920–85 period. What we have gained, of course, from more recent scholarship has been a greatly enhanced understanding of the character and micro-context of political action of a cohort of leading politicians, principally office-holders. But there has been no fundamental shifting of settled verdicts on leading figures. Thus, the more recent studies of de Valera, while more sympathetic to his achievements

---

12 Garret Fitzgerald, *All in a Life* (Dublin, 1991); Patrick J. Lindsay, *Memories* (Dublin, 1992); Thomas F. O'Higgins, *A Double Life* (Dublin, 1996); Conor Cruise O'Brien, *Memoir: My Life and Themes* (Dublin, 1998); Barry Desmond, *Finally and in Conclusion: A Political Memoir* (Dublin, 2000); Ruairí Quinn, *Straight Left: A Journey in Politics* (Dublin, 2005); Pádraig Faulkner, *As I Saw It: Reviewing Over 30 Years of Fianna Fáil and Irish Politics* (Dublin, 2005); Seán McBride, *The Day's Struggle: A Memoir 1904–1951* (Dublin, 2005); Albert Reynolds, *My Autobiography* (London, 2009); Nuala Fennell, *Political Woman: A Memoir* (Dublin, 2009); Mary O'Rourke, *Just Mary: A Memoir* (Dublin, 2013); Desmond O'Malley, *Conduct Unbecoming: A Memoir* (Dublin, 2014).

13 Cormac Ó Gráda, *A Rocky Road. The Irish Economy since the 1920s* (Manchester, 1997), pp. 31–34; Seán Ó Riain, *The Rise and Fall of Ireland's Celtic Tiger: Liberalism, Boom and Bust* (Cambridge, 2014).

14 For the consensus-maker *par excellence*, see Bertie Ahern (with Richard Aldous), *The Autobiography* (London, 2009).

(notably as a shrewd statesman and on the international stage), confirm earlier judgments on the essentially static, conservative nature of his social vision and the criticism of him for remaining too long at the helm. But the richer documentation has prompted the conclusion that he was even more ably manipulative of the ambitions and antipathies of his Fianna Fáil colleagues than was previously acknowledged. W. T. Cosgrave's solid, un-histrionic virtues and Seán McEntee's sharp tongue and hyper-cautious approach to spending and to the management of the state's finances have also been confirmed by recent research.[15]

Seán Lemass, perhaps, has attracted the most searching re-examination, with greater attention paid to his complexity and contradictions.[16] This is not to say that he had enjoyed uncritical approval in the prevailing historiography before 1990. Lee himself had acknowledged shortcomings. But such was the severity of the judgments on the economic and social crisis that marked the concluding phase of de Valera's long period at the helm, that Lemass's unequivocal prioritising of economic growth and increased employment earned universal plaudits. That Lemass's period as Taoiseach coincided with the new departure (towards greater free trade and away from protectionism) in economic policy, signalled by Whitaker's document of 1958, has resulted in the coupling of the two names – Lemass and Whitaker – in assessments of the launch and impact of the new departure of 1958–65. There is unanimity among commentators on the necessity of the policies, if not necessarily on their precise outcome.

Among recent commentators on Lemass, positive acknowledgment of his achievement is frequently marked by an adverse verdict, explicit or implicit, on de Valera. The differences in character and political style of the two men have, in fact, been a feature of political commentary from the time of the succession, at the latest. The pragmatic, urban Lemass, the quintessential Dubliner, brisk and business-like in speech and the conduct of politics, not given to eloquence or to the lengthy exposition of cultural visions, is an obvious counterpoint to de Valera. Though he lived all of his adult life in the capital, de Valera's cast of mind – no less than his cadence of speech – remained that of the countryman. The conviviality of the golf club and the poker game among friends, in which Lemass could relax, had no place in the life of Dev, for whom politics itself was an all-consuming passion. The constant exhortations of Dev on the need to restore the Irish language as a main vernacular, struck no chord with Lemass. And the list of contrasts might easily be extended further.

Yet while recent studies have not subverted or contradicted these established, contrasting profiles, they have given grounds for greater caution in resorting to stark, binary terms in assessing the two men as leaders. De Valera did not oppose or obstruct Lemass in the successive phases of the latter's drive for economic growth and 'modernisation' – either in the early zealously protectionist phase (from the 1930s) or in the later drive to dismantle

---

15   See Laffan, *Judging W. T. Cosgrave*; Feeney, *Seán McEntee*.
16   Michael O'Sullivan, *Seán Lemass: A Biography* (Dublin, 1994); John Horgan, *Seán Lemass: The Enigmatic Patriot* (Dublin, 1997); Robert Savage, *Lemass* (Dundalk, 1999); Brian Girvin and Gary Murphy (eds), *The Lemass Era: Politics and Society in the Ireland of Seán Lemass* (Dublin, 2005); Tom Garvin, *Judging Lemass* (Dublin, 2009); Bryce Evans, *Seán Lemass: Democratic Dictator* (Cork, 2011).

protectionism. Moreover, for all his visionary rhetoric, de Valera was the arch pragmatist when it came to maximising political advantage and keeping Fianna Fáil in power.[17]

As for Lemass, his loyalty to de Valera was unshakeable. He never concealed or repented his hopes for the ending of Partition. He was an orthodox Catholic, was careful and respectful in his relationships with Catholic bishops (notably McQuaid), and had misgivings about the potential impact of television and of other aspects of the consumerist culture that he was, in his economic policy, helping to bring to dominance in the life of the state. He was a private man with modest material and recreational needs. While at his ease in the company of businessmen, he did not covet money nor acquire wealth in office.[18]

The recent crop of studies of Lemass – notwithstanding the benefit of new sources, including interviews with Lemass himself and members of his family – has not unleashed a trove of new information on his political life. Tantalising questions remain regarding his relations with archbishop McQuaid and the influence on his thinking attributable to his business contacts. But where recent historians differ in their assessments of Lemass as a leader, the matter at issue is essentially one of judgement rather than evidence. For admirers, the break with de Valera's pastoral vision, with the economic protectionism of which Lemass had been the principal architect, the departure from the long-established response of Fianna Fáil to Partition – these changes of position are seen as altogether admirable and long overdue. The more critical assessment lingers on his impatience with the discursive or deliberative dimension of parliamentary politics, his instinct for control and executive discretion, his general *dirigiste* inclinations.[19]

What emerges from Mary Daly's study of the 1960s is the particular legacy that his style of leadership bequeathed to Fianna Fáil, more enduring and more deeply embedded in the party's culture, perhaps, than de Valera's visionary mode. His determination to position Fianna Fáil as the movement best equipped to serve the national interest required the smothering of class conflict and the integration of competing elements (employers, trade unionists, farmers) into a common strategy and effort for achieving economic progress from which all would benefit.[20] Locking the social partners (as they would later be styled) into a national policy that had a close regard for optimising the electoral prospects of Fianna Fáil was a development model in which Lemass saw the state (acting in the national interest) as the decisive fulcrum: in this it differed fundamentally from the competing versions of corporatism being canvassed (not least by certain Catholic bishops) in the second quarter of the last century.[21]

Political leadership across the main parties in the independent Irish state up to the 1980s is credited by virtually all recent commentators with providing remarkable stability in the state. Independent Ireland remained free of major convulsion in the decades after 1920,

---

17 Diarmaid Ferriter, at one with Lee, sees Dev's 'dignity' and 'nobility' of bearing – and not only in the international arena – as especially praiseworthy. *Judging Dev: A Reassessment of the Life and Legacy of Eamon de Valera* (Dublin, 2007) , pp. 258, 367.

18 Horgan, *Lemass*, is judicious in assessment.

19 See Garvin, *Judging Lemass*, and Evans, *Lemass*, for contrasting assessments.

20 Daly, *Sixties Ireland*, pp. 381–2.

21 J. J. Lee, *Ireland 1912–1985: Politics and Society* (Cambridge, 1989), pp. 271–293; 'Aspects of corporatist thought in Ireland: The Commission on Vocational Organisation 1939–43', in Art Cosgrove and Dónal McCartney (eds), *Studies in Irish History* (Dublin, 1979), pp. 324–346.

when instability, war, dictatorship, displacement and mass suffering was the experience of most Europeans across the continent. Moreover, despite the enactment of emergency legislation during the war (1939), this stability was maintained in an 'open' society. To this credit sheet of the political leadership should be added the overwhelming probity that marked the holding and exercise of public office. These, and a record of dignified, sensibly idealist, and constructive engagement in international affairs and institutions, must be included in any assessment of the performance of political leaders in the independent Irish state from 1922 to 1989.[22]

At this point, it may be objected that Lee's critique of shortcomings in leadership in independent Ireland was not directed exclusively, perhaps not primarily, at political leaders but at a wider constituency of leaders involved in shaping and implementing policy: key mandarins in the higher echelons of the civil service and the 'licensed' producers and trustees of ideas within the wider institutional framework of the state. It is not necessary to rehearse at length here the Lee charge sheet, but a central feature of it was a criticism of the continuing dependence of key elements of the decision-making elites on British standards, exemplars, models, ways of thinking and doing things. This postcolonial dependency syndrome had resulted in the targets of ambition for economic growth being set too low and in innovation and bold choices being set aside in favour of the preservation of established procedures, structures, and jealously guarded bailiwicks of authority. There had been a failure to learn from appropriate 'others', to be sufficiently discriminating in borrowing ideas and new ways of doing things. Lee identified, in particular, the oppressive influence of the 'Treasury mind' on the Irish Department of Finance, notably during the secretaryship of James McElligott.[23]

In the more than 30 years since 1989, a considerable body of official papers has become accessible under the 30-year rule. But the official archive for the early decades of the state (to the 1950s) was already being researched by the later 1980s. Since then, private papers of some public servants have been deposited in public archives, though they scarcely constitute a bonanza for researchers. A clutch of senior civil servants had been contributing to the public discussion of economic matters and public administration, principally in specialist journals, prior to the 1950s. And the founding of An Foras Riaracháin in 1957 (with its journal, *Administration*) gave heft to the self-appraisal of civil service performance. Moreover, a handful of public servants (Leon Ó Broin, Seán O'Connor, C. S. Andrews) had published memoirs or reflections relevant to their public careers. The past 30 years has not seen a major advance in the supply of this genre, though Deeny, Salmon, and, more recently, Dorr have published insightful books.[24] The major exception to these observations is T. K. Whitaker, whose significance and testimony will be considered presently.

---

22 E.G Michael Kennedy and Joseph Skelly (eds), *Irish Foreign Policy, 1919–66: From Independence to Internationalism* (Dublin, 1999); Michael Kennedy and Deirdre McMahon (eds), *Obligations and Responsibilities: Ireland* at *the United Nations, 1955–2005* (Dublin, 2005). The invaluable series *Documents in Irish Foreign Policy*, published by the Royal Irish Academy, began publication in 1998.

23 See especially, Lee, *Ireland 1912–1985*, pp. 279–288 and passim.

24 James Deeny, *To Cure and to Care* (Dublin, 1989); Patrick J. Sammon, *In the Land Commission: A Memoir 1933–1978* (Dublin, 1997); Noel Dorr, *The Search for Peace in Northern Ireland: Sunningdale* (Dublin, 2019). Former diplomats have become frequent contributors to public debate on current affairs in the past decade or so.

However, despite the relative dearth of direct testimony from senior mandarins, the mining of the official papers in recent years has revealed much about decision-making and responsibility for success or failure of government policy. In particular, recent publications have drawn attention to the shifting dynamics and rivalries between government departments and their heads. Mary Daly, from her close archive-based studies of the Department of Local Government and, to a degree, the Department of Agriculture, identifies as one of the factors obstructing or retarding policy innovation, interdepartmental turf wars – competing egos and silo cultures, and a pervasively cautious, not to say procrastinating, attitude to proposals involving change.[25] As Daly concludes: 'The evidence presented throughout this book suggests that interdepartmental rivalries often proved more significant barriers to implementing new policies than the opposition expressed by the Department of Finance'.[26] Garvin, for his part, concludes that, up to the late 1950s, as leaders in the republic were faced with such urgent issues as much-needed industrialisation, a new Northern Ireland policy, or demands for educational reform, there was 'a deep ambivalence and an almost pathological irresolution ... Eventually various Gordian knots were cut, but it took time; some would say that indecision and vacillation ... have become traditional and ineradicable traits of the Irish government'.[27] Reviewing the shortcomings of Irish government in the period from 1959 to 1985, Lee's own verdict from the gloomy mid-1980s was severe:

> The growth in the variety of vested interests, inside no less than outside the public sector, in the 25 years since *Economic Development* made it difficult for even determined and clear-sighted leaders, whether politicians or administrators, to slice their way through the intestinal intricacies of the institutional maze. Clear vision, and firm political leadership, may not suffice to attain national goals. Without them, however, paralysis prevails.[28]

Thus it was contended, not only vested interests but also chronic organisational fragmentation militated against intellectual coherence and prevented strategic thinking. It was this institutional proliferation that Louden Ryan had criticised as having congealed into 'a disorganised over-complexity of formidable vested interests'.[29] If to this we add the notorious localism sustained by the Irish electoral system, then the impediments to effective ('brave') decision-making for long-term strategic objectives seemed formidable.

'Cutting through the knots' of these formidable defences against change and innovation was the Lemass/Whitaker achievement that attracted the admiration of a cohort of academics concerned with Irish modernisation.[30] It is fair to say that the historiography of the Lemass/Whitaker demarche of 1958–65 has been rewardingly revisionist in recent decades. Indeed, almost simultaneous with Lee's landmark 1989 volume, or shortly thereafter, the genesis and the legacy of *Economic Development* were being closely evaluated, initially in a 1990

---

25 Mary E. Daly, *The Buffer State: The Historical Roots of the Department of the Environment* (Dublin, 1997); Mary E. Daly, *The First Department: A History of the Department of Agriculture* (Dublin, 2002).
26 Daly, *Buffer State*, p. 531.
27 Tom Garvin, *News from a New Republic: Ireland in the 1950s* (Dublin, 2010), p. 5.
28 Lee, *Ireland 1912–1985*, p. 555.
29 Cited in Lee, *Ireland 1912–1985*, p. 635.
30 In his contribution to John F. McCarthy (ed.), *Planning Ireland's Future: The Legacy of T. K. Whitaker* (Dublin. 1990), Ronan Fanning lists the positive assessments, pp. 74–76.

festschrift for Whitaker, and in a steady flow of reassessments that followed.[31] It had already been acknowledged – by Lee and others – that a cadre of change-advocates working with Whitaker had identified many of the blockages to sustained economic growth, together with the measures that were needed to address them, later encapsulated in *Economic Development*. Also acknowledged was the significant gallery of organisational innovations from the late 1940s through the 1950s that not only identified but sought to correct the shortcomings that were retarding growth: the CSO, IDA, Córas Tráchtála, IMI, Foras Riaracháin. The strong 'outward' orientation signalled by membership of the IMF, World Bank, Irish officials travelling to meetings of emerging European institutions post-1945, the participation in the Marshall Plan: all these pointed to a growing acceptance of the need to actively engage with post-war structures and shared international responsibilities.[32]

As far as the impact of Whitaker/Lemass is concerned, Daly's recent revisionist study of the 1960s has sought to temper claims for an immediate and decisive shift in attitudes or even in actual economic performance. Improvements there were: population stabilisation, economic growth in the early sixties, greater inward investment and industrial startups, and moves towards dismantling protection, which led to the Anglo-Irish agreement of 1965, with membership of EEC set as a firm state objective. But agricultural productivity remained disappointing, likewise employment growth. The shadow of Britain – as comparator/exemplar – continued to dominate throughout the 1960s. Planning encountered difficulties, even as educational access widened, education now being viewed as the key to capacity-building. But embedded social attitudes and vested interests remained strong through the 1960s. In short, the transformation from darkness to light was neither a sudden nor a dramatic episode.[33] Viewed from the mid-1980s, however, with disillusion widespread and the state seemingly succumbing again to special interests, factionalism, and incoherence, it shouldn't surprise that there was a certain degree of nostalgia for the clarity and decisiveness in leadership attributed to the Whitaker/Lemass 'moment'.[34]

Central to these debates on leadership and changes in strategic direction in 1958–66 is the towering historiographical presence of T. K. Whitaker. The career in public service and the influence on Irish public life of T. K. Whitaker has been subject to a critical scrutiny accorded to no other public servant in Ireland. Over a long, distinguished career in various public offices, Whitaker himself contributed a substantial body of writings and commentary on public policy, current and historical. A sympathetic biography and several festschriften have examined the man and his work, while an expanding platoon of historians and economists, concerned with the evolution of Irish economic policy and of policy towards Northern Ireland from the 1960s to the 1980s, have been evaluating his role and influence.[35] It is not intended here to discuss in detail this considerable body of

---

31   McCarthy, *Planning Ireland's Future*.
32   For a positive reading of new ideas fermenting prior to 1959, see Gary Murphy, *In Search of the Promised Land: The Politics of Post-War Ireland* (Cork, 2009).
33   Daly, *Sixties Ireland*, passim.
34   For a later revisionist reading, see Kevin O'Rourke, 'Independent Ireland in comparative perspective', in *Irish Economic and Social History*, 44 (2017).
35   McCarthy, *Planning Ireland's Future*; Fionán Ó Muircheartaigh (ed.), *Ireland in the Coming Times: Essays to Celebrate T. K. Whitaker's 80 years* (Dublin, 1997); Anne Chambers, *T. K. Whitaker: Portrait of a Patriot* (London, 2014); Graham Brownlow, 'T. K. Whitaker: Engineering prosperity

work. But it may not be unfair to conclude that the weight of recent research suggests that his genius lay in his political judgement, in its widest dimensions: sharp analytical capacity, diplomatic finesse, shrewd timing, exemplary administrative skill and a fine command of language. These political assets, rooted in a rock-like integrity, were the source of his influence and authority, rather than any striking originality in thought or ideas.[36]

Specifically, in the area of economic ideas and policy, it is contended that in the 1950s and early 1960s Whitaker was a pragmatist and a skilful synthesiser of an emerging conventional wisdom on what needed changing in Irish economic policy. Cautious by temperament, his was an impressively ordered mind rather than one generally indulgent of speculation.[37] What is significant, however, is that the close attention given to Whitaker has reinforced an understanding of Irish economic development since the 1950s as a 'top-down' project, pivoting on the decisive influence of the mandarinate. Indeed, by signing his own name to *Economic Development* in 1958, Whitaker hoped that the civil service could make a more direct contribution to the shaping of public opinion on the options for economic growth and improved living standards.[38]

The dramatic effect of a single-author (as it seemed) intervention may have resulted, however unintentionally, in the collapsing of a more extensive and protracted chain of antecedent interventions and their begetters into a later historical narrative of heroic rescue. The notion of the saviour-mandarin became embedded in the myth of the 'resurrection of 1958–9'. While Whitaker himself was always scrupulous about crediting the efforts of his collaborators and others, the fact that he lived so long, wrote and, in interviews, spoke so eloquently and persuasively on the 'new departure' and of his own memories of the 'darkness-into-light' shift from fatalism to purposefulness inevitably involved a kind of curating of his own reputation and historical role.

What recent research has confirmed, however, is how much of a traditional 'Finance man' Whitaker was: cautious, orderly and prudent. Indeed, even in fundamentals – an aversion to the downside of protectionism and a belief in a competitive economy as the key to prosperity – the line of succession from McElligott to Whitaker has been emphasised in recent research.[39] This 'Finance mind' would endure.[40] Indeed, in the late 1980s (as Lee was published), the secretary general of finance was the Finance man par excellence, Seán Cromien, virtually a 'lifer' in the department.[41] Cromien wrote the entry in the DIB for his predecessor. While conceding that McElligott remained 'negative' too long – when pump-

or preventing the future?', *Irish Economic and Social History*, 42 (2015), pp. 93–103; T. K. Whitaker, *Interests* (Dublin, 1983).

36 Brownlow, 'T. K. Whitaker' is especially corrective. Surprisingly, the role of Patrick Lynch remains underexamined since Lee's perceptive appraisal, but see Miriam Hederman (ed.), *The Clash of Ideas: Essays in Honour of Patrick Lynch* (Dublin, 1988).

37 Brownlow, 'T. K. Whitaker', pp. 93–103.

38 There had been earlier signed contributions to public debate by, for example, Tom Barrington and Patrick Lynch.

39 Anna Devlin and Frank Barry, 'Protection versus free trade in the Free State era: The finance attitude', *Irish Economic and Social History* 46 (2019), pp. 3–21.

40 See obituary for Maurice O'Connell, *Irish Times*, 20 Apr. 2019; and for gentle memoir, Maurice O'Connell, *No Complaints: A Memoir of Life in Rural Ireland and in the Irish Public Service* (Dublin, 2020).

41 See obituary for Seán Cromien, *Irish Times*, 18 Aug. 2018.

priming and deficit spending was called for – Cromien stoutly defended the traditional finance role, as a bulwark against fads, ministerial pet schemes and all hints of extravagance:

> He (Jimmy McElligott) has been strongly, indeed harshly, criticised by J. J. Lee, for his conservatism. Such criticism does not take into account the contribution he made in the 1920s to the continuity of public administration and the establishment of the financial standing of the new state. It also fails to recognise the role of devil's advocate which a department of finance must play in criticising proposals for increasing expenditure, and which is part of the system of checks and balances that must operate in a parliamentary democracy.[42]

In passing, we may look forward to the examination of Seán Cromien's diary, kept from his first day in Finance and now deposited in the NLI, for a unique insight into the private world of the archetypal 'Finance mind'.

However, even if personal papers relating to senior mandarins – revealing something of their routines, reflections, rivalries, relations with individual ministers and with others – were to become accessible and to prove copious, there remains the underlying issue of the 'institutional culture' of the civil service and how best this might be explored. Here we need more than a shelf full of worthy festschriften or such short biographical profiles as can be provided in official histories of individual departments, valuable though such information may be.[43]

What is required is a more systematic historical sociology of the mandarinate; a prosopography covering family and social background, education, qualifications and experience, recruitment, career progress, in-house training and promotion, for a sizable cohort of senior public servants. Ideally, a longitudinal dimension would permit consideration of mobility across and from outside the sector, the effects of the Boland reforms of the 1980s and of revised recruitment competition for fixed-term appointments as secretaries general in recent decades. Barrington in the 1950s and Devlin in the 1960s provided important data on the profiles of various grades in the civil service. Such data needs to be refined for later decades. Moreover, and particularly for recent decades, in considering the wider context of policy-formation and decision-making, it would be useful to track the later career of top mandarins – on the boards of companies or in consultancies – after they had left the service.[44]

A similar investigation of key vested interests or lobbies, whose influence on decision-making and policy-implementation has long been assumed, would also have value for any consideration of leadership: the professions (medical, legal and accountancy), the trade union leadership, business leaders.[45] In the wider society the market for ideas in independent Ireland was never stagnant; indeed, so far as discussion of public policy on

---

42 See 'James John McElligott (1893–1974)', in James McGuire and James Quinn (eds), *Dictionary of Irish Biography*, Vol. 5, pp. 990–1.

43 Daly, *Buffer State*; Daly, *First Department*; and Fanning, *Planning Ireland's Future* all provide valuable biographical notes on leading civil servants in Environment, Agriculture, and Finance respectively. Also, Ciarán Casey, *The Irish Department of Finance 1959-99* (Dublin, 2022).

44 The Devlin Report (1969) and the Boland reform initiative (1984) had both been evaluated by Lee: *Ireland 1912–1985*, pp. 548–59.

45 Suggestive insights in, e.g., Eugene McCague, *Arthur Cox, 1891–1965* (Dublin, 1994); Tony Farmar, *The Versatile Profession: A History of Accountancy in Ireland since 1850* (Dublin, 2014); Ruadhán MacCormaic, *The Supreme Court* (Dublin, 2016).

economic and social development is concerned, there was a quickening of public debate in the post-1945 decades. Lee had contended that it was the demand side that was weak in the ideas market. The work in recent decades of Bryan Fanning, Tomás Finn, Tom Garvin, and others demonstrates clearly that the market was indeed lively – in journals, pamphlets, conference proceedings – from the 1950s. The issue is not the absence of debate in the public square, but the underlying reasons for the hegemonic ideology being so conservative. [46]

A central element of the answer to this question is emigration: the seemingly relentless outflow of disproportionately young men and women who might otherwise have constituted a challenging collectivity to the status quo in Ireland. But the answer must also focus on the influence of the church of the majority, the Catholic Church. How one approaches the place of the Catholic Church in the changing historiography on leadership and decision-making in independent Ireland depends on what one considers the basis of its influence. Is it best seen as a powerful vested interest with formidable resources – personnel, institutions, physical infrastructure in education, health and welfare – and privileged access to political leaders, or as the ideological behemoth defining and, when under pressure, fiercely defending the parameters within which ideas on social progress or change could or should be discussed? In fact, it was both.[47]

By the time of Lee's volume, the late 1980s, its powerful position was being increasingly challenged, a challenge that had been gathering momentum since the 1960s. The visit of Pope John Paul II in 1979 had given committed Catholics a morale boost and may have emboldened those who successfully launched the campaign for the Eight Amendment (to prevent abortion) in 1983. Moreover, the opposition to demands for the introduction of divorce or to liberalisation of sexual freedoms remained formidable throughout the 1980s. Indeed, while the public mood was shifting, the retreat of the Catholic hierarchy from its powerful position in the face of the advancing demands for greater individual rights and choices, notably in reproduction and sexual areas, would be protracted. And by the mid-1980s the avalanche of scandals involving religious persons, sexual abuse and church-run custodial institutions in Ireland was yet to unfold. The revelations, when they came, constituted a severe indictment of church leadership over many decades.

The historiography of the past 30 years has, inevitably, retraced the roots and, now more clearly evident, the staging posts – remote and proximate – for the recent collapse of the authority of the Catholic Church and its influence on the debate on the relationship between the state and public and private morality. Inevitably, this revaluation has been conducted in the context of the long-term frame of church-state relations in independent Ireland.[48] Thus, for example, Bryan Fanning, in his study of *Christus Rex* and of the mission

---

46 Bryan Fanning, *The Quest for Modern Ireland. The Battle of Ideas 1912–1986* (Dublin and Portland, 2008); Tomás Finn, *Tuairim, Intellectual Debate and Policy Formation Rethinking Ireland 1954–1975* (Manchester, 2012); Tom Garvin, *News from a New Republic: Ireland in the 1950s* (Dublin, 2010).

47 John Whyte, *Church and State in Modern Ireland 1923–1970* (Dublin, 1971); Tom Inglis, *Moral Monopoly: The Rise and Fall of the Catholic Church in Ireland* (Dublin, 1998); Louise Fuller, *Irish Catholicism since 1950: The Undoing of a Culture* (Dublin, 2002).

48 For a concise overview, see Daithí Ó Corráin, 'Catholicism in Ireland, 1880–2015: Rise, ascendancy and retreat', in Thomas Bartlett (ed.), *The Cambridge History of Ireland*, vol. 4: *1880 to the Present* (Cambridge, 2018), pp. 726–64.

of Catholic sociology, confirms Lee's verdict on the campaign for vocationalism in the 1940s, that the Catholic Church's preferred model of social harmony, order and progress – based on the family and natural law and resistant to state intrusion – was emphatically a lost cause in Irish political debate long before the 1960s.[49] Political leaders did not entertain Church intrusion on, or attempts to limit, state initiatives, when convinced that it was right and timely for the state to act. The Mother and Child Scheme debacle in 1951 was an exceptional episode. And continued Church control of swathes of institutional terrain in education, health and welfare was the outcome of political willingness, for cost and other reasons, to have it so.

Much remains to be uncovered in the files of various government departments and in institutional archives for a thorough examination of how influence was exerted, on politicians and public servants, by a range of powerful interests, including all the churches. But the returns on the expanding access to archives are already evident in the reappraisals of church-state relations and, however unevenly, in new perspectives on diocesan religious activities and episcopal stewardship.[50]

Finally, the debate on leadership as a factor in the performance of the Irish state must be conducted in the wider frame of the deep structures of Irish society. Here, the longer perspective may be useful. In his first book, Lee addressed the 'modernisation' model in interpreting the directions taken by Irish society in the six decades after the Famine.[51] Two major socio-cultural processes that independent Ireland inherited from those decades were, firstly, the huge accretion of social and cultural influence that marked the Catholic Church's expansion in these decades, and secondly, the creation during 1880–1914 of a largely peasant proprietorship in the countryside, with widely-distributed ownership of farms of various sizes and land quality.

By the end of the second decade of the twenty-first century, the Church's cultural influence had dramatically shrivelled. Irish society had been gripped by a housing crisis, confronted by a global climate emergency, and, in 2020, paralysed by a world pandemic. But property rights endured, and political leaders still needed to tread warily in disturbing them. In this sense, the possessor principle remains a presiding concern of political leadership and of decision-making in contemporary independent Ireland.

---

49   Fanning, *Quest for Modern Ireland*, pp 114–137; Bryan Fanning, 'Jeremiah Newman and Catholic decline', in *Histories of the Irish Future* (London, 2015), pp. 169–86.

50   Daithí Ó Corráin, *Rendering to God and Caesar: The Irish Churches and the Two States in Ireland, 1949–73* (Manchester, 2008); Thomas Bartlett, 'Church and state in modern Ireland, 1923–1970: An appraisal re-appraised', in Brendan Bradshaw and Daire Keogh (eds), *Christianity in Ireland: Revisiting the Story* (Dublin, 2002), pp. 249–58; James Kelly and Daire Keogh (eds), *The Catholic Diocese of Dublin* (Dublin. 2000).

51   Joseph Lee, *The Modernisation of Irish Society: 1848–1918* (Dublin, 1973).

AFTERWORD

When its pugnacious editor D. P. Moran launched his Irish Ireland journal, *The Leader*, in 1900, he set out to look at 'the facts, the possibilities and the limitations of Irish national life'.[1] In combative prose, Moran let fly at the machinations of 'the English mind' in Ireland and sought to supplant it with 'a real and virile national spirit'.[2] Moran's recipe for success was for the Irish mind to turn its back on English influences and embrace an exclusively Gaelic and Catholic ethos. For his part, Joe Lee attributed the inadequacies of the Irish mind to desultory economic literacy rather than to any lack of Gaelic pedigree. I make no comparison between Joe Lee and Moran, 'the dark genius of Catholic nationalism' as Conor Cruise O'Brien dubbed him,[3] but Joe would surely have gone along with Moran's emphasis on economic self-sufficiency and with his contention that 'the age of economics has come.'[4] Joe Lee's key publications, *The Modernisation of Irish Society* and the focus of this volume, *Ireland: 1912-1985*, put Ireland's failings and foibles under an exacting microscope while also eyeing the country's promise if the Irish mind could somehow be directed into more performative, productive channels.

My life as a student, a diplomat and, latterly, in academia has circled around Joe Lee's long and distinguished innings as historian and public figure. I had the good fortune to be Joe's first postgraduate student at University College Cork in the mid-1970s. Four plus decades later, while I was the Irish Ambassador to the United States, I spoke at a seminar marking Joe's retirement from New York University's Glucksman Ireland House, where I later taught for a semester following my retirement in 2022 after 44 years with the Department of Foreign Affairs of Ireland. Facilitated by Joe's Cambridge connections, I was primed to study there in the late-1970s, but took the diplomatic route instead. In 2022/23, I became the Parnell Fellow at Magdalene College, Cambridge, a position Joe was the first to occupy in 1992.

I entered secondary school just after Education Minister Donogh O'Malley's landmark decision to introduce free secondary schooling, which greatly expanded educational access. Thus, when I arrived at UCC in 1972 to study History and Literature, I was part of an enlarged cohort of university students, many like me being the first members of their families ever to go to university. It was in Cork that I discovered the appeal of history as an intellectual discipline, which has given me lifelong satisfaction. The History Department had a strong line-up with the lively historian of early Ireland, Donnchadh Ó Corráin, the late-medievalist, Kenneth Nicholls, the modern Irish specialist, John A. Murphy, and Oliver MacDonagh, who was known for his excellent short study, *Ireland: The Union and its Aftermath* (1977).

---

1   D. P. Moran, *The Philosophy of Irish Ireland* (UCD Press, 2006), p. 120.
2   *Ibid.*, p. 2.
3   Patrick Maume, *D. P. Moran* (Dublin: Historical Association of Ireland, 1995), p. 53.
4   Moran *op. cit.*, p. 15.

When MacDonagh left for the Australian National University, Joe Lee was recruited from Peterhouse College, Cambridge, and turned out to be an outstanding addition to the academic community in Cork. He hit the UCC History Department like a whirlwind and I can still remember his effervescent lectures on modern European history, which brought the subject vividly to life. Delivered with energy and humour, they were a highlight of my undergraduate years. A line Joe wrote for the Preface to my first book in which he described Queen Victoria's visit to Ireland in 1900 as giving her 'Hibernian subjects' an opportunity for 'feasting their eyes upon their monarch'[5], made me chuckle in remembrance of Joe's lecturing style, for he is someone who possesses the ability to write exactly as he speaks.

I also remember Joe's capacity to make things happen. I was among a group of students who complained about the poor quality of a course that had been taught by a temporary lecturer in the interregnum prior to Joe's arrival in Cork. He responded by arranging for the renowned James Joll to come over from the London School of Economics to give a stellar, intensive weekend course on the renaissance. I had the privilege of having Joe Lee supervise my M. A. thesis and retain happy memories of the stimulating exchanges I had with him during those two years of postgraduate study. My thesis explored the evolution of nationalist Ireland through the work of the writers, W. B. Yeats, George Russell (AE) and Seán Ó Faoláin.

As a product of the 1960s and early 1970s, I shared their critique of the preponderant, conservative ethos of the Ireland of their time and mine. Without in any way discounting its many deficiencies, I now look with greater indulgence at that fledgling phase of Irish independence, valuing the attainment and maintenance of political stability in the troubled, tempestuous world of the 1920s, 1930s and 1940s. But I was always aware of Ireland's economic frailties, and one of my earliest memories of Irish public life is hearing on RTÉ radio about the Second and Third Programmes for Economic Expansion. The titles of those documents had a ring to them, offering the prospect of advancement to an Ireland unaccustomed to such vistas.

Joe Lee's 1973 volume in the Gill History of Ireland, *The Modernisation of Irish Society, 1848-1918* was the first Irish history book I ever bought. Its title sets it apart from the other volumes in that series, most of which have purely chronological markers–*Ireland before the Vikings, Ireland before the Normans, Tudor and Stuart Ireland, Ireland in the Eighteenth Century, Ireland before the Famine*, and *Ireland in the 20th Century*. The gist of Joe's thesis was that those decades between the Famine and the advent of independence were ones during which Irish society was, despite all of its many travails, successfully modernised. Looking back, it was indeed something of a miracle that such a damaged, depleted people managed to assert themselves and wrest independence from one of the world's premier powers that had just emerged victorious from World War I. Irish independence was the product of a thoroughly modern freedom struggle.

The book begins with a summary of the disastrous effects of the Famine, the scale of the mortality wrought by hunger and disease, and the further diminution of Ireland's population because of emigration. It moves swiftly on to an analysis of the underlying trends that helped to transform post-Famine Ireland, insisting that it was not the Famine

---

5   In Daniel Mulhall, *A New Day Dawning: A Portrait of Ireland in 1900* (Cork: Collins Press, 1999), p. *ix*.

that was unique, but rather 'the long-term response of Irish society to this short-term calamity'. The upshot was that Ireland became a 'demographic freak', characterised by a declining population and low rates of marriage coupled with the frequent deferral of marriage until family farms had been safely inherited.

His analysis is gently subversive. For example, bucking an emerging, liberal consensus, he relieves the Catholic Church of responsibility for 'the unnatural marriage patterns in post-Famine Ireland'. Priests and parsons, 'products and prisoners of the same society', were, he argues, 'powerless to challenge the primacy of economic man over the Irish countryside'. This use of 'economic man' with reference to rural Ireland in the nineteenth century was in its own way daring!

Joe sought to dig into the roots of Ireland's economic frailty. For that time in Ireland, this unusual focus on 'economy and society' reflected Joe's priorities and preoccupations. His analysis was characteristically persuasive and provocative. It wasn't that Ireland was too Catholic or not Catholic enough, or too oppressed, or not oppressed enough, but rather that both sides of the political divide were blinkered and inhibited in their thought processes. Ireland missed the boat not because it was deliberately held back, but because there were not enough talented Irish people willing to commit themselves to the ups and downs of a life in business, preferring instead the social status associated with entry into the professions. For their part, the rising Irish middle classes were too imitative of British models to be able to come up with a dynamic that might have transformed Ireland's circumstances and made emigration less of a necessity than it came to be for the post-Famine generations

In 2016, when preparing a collection of essays on the period between 1890 and 1922, my co-editor, Eugenio Biagini, and I saw the need to examine it from an economic angle, and asked Joe to contribute an essay on the Guinnesses and the biscuit makers, Jacobs, two conspicuous – and rare – nineteenth century Irish success stories in business. In his contribution, Joe bemoaned the lack of attention to Irish business history, which involved the neglect of 'a crucial factor in the quality of not just economic, but overall, national performance.'[6] Above all else, Joe Lee always desired an Ireland that could perform.

The Modernisation of Irish Society argued that Ireland was afflicted by policies that had proven successful in Britain, but were unsuited to the very different circumstances applying in Ireland. In a phrase characteristic of his inimitable effervescence, he observed that: 'Not the malevolence of the English mind, but the irrelevance of its preoccupations, impeded Irish progress.'

On the spectrum that divided historical revisionists from traditionalists in Ireland's history wars, Joe Lee occupied an outlying perch, suggesting as he did that a lack of independence of mind may have been more debilitating to Ireland than the absence of self-government. It could, of course, be argued that political independence might have spawned ancillary virtues of the mind, but that's an argument for another day.

Despite Ireland's lack of economic advancement, Joe Lee argued that 'Southern Ireland modernised as quickly as any other European society' in the late 19th and early 20th centuries. And he identified some unlikely modernisers, among them Cardinal Paul Cullen,

---

6   J. J. Lee, 'The Guinnesses and beyond' in Eugenio Biagini and Daniel Mulhall (eds), *The Shaping of Modern Ireland: A Centenary History* (Dublin, 2016), p. 211.

'the Pope's chief whip in Ireland', to whom Joe attributes a degree of pragmatism and even a liberal Catholic outlook at variance with his domineering 'Prince of the Church' image. This benign assessment of the leading Irish churchman of the late-nineteenth century was somewhat out of tune with the zeitgeist of the early 1970s, but Joe always liked to stir up his readers and listeners.

The Fenians are credited with a modernising role as 'the first nationwide lay secular society' that 'helped broaden the petty horizons and foster a sense of national political consciousness.' The emergence of the Land League was also seen as 'a major milestone on the road to modernisation', on account of the way in which it transformed an economic crisis in the west of Ireland into 'a political problem for the government.'

The Modernisation of Irish Society was written in 1973, the year Ireland joined what has since become the European Union, membership of which turned out to be a game-changer in so many ways. In Joe's analysis of post-Famine Ireland, there was at least a hint of warning about the need for Ireland to get a grip on those attributes that would strengthen its viability in the new European venture on which it had just embarked. Fast forward to the publication in 1989 of his great work, *Ireland: 1912-1985, Politics and Society.* Here his critique of contemporary Ireland is much more explicit. Not only was Joe by that time older and more assured in his analysis, but the circumstances in which he wrote were dramatically more negative than they had been in the comparatively starry-eyed early 1970s.

I returned from a career break in Australia early in 1987, when Joe was already at work on his magnum opus, and can vividly recall the parlous situation in which Ireland was mired. Those I met at home often questioned my sanity in returning from Australia, a country to which so many Irish people seemed keen to emigrate. The economic backdrop was indeed alarming. In sorting out some of my papers in recent months, I came across a National Economic and Social Council report from 1990 entitled *A Strategy for the Nineties.*[7] While its main focus was on setting out a vision for Ireland's near future, it also contained a review of its then recent past. It makes for salutary reading.

Between 1980 and 1986 Ireland's average annual GNP growth had been barely above zero, while employment had fallen by 75,000 (at that time the workforce was much smaller than it is today). The unemployment rate in 1986 was a whopping 18.1 per cent and there was also significant net emigration. At the same time, the public finances were in serious strife. The Exchequer Borrowing Requirement in 1986 was running at 13 per cent of GNP. Thus, in the late 1980s, the bright promise of EU membership appeared to have evaporated into thin air. Those were hard times for Ireland when Joe was at work on *Ireland: 1912-1985.*

He set out his stall in the book's opening pages, seeking to focus 'more on the relationship between the potential and the performance of sovereignty' and to evaluate 'the performance of a sovereign people'. His point was that sovereignty is not something abstract to be admired for its own sake. It needs to be deployed to produce outcomes for the benefit of society. Sovereignty is a performance art rather than a pictorial one. Joe's focus on performance was characteristic of his thinking throughout his life. I recall another

---

7   National Economic and Social Council, *A Strategy for the Nineties: Economic Stability and Structural Change* (Report Number 89, October 1990).

essay of his in which he reflected on the lack of a 'rat race' in Ireland prior to the 1960s/70s. It was not, he said, that there was any dearth of rats in the country, but that they were unable to race!

In *Ireland, 1912-1985*, he offered some 'meditations on *mentalité*', which brings us back to his enduring critique of the Irish mind, but this time his analysis has a more trenchant, contemporary edge. His key point is again an economic one; that independent Ireland had 'a most unusual economic history', recording the slowest growth rate of any European country in the twentieth century. The most compelling part of Joe Lee's analysis comes when he offers reflections on twentieth- century Ireland under the headings of Performance (that word again), Potential, Institutions, Intelligence, Character and Identity. A conspicuous feature of his analysis is an urge to make comparisons with European countries other than Britain. That was a very valuable approach, an antidote to a perhaps understandable tendency to measure ourselves with reference to our nearest neighbour. He pointed out that the country had in 1910 been slightly wealthier than Norway and Sweden, and way ahead of Italy and Finland. By 1985, it was well behind those countries. His question was why? He put Ireland's inadequacies down to inertia rather than any lack of potential and saw 'an absence of an adequate performance ethic in the society', and a lack of respect within Government and in society for intellect and innovation.

Ireland 1912-1985 acted as a kind of wake-up call for an underperforming Ireland. It is, of course, impossible to judge the impact of a single publication on the society to which it is addressed, but Joe's book was widely read, and its analysis attracted serious attention. As it happens, it was not long before the gloomy scene he sketched with his usual vigorous candour began to change. By the second half of the 1990s, Ireland was growing economically at a rate of knots, a process that continued until 2008. Looking back, it is clear to me that this overhaul of our economy and society had a great deal to do with a more determined embrace of the opportunities provided by EU membership. After a generation of membership, it was high time for us to make a good go of it. The greatly expanded EU structural funds and the advantages of the single market gave Ireland opportunities that had not been available to previous generations. The Maastricht Treaty and its provision for the creation of an economic and monetary union involved an irrevocable commitment to EU integration, one that our nearest neighbour felt unable to make.

I wonder if Joe would agree with me that Brexit may come to be seen as a major milestone in the Europeanisation of the Irish mind? When the tsunami of the Great Recession hit Ireland in 2009, there were those who believed that we were destined to be hurled back into an underachieving past, but the rapid development Ireland had experienced during its 10-year boom had inoculated the country to some extent from the worst effects of the downturn and, for example, population continued to grow during that crisis, which was quite unlike what occurred during the economic adversities of the 1950s. Stoicism rather than angry despair characterised the public mood. Especially after Ireland entered the EU-IMF bailout programme in 2010, there was, I think, a strong, collective determination to extract ourselves from its restrictive, embarrassing grip.

If Joe Lee were to re-examine the Irish mind in 2023, what might he conclude? He would surely laud Ireland's economic transformation since 1985. The performance ethic he pleaded for has probably been more in evidence in recent decades than at any other time in the twentieth century. But, being Joe, he would want more and would have critical things to say and new goals to set. I cannot speak for Joe but, almost a decade-and-a-half on from the traumas of 2009/2010, and three-and-a-half decades since the publication of *Ireland: 1912-1985,* it seems to me that the challenge today is to avoid succumbing to lazy assumptions that all will always be right with our island economy, or to fatalistic prognoses of powerlessness in the face of the grand global forces at play today. External conditions are changing and we need to be ready to make judicious adjustments of our own.

We may be corks bobbing on the global ocean, but the Irish have shown through the centuries that we also have 'bottle' to make our way in the world. We are responsible for making our own luck. That's the way it has always been and that's how it will always be. Today, we have more to lose than was the case either in the era surveyed in *The Modernisation of Irish Society,* or in the straitened economic circumstances of the late-1980s that formed the backdrop to *Ireland, 1912-1985.* But we also have more resources with which to gird ourselves for an always uncertain future. I hope that, in Yeats's phrase, 'Ireland in the coming times' will produce public historians of Joe Lee's calibre to enlighten us, and goad us intelligently into realising our full potential.

Daniel Mulhall
Cambridge
July 2023

Appendix

Peripatetic Professor
An Interview with Professor Joe Lee

GH: Tell us about your background.

JL: I was born in Tralee, County Kerry, in 1942. I spent my first nine years in the tranquil environment of Castlegregory, a village 16 miles west of Tralee on the north side of the Dingle peninsula, where my father was a guard. We then moved to Ballinasloe, and four years later to Dublin.

GH: Where did your love of history come from?

JL: I don't know. My parents encouraged me enormously in education in general—otherwise I could hardly have got to secondary school, much less to university—but they did not direct me towards history specifically. My father had vivid recollections of the early days of the state, when unarmed guards faced many difficult situations. Maybe those memories influenced me. I may have been fortunate too in going to Gormanston, not only because of the fine teachers there, but because we were lodged in the handsome castle of the Prestons, a Norman family. I don't want to launch into a Trevelyan-type rhapsody on the power of place to inspire the historical imagination, but I do remember the sense of curiosity about the past the castle roused in a boy of 12.

GH: When you went to university did you always intend to study history?

JL: Yes. My entrance scholarship to UCD was actually in Irish, English and Latin, but history was my first love. I was also interested in economics, but I knew nothing about it. I had a sense, however, that in order to understand history, one ought to have some grasp of economics.

GH: You were a student at University College Dublin. How did you find your time there?

JL: I was fortunate to become a student in a great history department. The two senior, if somewhat idiosyncratic personalities, Dudley Edwards and Desmond Williams, both had first class historical minds, although of very different types. The sometimes explosive, but remarkably stimulating, chemistry of their relationship has yet to be fully reconstructed. Edwards could have his erratic moments, but I always found him exceptionally supportive. Aidan Clarke's handsome valedictory tribute to him at a memorable meeting in UCD, where the late Liam Hourican and Denis Bethell also spoke perceptively, was well-deserved. Williams used generously for his students his exceptional range of international connections, and brought a cosmopolitan perspective to his teaching, at least on those occasions when his physical presence chanced to coincide with that of his class. He was such a wonderful educator that we adapted to his wayward sense of time. Some of us even stopped taking notes in his class, just to listen to him! He was a particularly acute observer of personality, and in my year his American history class sat spellbound as he probed the personalities of Jefferson, Hamilton, Jackson and Lincoln. The European perspective brought by Kevin Nowlan, a most accomplished lecturer, reflected his studies in Marburg as well as Cambridge. It was only when I joined the lecturing staff myself that I realised how essential Kevin was to the effective running of the department. Undergraduates have no idea of the amount of work involved, and given that neither Desmond nor Dudley were at their best on matters of administrative detail, the department was fortunate to find such organisational ability in Kevin, together with Paddy Ann O'Sullivan, a wonderful secretary who died tragically young. I can vouch from my own experience of 20 years in Cork the crucial role played by good secretaries. Hugh Kearney, who had just published his seminal study on Strafford, was already locating Irish history in a wider context, anticipating much of his subsequent work, as was Jack Watt, who enthralled large classes in medieval history. John Morrall, my first Tutor, had a rare gift for elucidating complex concepts in ancient and medieval political thought, and even raw undergraduates could appreciate something of F. X. Martin's remarkable range over medieval and modern. Maureen Wall, who also died tragically young, was an incisive lecturer with a very sharp historical mind indeed, revisionist in a genuinely historical rather than political propagandist way. I was also fortunate that some senior people in Economics, James Meenan, Paddy Lynch and Alexis Fitzgerald, brought a highly-developed historical sense to their teaching. Whatever criticisms may be made of that generation of Irish scholars, we should not underrate the quality of their teaching, which was at least as good as any I have met anywhere since. I hope, and believe, that good teaching remains one of the great, if under-recognised, strengths of historical studies in Ireland.

GH: Are there any periods or issues in Irish history of particular interest to you?

JL: I am fascinated by every period or issue I have had time to think about. The main challenge is to acquire historical perspective by grasping the linkages between as many periods and issues as possible, so that we are constantly alert to the danger of thinking that whatever period we ourselves are most familiar with must be the most important. The moment you find anybody assuming that their period is the more important, you know that, however competent they may be at a monographic level, they lack historical perspective.

GH: But you prefer modern history?

JL: No. I am attracted by all periods and I have taught every century since the twelfth. But you can't do everything yourself. I am hoping to find more time to read, or re-read, the classics of ancient and medieval history. It is unfortunate that we teach such little ancient history in history departments. I remember beautiful lectures on Roman and Byzantine history by John O'Meara and Donald Nicol in my Latin course.

GH: Why did you opt for modern history?

JL: It was almost accidental. I was looking for a good MA topic, when Kevin Nowlan, knowing I had graduated in history and economics, suggested that I work on the early history of Irish railways. The next big jump for me was geographical. Desmond Williams nominated me for a place at the Institute of European History in Mainz. It was daunting enough to change country and language without changing period as well, and I decided to work on the history of German urbanisation, particularly on the building industry. That involved concentration on the period from 1860 to 1914. In my subsequent research on labour in German industrialisation, for the Cambridge Economic History of Europe, I did a good deal of work on the eighteenth century also, increasingly convinced as I became of the continuities between pre-industrial and industrial history, despite the apparent rupture brought by industrialisation. Anyone, like myself, who has an abiding interest in rural history in general, and the history of the peasantry in particular, will find their reading taking them across centuries and cultures in the search for understanding.

GH: How did you find your time at the Institute?

JL: The Institute had an enormous influence on my development as a historian. Under the benign direction of Martin Göhring, it brought together graduates and established scholars from nearly every European country, including several Eastern European ones. There was no formal teaching, but the daily coffee round after lunch created an exhilarating atmosphere of scholarly exchange. The experience introduced me to the diversity of European historiographical traditions. When I went from there to Cambridge I found myself withdrawing into a highly Anglocentric world. Cambridge had Commonwealth and American students, but very few continental Europeans. I enjoyed Cambridge enormously, but I missed the intellectual diversity of Mainz. However, I was fortunate in that the four senior historians in my college, Peterhouse—Butterfield, Postan, Knowles and Brogan— did have a familiarity with European scholarship. It was my great good fortune that Peterhouse also had such a galaxy of younger historical talent at the time. There was a fine, if occasionally caustic, camaraderie there at that time, a true collegiality. Collegiality is the most difficult ethos of all to foster in a college, but the Masters in my time, Butterfield, the mathematician Charles Burkill, and the archaeologist, Grahame Clark, were devoted to sustaining it.

GH: Do you have a favourite historian?

JL: No, but I have learned from many. Any shortlist of my favourites would include Burckhardt, Nipperdey and Vann Woodward.

GH: Your own book, Ireland 1912-1985: Politics and Society (1989), was criticised for its lack of socio-economic material.

JL: There was as much socio-economic material as I deemed necessary to understand the quality of national performance. My main object in that book was to assess the performance of an independent state in Irish circumstances, particularly as influenced by public policy. Most histories of public life down to 1921 revolved around Anglo-Irish relations. That could no longer be the organising principle of the history of an independent state, important though the Anglo-Irish dimension remained. It is not for me to judge how far I succeeded. There are many different ways of approaching this type of subject. I have actually heard the book criticised for containing too much socio-economic material. You can't please everybody, and you shouldn't try, because you will simply finish up in a morass of mediocrity. There is always a danger as well of chasing the latest 'politically correct' fashion, which would be to prostitute history to propaganda. I don't set out to be unfashionable, but I would have to examine my conscience if I found that everything I said was fashionable. But there is not much danger of that! Within the limits I set myself, I haven't seen any criticisms yet that would convince me of the need to change the balance of the contents.

GH: So it was the public sphere that you were writing about?

JL: Yes, of course, as my preface said. Most of the criticisms I have seen were of the book the critics felt I ought to have written. I will naturally try to take cognisance of intelligent criticisms in any further writing I may do on the topic.

GH: And the lack of women?

JL: There was a lack of women in public policy-making. The history of public policy is essentially the history of political power, however much that may be embedded in social structures and social values. It was overwhelmingly men who exercised that power at that time, at least men from the lower middle class upwards. Working-class men feature little. I am a fervent believer in equality of opportunity at all levels—it would be surprising if I weren't, given my own experience of the obstacles posed by inequalities of income and place—but I try to write history as it was, as best I can, not as I would wish it to have been. Of course I may get it wrong. One of my current enterprises is a general social history of Ireland, which devotes at least as much attention to women as to men. But that involves no change of perspective on my part. It picks up on topics, including the history of women, and labour history, on which I have written or lectured, sometimes many years ago, but in which I have always retained an interest. As far as I am concerned, this type of history is neither better nor worse than other types, simply different, based essentially on different types of sources from my last book.

GH: How do you manage to combine your academic career with your position in the Senate?

JL: I have an intense interest in policy-making processes, on which I lecture in UCC anyway. In the Senate I speak on issues that I find of intrinsic interest, and on which I would be striving to keep myself informed in any case. There is a fair amount of physical wear and tear, and of sheer waste of time, in travelling regularly between Cork and Dublin. But that is nothing new for most historians living outside the capital. I had to make more than 300 trips to Dublin archives and libraries when writing my last book, or roughly 2,400 hours spent in travel alone. The bulk of our source material on Irish history is in Dublin. If you are located in any centre lacking extensive primary sources, or even adequate secondary ones, you have to resign yourself to the hacking of regular travel unless you propose taking early retirement from research. And premature retirement from research is not part of the present ethos of Cork history, or indeed of Galway history, even though it has been suggested to me that our teaching loads tend to be relatively heavy. Whatever about that, to be productive, we must be peripatetic. What is really soul destroying for a head of department is departmental administration, and the associated college activities. Several Irish historians would probably have published more but for these calls on their time. This is not, however, necessarily all loss for the historian. One learns a great deal about human nature, and the relationship between individuals and institutions. Having said that, I am tempted to feel that I may have enjoyed an embarrassment of educational riches in both these matters by this stage!

GH: Do you think that historians have a role in political life?

JL: Not particularly. An informed historical perspective should obviously deepen one's understanding of public affairs, but no historical education in itself can compensate for inherent limitations of temperament or judgement. There is sadly little evidence that the personality types attracted to history are exceptionally equipped for political life.

GH: Both revisionists and anti-revisionist historians have claimed you as their own.

JL: So I have noticed.

GH: Does this mean you have hit the ideal middle ground?

JL: I fear not. Obviously some views of mine must happen to coincide with some held by revisionists, and others held by anti-revisionists. But I do not think much in terms of revisionist and anti-revisionist. The sad thing is that there is so little middle ground between the protagonists, largely because of the unusual direction revisionism has taken in Ireland. In the nature of the subject, much historical writing is likely to contain an element of revisionism. One would have expected some revisionist turn to have come in the 1970s, when the great founder generation of Irish Historical Studies was reaching its natural span. Unfortunately, the outbreak of the Northern conflict helped promote a revisionism that, for the most part, and despite some impressive individual contributions, proved to be simply the opposite side of the same coin, when the more constructive revisionism that might normally have emerged would have required the minting of a new coinage. However, if the peace process can continue, maybe some of the self-delusion can be overcome and a more mature attitude may emerge. In any case, authentic scholarly revisionism, as distinct from propagandistic revisionism, still lies, for the most part, in the future.

GH: You have always regarded James Connolly as important. Why?

JL: I admire Connolly because nobody has overcome so many material obstacles to write

so illuminatingly about Irish history. The quality of his insights obliges one to continue to wrestle with him, however much one may dis-
agree with his interpretation. He asked big questions, which remain of enduring relevance.

GH: Recently you have been giving a series of lectures on F. S. L. Lyons and some other prominent historians. Are you going to publish these?

JL: I hope so, once I'm satisfied that they have a contribution to make to our self-understanding. The use of evidence is central to scholarly historical writing, and I'm trying to recreate the mindsets of some Irish historians in order to better understand the way they use evidence. I reject the view that history is simply another form of fiction. But study of the use of evidence cannot be confined to checking the accuracy of footnotes, useful though that exercise can sometimes prove to be. It is essential that we historians interrogate our own assumptions, including especially our silent assumptions. It is quite remarkable how limited has been the systematic analysis of the use of evidence from that perspective by historians of Ireland.

GH: Would your questioning of the assertion that the 1916 Rising had little popular support be an example of that?

JL: Yes, especially as there I was testing an assumption that I myself shared. It did strike me, however, in the light of the claims vigorously advanced in the propaganda campaigns inspired by the Northern conflict, that the basis of our evidence for our assumptions about public opinion in 1916 was extraordinarily fragile. My concern was not to prove any particular thesis, but to explore the use of evidence underlying our dominant assumptions. What I did was very elementary, and much more can be done. But it does suffice to show, I think, how uncritical our assumptions can be about even central issues unless we remember to keep asking the question, 'how do we know?', as well as 'what do we know?'. What I am engaged in is not, incidentally, a destructive exercise. There is a distinct shortage of constructive criticism in writing on Irish history. I am confining my critique largely to writers I admire, and I hope that whatever is published may help us understand our subject, and the history of this country, a little bit better.

Interview conducted by Gráinne Henry
First published in *History Ireland*, Issue 2 (Summer 1995), Volume 3
Reproduced with kind permission of *History Ireland*

ACKNOWLEDGEMENTS

This book is just a small manifestation of the esteem in which Joe Lee is held in academia and beyond and the international reach of his energies. When Joe retired in 2018 New York University fittingly marked the occasion but the idea of celebrating the impact of Joe's work on Irish soil was first suggested by Richard McMahon and Niall Whelehan and culminatined in a memorable day-long event at the Royal Irish Academy in 2019. The milestone was also memorialized more widely with commentary by Diarmaid Ferriter in *The Irish Times* and by John Bowman on RTÉ's Bowman Sunday. Soon thereafter events of massive historic import, a global pandemic, took over and slowed the pace of a fitting publication to reflect on Joe's impactful monograph. I am grateful to the contributors for their forbearance and to New York University's Glucksman Ireland House for their ongoing support. Special thanks are due to Loretta Brennan Glucksman, along with the entire Glucksman advisory board, and to Kevin Kenny and the team at Glucksman Ireland House. The collaboration with UCD Press led by Noelle Moran has been another productive, professional and convivial one. Thanks are also due to Michael D. Higgins, Mick O'Dea, Bernadette Whelan, Úna Ní Bhroiméil, Eli Diner, Iarla Ó Lionáird, Dan Mulhall, Fintan O'Toole, Hasia Diner, Gearóid Ó Tuathaigh, Tommy Graham, Carla Capone, Christine Kinealy, Judith McGuire, Ted Smyth, Sophie Sweetman McConnell and Marion R. Casey. In no small part has Joe made his mark on the world as a result of the love and support of his family and especially his loving wife, Anne, to whom this book is dedicated. For my own part, I am fortunate to count on the support of all the Nyhans and Greys in all these endeavours. Is mór iad na beaganna i dteannta a chéile.

Miriam Nyhan Grey
September 2024

Index